SHIFTING ALLIANCES

CHURCH AND STATE IN ENGLISH EDUCATION

PRISCILLA CHADWICK

CASSELL

DEDICATION

Matri dilectissimae necnon magistrae.

Cassell
Wellington House, 125 Strand, London WC2R 0BB
PO Box 605, Herndon, VA 20172, USA

© Priscilla Chadwick 1997

First published 1997

British Library Cataloguing-in-Publication Data
A catalogue record for this book is available from the British Library.

ISBN 0-304-70124-6

Typeset by Yorkhouse Typographic Ltd, London
Printed and bound in Great Britain by Biddles Ltd, Guildford and King's Lynn

CONTENTS

FOREWORDS

The relationship between Church and State in education in modern England is a strangely neglected topic. The position in England is quite different from what has developed in other countries, but it tends to be taken for granted rather than analysed.

Dr Priscilla Chadwick has now filled the gap admirably with a book which is both scholarly and very readable. Much of the book is concerned with issues that have arisen since the 1988 Education Reform Act: I found the account of the clash between Christian values and the market particularly illuminating.

Professor Denis Lawton
Institute of Education, University of London

The debates on religious education have left a remarkable imprint on the legislative changes of the past two centuries and still attract headline news. This timely and scholarly book is written from the standpoint of an experienced RE practitioner and headteacher who has lived through the recent debates and understands their significance. By placing them in their historical context, the author offers us a valuable perspective on developments, particularly during the Thatcher era.

Priscilla Chadwick's comprehensive knowledge and excellent grasp of the issues provide a fascinating insight into the world of church politics and education. Readers, whether experts in the field or not, will enjoy tracing the extraordinary pattern of shifting alliances in Church and State into the twenty-first century.

Barbara Wintersgill, HMI

LIST OF ABBREVIATIONS

CES	Catholic Education Service
CTC	city technology college
CVCP	Committee of Vice-Chancellors and Principals
DBE	Diocesan Board of Education
DES	Department of Education and Science
DFE	Department for Education
DFEE	Department for Education and Employment
FAS	Funding Agency for Schools
GLC	Greater London Council
GM	grant-maintained
GMS	grant-maintained status
HMI	Her Majesty's Inspectorate
ILEA	Inner London Education Authority
LEA	Local Education Authority
LMS	local management of schools
NAHT	National Association of Head Teachers
NASUWT	National Association of Schoolmasters Union of Women Teachers
NCC	National Curriculum Council
OFSTED	Office for Standards in Education
PFI	private finance initiative
PSE	personal and social education
SACRE	Standing Advisory Committee on Religious Education
SCAA	School Curriculum and Assessment Authority
SCITT	school-centred initial teacher training
SEAC	School Examination and Assessment Council
TES	*Times Educational Supplement*
TTA	teacher training agency

PREFACE

In historical terms it is not so long ago that the State had no schools. Those with money paid for education; for those without resources it was provided mainly by the Church of England, which used the Prayer Book Catechism to teach the young to keep their hands from 'picking and stealing'. Since the Victorian era, central government has taken an ever-increasing financial responsibility for schools, including those with denominational foundations, the Churches no longer having the resources to maintain the system which they created.

This survey explores the shifting alliances and polarities within the partnership of Church and State in education over more than a century. It traces the relationship between the main Christian denominations, particularly the Anglican and Roman Catholic Churches, which have long been committed to their own church schools within the state system. Many contemporary issues have their roots in the conflicts and compromises of the past and cannot be fully understood without reference to their origins. This book aims to set these debates in context and point the way forward for the new millennium.

As a church school headteacher throughout the reforms of the Thatcher era, I became increasingly aware of how little policy-makers, both local and national, understood or sometimes even cared about the impact of legislation on the Churches' distinctive contribution to state education. The Churches themselves are in the process of reappraising their approach to educating children for an increasingly secular, multicultural and technological society, whilst seeking to retain traditional Christian culture and values. For both policy-makers and the Churches, religious education remains a central issue in this discussion.

The Churches' historical associations with both the independent school sector and higher education are necessarily beyond the scope of this book. The focus here lies primarily on church primary and secondary schools in the state sector during the period since 1870, in order to clarify the critical factors in the partnership between Church and State in the evolution of education policy. The introduction of grant-maintained status in 1988, for example, proved controversial within and beyond denominational loyalties.

Labour's 1997 election victory not only marked the end of 18 years of Conservative leadership; it also allowed educationists to assess the reforms of the late twentieth century more objectively. As we move into the third millennium with commitment to greater consensus in education, there is an opportunity for both Church and State to evaluate and reflect on the purpose of church schools and religious education for the next generation.

INTRODUCTION

In European countries other than Britain, nineteenth-century secularization meant that the Church's role in education (entirely dominant at the primary level) was the subject of fierce controversy between Church and State. In England, however, the conflict was not so much between Church and State, perhaps because, even after the constitutional revolution of 1828–32, the distinction could be blurred in the minds of many. The basic conflicts were between the different Churches, among which the Church of England possessed a dominance resented by the other bodies. Initially the state system (from 1833 onwards) was brought in to supplement rather than supplant what already existed.[1] Hence the 'dual system'. The State built schools where the Church was not already providing them, and it was only by a slow process that the State, with the revenue of taxation behind it, came to possess schools and school buildings that were better than the older church foundations. For more than a century, education provided the chief arena in which the various religious denominations in England and Wales 'exerted their political muscle'.[2]

When one considers the violent antipathies provoked in France, Germany, and Italy by the mere existence of any education in which the Church had a hand, the moderation and capacity for compromise of the English people seems striking. Indeed, Anglicans and Roman Catholics shared their concern for 'Sunday schools for all denominations' and worked together in non-denominational schools.[3] Not that there were no secularists in England anxious to exclude all religious education from the minds of the young. But in England in the nineteenth century the secularizers (mostly 'philosophical' radicals) were sufficiently weak in numbers and voice for the central controversy to be not whether there should be religious education but whether those who were concerned to provide it could reconcile their differences.[4]

The dual system was a compromise with great pragmatic virtues, even if it did not and does not leave everyone completely happy with the result. Its consequences continue to the present day. It is worth recalling a penetrating comment written in 1939 by one of the most critical minds in the Church of England at that time:

> The Dual System, as it now exists, obstructs the complete triumph of the secularising tendency. It affirms an educational ideal which is larger in range, more intelligently sympathetic in temper, more congruous with human nature, than that which secularism embodies. It is a rallying point, to which all the higher factors in the community can gather, and by means of which they can affect more or less directly the whole educational process. (Henson, 1939, p. 204)

The words come from the trenchant pen of the man who served for nearly twenty years as Bishop of Durham (1920–39), writing in the period leading up to the Butler Education Act of 1944. He was noting the chief educational justifications advocated by supporters of the dual system, whereby church schools operate in parallel to state-maintained schools at both primary and secondary level,[5] even if he himself questioned its value.

It would be wrong to suppose that the Church's role and influence in education are to be taken for granted and accepted without question.[6] The historical legacy of Christian commitment to education does not ensure that the Church automatically has a permanent role in the education of the future; nor perhaps should it. Just as church leaders (particularly Anglican and Roman Catholic) have had to justify their endorsement of church schools in the past, so also their successors need to face squarely the often vociferous arguments put forward by those (for example the Socialist Education Association) who strongly oppose the so-called 'privilege' and 'divisiveness' created by specifically Christian schools. They also have to address more recent issues such as the position of ethnic minorities and multicultural education, examined for example in the Swann Report 1985 (chapter 8). Nevertheless it is of some importance to look back on the arguments exchanged in the debate leading up to the 1944 Act and to observe that the fundamental questions remain remarkably unchanged.

The Church of England (as medieval Lollards complained)[7] has been both a social and religious body, identified by government and by society at large as possessing responsibilities and corresponding privileges which mark it out from other groups in England. The actions of Henry VIII and the Reformation did not alter that; but they narrowed the number of citizens for whom the reformed Church of England represented the *ecclesia catholica,* excluding those who, whether as Roman Catholics or as Puritan Dissenters, rejected the role played by the Crown and Parliament in determining the character of the national Church. The royal ecclesiastical supremacy, which in the sixteenth century marked out the Church of England from Christians who looked towards Rome for the preservation of the authentic tradition, paradoxically became the conserving force which upheld the episcopal succession and the Book of Common Prayer and Ordinal against the Puritan Dissenters for whom the liturgy and episcopal order were irredeemably Catholic.[8] The phrase 'The Church of England' thereby became narrower and more specific. Similarly, the Established Church's view of Anglican schools, as central to the education of the nation, has long been qualitatively different from that of other ecclesial bodies. On the one side, Protestant Nonconformists have historically been opposed to church schools on the principle that denominational education should not be supported by the nation's rates. On the other side, Roman Catholics have vigorously defended their own schools to ensure the security and survival of their minority interests in a society which (in consequence of the papal excommunication of Elizabeth I in 1570) long identified Roman Catholicism with too faint loyalty to the Crown.[9] Against this background the debate leading up to the 1944 Act was bound to be stormy.

NOTES

1 Acknowledged by government in 1995: 'Historically the State has been the junior partner' (*Consultation Paper on Self-government for Voluntary-aided Schools,* DFEE, October 1995).

2 A. Howard (1987) *RAB: the Life of R. A. Butler* (London: Jonathan Cape), p. 111.

3 Cf. J. D. Holmes (1978) *More Roman than Rome* (London: Burns & Oates), p. 205. G. Connelly (1984) 'The transubstantiation of a myth', *Journal of Ecclesiastical History* **35**(1), pp. 78–104.

4 See E. R. Norman (1977) *Church and Society 1770–1970* (OUP), p. 6. These differences are analysed in M. Cruickshank (1963) *Church and State in English Education* (London: Macmillan), pp. 4–5. She continues: 'Despite their differences, denominationalists were united in their belief that religious and secular education were inseparable, united also in their faith in the philanthropic and personal value of voluntary work and in their distrust of the bureaucratic powers of the State' (p. 7).

5 The sentiments quoted would not be far removed from more recent thinking among Anglican educationists, as may be seen in a statement from the National Society (Church of England) for Promoting Religious Education, endorsed by the General Synod in 1985; R. Waddington (1984) *A Future in Partnership*, pp. 40–1.

6 The ancient Church had no Christian schools until after the barbarian destruction of the Roman empire; St Augustine regretted that the Bible had been no part of his education and that the literature he learned by heart was entirely pagan (*Epistle to Nectarius*, 104.3).

7 The texts in Anne Hudson's *Wycliffite Writings* (1978, CUP) show how many such attitudes antedate the sixteenth-century upheaval.

8 Even in November 1995, the Church Society regretted the Queen's attendance at the Roman Catholic service of vespers to celebrate the centenary of Westminster Cathedral and 500 protesters outside accused her of 'betrayal'.

9 Roman Catholic Churches have not traditionally observed two minutes' silence on Remembrance Sunday, since such rituals were seen to belong to another 'tribe'; the IRA bombers would have assumed that no republican sympathizers were present at Enniskillen's war memorial in 1987.

1

A HISTORICAL PERSPECTIVE ON THE CHURCHES AND EDUCATION IN ENGLAND PRIOR TO 1944

EARLY DEVELOPMENTS

To understand the differing perspectives of those debating the enactment of such momentous legislation, it is important to consider the position as it was prior to 1944. The aims of any national system of education have rarely achieved wholehearted consensus at any time, the post-Reformation period being no exception. The very idea of 'education for all' triggered horrifying visions of violent revolution and usurpation of power. Herbert Hensley Henson commented:

> The ignorance of the masses was thought by the ruling class to be the best protection of society against the destructive idealism of minds which had been so far enfranchised by knowledge as to feel hardship and to resent oppression. (Henson, 1939, p. 189)

At the same time the only guarantee of moral order and social stability seemed to be the inculcation of Christian values: how else were people to learn to distinguish right from wrong, law from lawlessness, good from evil?[1] The very survival of human society is involved in respect for such precepts as those of the Decalogue forbidding murder, adultery, and theft. Religious foundations had long been in the business of educating the élite. But it was not effectively until the nineteenth century that education for the people at large came to be offered by other than charity schools.[2] With the creation of the British and Foreign School Society in 1807 (adopting Joseph Lancaster's 'unsectarian' monitorial system) and the National Society in 1811 (based on Andrew Bell's educational methods), Dissenting bodies and the Church of England respectively took substantial steps forward in encouraging the country to take seriously the education of all its people.[3] Utilitarian radicals such as Lord Brougham who wished to see a state system of education were realistic: 'nothing will be admitted offensive to any religious opinions, while care must by all means be taken that nothing be allowed to interfere with the just privileges of our national Establishment' (quoted in Norman, 1977, p. 57). Yet his attempt in 1820 to have a national system of parochial schools on the local rate was attacked by Anglicans for excluding the catechism and by Dissenters for allowing clergy a veto over teacher appointments.

The 1832 Reform Act extended the popular franchise and thereby added weight to the argument that an educated society was less dangerous than an illiterate one. The State offered the first grant towards school building costs to the two societies in 1833, £11,000 for the National Society's 690 schools, £9000 for the British and Foreign Society's 190 schools; it no longer seemed satisfactory that so major a task as education should be left to religious and charitable foundations.

Even in the nineteenth century, the problems raised when the only available school belonged to the Church of England were noted by the Parliamentary Select Committee of 1818. The committee envisaged places with two schools, one for children of the Established Church, a second for 'children of all sorts'. But in places where only one school could be supported, regulations which excluded Dissenters deprived the Dissenting poor of all means of education. The committee, however, thought it saw a solution:

> Your Committee, however, have the greatest satisfaction in observing that in many schools where the national system is adopted, an increasing degree of liberality prevails, and that the Church catechism is only taught, and attendance at the established place of public worship only required, of those whose parents belong to the Establishment; due assurance being obtained that the children of sectaries shall learn the principles and attend the ordinances of religion according to doctrines and forms to which their families are attached. (Maclure, 1979, pp. 19–20)

Such tolerant arrangements clearly impressed the Select Committee to such an extent that, in their recommendations 'for promoting universal education', they advocated capital grants in areas 'where the poor are manifestly without adequate means of instruction', with the proviso that links to the Parish School system should be retained. As long as children of Dissenters were provided for in the way here envisaged, such arrangements seemed to be 'the safest path by which the legislature can hope to obtain the desirable objects of security to the Establishment on the one hand, and justice to the Dissenters on the other' (*ibid.*, p. 21). Such optimism seemed misplaced. As Cruickshank observed, 'the Dissenters were never reconciled to the Anglican monopoly of the village schools and right into the twentieth century they had good cause to regard it as the most humiliating of their injustices' (1963, p. 10).[4] Lord Russell's proposal (12 February 1839) to increase the Whig government's contribution to schools of the National and British and Foreign Societies, far from being welcomed, raised anxieties because grants were also to be paid to 'reputable' schools run by strict Nonconformists and Roman Catholics and the grants were dependent on state inspectors supervised by a Board of Education consisting of lay Privy Councillors. As Machin commented,

> People of widely differing opinions were unhappy with the plan. To Voluntaries it was a step towards centralised control; to evangelical Anglicans and Wesleyans it was a dangerous encouragement to Roman Catholicism; to conservative churchmen a further move away from education under Church auspices; to high churchmen an unpalatable extension of undenominational education. (Machin, 1977, p. 65)

Although Russell had to give way on grants to other denominations' schools (after 30,000 hostile petitions),[5] the secular Board's powers remained; the National Society only renewed its application for state grants after a 'concordat' in July 1840 when the archbishops' right of veto over the appointment of inspectors for the schools was negotiated, a concession extended to the Nonconformists' British and Foreign Society schools in 1843.[6]

The attempt by the Conservative Home Secretary, Graham, to introduce new factory schools in 1843 also exacerbated denominational tensions; his proposal to limit children over the age of eight who worked in factories to a maximum of six and a half hours a day to enable them to attend school for three hours, foundered on the issue of church control and religious education. Anglicans like Sir Robert Inglis MP felt that national education should be the prerogative of the national Church rather than the State,[7] while W. F. Hook, Vicar of Leeds, being more sympathetic to Graham's bill, considered the church's predominant influence should be reflected in greater financial contributions.

Wesleyans objected to control over religious education being granted to a church steeped in Tractarian theology, but later acquiesced to modified proposals. Other Dissenters adamantly refused to accept any extension of influence for the Established Church, exercised for example through episcopal control of the appointment of schoolmasters; they also feared that 'social pressure' would restrain Dissenting parents from exercising their conscientious right to exempt their children from religious instruction. Roman Catholics feared that the poverty of most Catholic families and the serious shortage of Catholic schools[8] would allow Catholic children to be 'perverted through [the Bill's] active malignity or allowed to grow in vice through its positive neglect' (Machin, 1977, p. 96). An unusual coalition of Catholics and Dissenters even resulted in a joint petition to the Queen in June 1843, unusual since 'one of the reasons for Dissenting protest was Romanisation in the established Church' (*ibid.*, p. 158). Roman Catholics were as anxious as Protestant Dissenters that factory children should not be given non-denominational education supervised by the Church of England and using the Authorized Version of the Bible which they considered far from neutral. Roman Catholic bishops were prepared to jeopardize government grants for Catholic schools rather than meet the State's wish to have the Authorized Version used in Catholic classrooms.[9] Although Graham managed to salvage the reduction in factory labour hours, his failure in establishing schools which combined Church and State involvement gave fresh impetus to voluntary denominational education.[10]

The State continued to improve educational provision throughout the mid nineteenth century, for example raising teachers' qualifications and increasing building grants. Russell's 1846 proposals to send the best apprentice 'pupil teachers' to training colleges, while opposed by militant Dissenters, gained support from Anglicans and Wesleyans, the latter on the understanding that Catholics were excluded from the scheme, although by a year later Catholic schools were also included. In 1847 the Privy Council Educational Committee also proposed to encourage more lay participation in school management, thereby limiting clerical control in schools. The Wesleyans accepted this without demur. The Roman Catholics (by then desperate to claim building grants to provide Catholic schools to educate the influx of Irish immigrants) agreed, since their laymen were under episcopal authority and offered no threat to Church control of their schools.[11] Anglicans, on the other hand, were divided, the majority in the National Society wishing to accept the proposal that their schools could be managed by lay Anglicans chaired by the parish incumbent; however, the Tractarians, especially Archdeacon Denison of Taunton, insisted that the National Society should not submit to creeping Erastianism.[12] When the government in the 1860s, however, attempted to give parents the right to withdraw their children from all religious instruction on grounds of conscience (*Hansard*, cxl, 1965–7), both Anglicans and Dissenters were united in opposition. It is interesting to reflect that the Dissenters' opposition to the Church's control of education led to increased demands for a secular educational system (Norman, 1977, p. 115). Robert Lowe's Revised Code[13] of 1862 advocating payment by results was also condemned by all denominations as a deliberate policy of secularization and curriculum control.[14]

The Newcastle Commission of 1861, in recommending a national system of schools, nevertheless recognized the essential role of church voluntary schools in government policy to extend elementary education to all social classes. The Church of England had provided, through voluntary contributions, twice as much money as the State for its schools since 1833, alongside the work of Nathaniel Woodard[15] for lower middle-class boys and the established public schools led by distinguished clerics such as Thomas Arnold.

While universal education was recognized as desirable, its scope was limited. How limited can be seen in the Duke of Newcastle's Report:

> With a view to the real interests of the peasant boy . . . we must make up our minds to see the last of him, as far as the day school is concerned, at 10 or 11. Once he can 'read a common narrative', 'knows enough of ciphering to make out or test the correctness of a common shop bill', and has sufficient recollection of Holy Scripture and catechism 'to know what are the duties required of him towards his Maker and his fellow man', he will have had sufficient elementary education. (Chapter 4, p. 243)

At that time ideas of compulsory education were viewed sceptically. Not only could such a possibility give rise to religious and political objections, but the Newcastle Commission considered that education was advancing successfully without it (Chapter 6, p. 300).

THE 1870 EDUCATION ACT

By 1870, the government was convinced that more direct intervention could not be deferred. As Gladstone was preoccupied with the Irish question, the Education Bill was entrusted to Thomas Arnold's son-in-law William Edward Forster (1818–86), a former member of the Society of Friends until he married Arnold's daughter. He argued persuasively in Parliament not so much for the justice of elementary education as for its utility for the country: 'Upon the speedy provision of elementary education depends our industrial prosperity'.

To bring about the improvement necessary for commercial success, the Act established school boards based in local districts, which were empowered to set up board schools in areas where elementary education was insufficient and encouraged to provide schooling for children aged 5–13. Although school fees were not abolished, the boards could set up special free schools and provide needy families (unable to afford ninepence a week for fees) with free tickets for schooling. The principle of educational support from local rates and central government grant was thus established. The Forster Act marked the moment when the State accepted its responsibility to run schools.

The changes made by the Act were far-reaching, even if Forster aimed 'not to destroy the existing system in introducing a new one' (*Hansard*, 17 February 1870, 439–40). But the passing of the Act ultimately hinged on agreement concerning the religious issue. The proposals for maintaining secular efficiency through inspection were readily accepted, even the inspection of secular subjects in church schools receiving state aid; a conscience clause enabled parents to withdraw their children from religious instruction and where a school board did not teach religion, it had to teach morality, even though the feasibility of teaching morals outside a religious context is still debatable.[16] But it remained a question what kind of religious instruction would be generally acceptable in rate-aided board schools.

Though the consequences of the constitutional changes of 1828–32, with Roman Catholic Emancipation and the Reform Act, were slow to penetrate the Victorian mind, it was becoming gradually more evident that in religion, and eventually in matters of morality other than theft, murder, sex and marriage, the stance of government was neutral. The Protestant Nonconformists were forceful and persuasive in advocating free, compulsory, rate-supported non-denominational elementary schooling; they took it for granted that what was non-denominational was sure to be Protestant in its general standpoint, this latter view being shared by Roman Catholics. Having accepted that he was not likely to gain acceptance for a fully state-controlled educational system where denominational teaching was left to local discretion (as in Scotland), Gladstone's problem was to find a way of securing national agreement on a non-denominational religious instruction. At the same time the Established Church would feel understandable grievance at having to provide substantial funds to maintain its own parish schools if it were hindered from teaching the Prayer Book catechism in them, while the Protestant Dissenters were adamant that no state aid could be given to parish schools where denominational instruction was the norm. 'The seeds for the last great battle fought on behalf of the historical forces of Dissent in Britain had been sown' (Howard, 1987, p. 111).

The final compromise was enshrined in the clause put forward by William Francis Cowper-Temple (1811–88). This laid down that in schools 'hereafter established by means of local rates, no catechism or religious formulary which is distinctive of any particular denomination shall be taught'. This was agreed, or rather submitted to, only after fierce opposition and acrimonious debate; one amendment alone was debated in Parliament for four consecutive nights. It was in any event a compromise tending to gloss over fundamental differences of approach between the Church of England and the Dissenting bodies, not only in theology but in political and social tradition.[17] The effect of the Cowper-Temple clause was to limit religious instruction in all state-funded schools to Bible stories, not all of which, without the gloss of later Christian interpretation, were necessarily edifying or productive of the kind of morality which would help the government to keep down the crime rate. The clause implied a divorce of the Bible from the living community of faith. Disraeli even feared that schoolmasters responsible for interpreting the scriptures would become 'a new sacerdotal class'.[18]

There was a further difference between the Church of England and Dissenting bodies such as the Baptists. Anglicans accept infant baptism, and think of the Christian nurture of the child as a long process of character training. Much Anglican religious instruction in schools tended to presuppose that the children came from homes with a Christian affiliation and allegiance, and did not present the young with urgent exhortations to a conversion experience. By contrast, some of the Dissenting bodies, having a darker conception of the effects of original sin in producing 'total depravity' in unredeemed human nature, had less interest in transformist understandings of the operations of divine grace, and sought rather to invite the child, often in early adolescence, to accept salvation through a personal and conscious act of commitment. Catechism was accordingly less significant for the Nonconformist bodies.

The Dissenters fought hard for the Cowper-Temple clause. They had long felt that any specific catechetical instruction should be left to the minister on Sundays, not brought into the nation's classrooms on weekdays. If the clause left nothing to religious instruction other than the Bible alone, they above all knew that the Bible only was the religion of Protestants and a book which individual Protestants claimed to be at liberty to interpret as they willed, altogether apart from the 'tradition' of the community of faith. The clause could be accepted as enshrining the principle of religious freedom. If it was impossible for the State to take all voluntary schools under its direct control,[19] then the government must ensure religious freedom in its own schools.

By long tradition, Dissenters tended to be drawn from the lower middle classes,[20] and were Whig in politics. The Established Church retained the loyalty of the ruling classes in society and was for the most part Tory. This political division did not assist the formation of a common mind. The Dissenters resented their exclusion from admission to Oxford and from graduation at Cambridge; until the year 1871, subscription to the Thirty-nine Articles was a condition for obtaining a degree at Oxford or Cambridge. Nonconformists had to look elsewhere for higher education, to Scotland, the Netherlands, or their own dissenting academies established by the Presbyterians and Congregationalists. The dissenting academies tended to allow greater room for diversity of opinion and in some cases encouraged the Enlightenment spirit of free enquiry. In philosophy John Locke was their model; in theology Socinianism was never far away.[21] The Presbyterianism of the seventeenth century rid itself of orthodox strictness and by 1730 was moving into Arianism and Unitarianism. If the spirit of the Reformation was, or became by 1600, the exaltation of private judgement and liberty, then congregations could hardly assert the right to impose creeds on ministers.

The Methodists stood apart from the older Dissenters; John Wesley had found equally uncongenial the Calvinism of many Congregationalists and the rationalistic Socinianism current among the Presbyterians of his time. Moreover, the older Dissenting bodies and the Methodist societies had very different forms of organization, the Wesleyan tradition being far more autocratic and authoritarian. Nevertheless, the Methodists after their separation from the Church of England found themselves willy-nilly adopting Dissenting attitudes, consequent on their rejection of the principle that the Church of England was the Church of the nation. On the question of the Cowper-Temple clause, therefore, the Methodists joined forces with the other Protestant Nonconformist bodies, although they were also relieved when the 1870 Act allowed state capital grants for their denominational schools.

The Church of England inherited a deep sense of responsibility for education at all stages from parish school through to the university, with a duty to ensure that Christian doctrines and moral values flowed in the life-blood of the nation. The bishops of the Church of England retained their very ancient, pre-Reformation position in the House of the Lords. Yet within the Church of England, among the liberal and evangelical groups, there could also be supporters of the view that religious education need not include the catechism.[22] At the time when Parliament was carrying through a constitutional revolution utterly transforming the alliance of Church and State in England, Thomas Arnold in 1833 published his *Principles of Church Reform*, arguing for a retention of the identification of the liberal State with a liberally interpreted Church of England. Arnold at Rugby saw his task as educating children to serve God in both Church and State, the Christian school being directed towards the public service of the body politic.[23] In the nineteenth century there were Anglican minds who could find it possible to come to terms with the Cowper-Temple clause, because they thought that it was a historic obligation for the Church of England to reflect the religious attitudes of the English people, especially as expressed through Parliament, inheritor of the royal ecclesiastical supremacy asserted by Henry VIII. More conservative Anglicans concentrated on expanding the number of church schools (the total number of all voluntary schools peaked in 1890 at 14,479) and on lobbying[24] for rate aid for denominational schools and against the conscience clause (by 1887, only 2,200 out of 2,000,000 children had claimed exemption).[25]

Meanwhile, the Roman Catholics, though preoccupied with developments at the First Vatican Council (1870), were keen to safeguard their own concerns. While the Anglicans emphasized the education of the English nation as a whole, the Roman Catholics were insistent that their parents should have the right to Catholic education for their children.[26] Archbishop, later Cardinal, Manning was keen to extend this principle to all. But he also warned Gladstone 'that integrity of our schools as to i) Doctrine, ii) religious management, and the responsibility of the Bishops in these respects, cannot be touched without opening a multitude of contentions and vexa-tions'.[27]

Their main concern as a minority was a fair share of government capital and maintenance grants for their schools, particularly as the social deprivation of many Catholic communities, arising from Irish immigration after the famine of 1846–8, made any expectation of voluntary contributions for schools unrealistic. The principle that 'religion pervades all aspects of Catholic education' was very differ-ent from the State's policy of demarcating secular from religious instruction, and reinforced the claim for distinctive Catholic schools. They were apprehensive about the establishment of school boards over which they had no control (though some priests were elected on to their local boards in, for example, Manchester) and yet on which, under Section 75 of the 1870 Act, they were dependent to pay the fees of poor children otherwise unable to attend Catholic schools – a responsibility taken over by the Poor Law Guardians in 1876. The bishops' suspicion that board schools were Protestant institutions was hardly lessened by the Church of England's willingness to transfer more than 600 schools to the control of sympathetic local boards by 1884.

The Forster Bill was finally enacted on 9 August 1870, but only with the support of the Conservative opposition; the bitterness engendered by the debates contributed to the Liberals' electoral defeat in 1874. The compromise of the dual system papered over the cracks of a society divided by sectarianism and religious defensive-ness. It meant that Church and State were to operate parallel if not rival educational systems, distinctive in their religious teaching and their management structure even to the present day. Yet the Cowper-Temple clause, at all stages controversial, survived through successive attempts at educational legislation to underpin religious education even in the 1944 Butler Act and the 1988 Education Reform Act.

THE 1902 EDUCATION ACT AND ITS AFTERMATH

The period between 1870 and 1902 saw repeated attempts (e.g. Sandon's Education Act 1876) to improve the financial position of church schools,[28] especially since the State was now providing sub-stantial support for its board schools. Anglicans and Roman Catholics, united in the Voluntary Schools Association of 1884, lobbied both for increased grant and for the abolition of rates paid by voluntary schools to support board schools. (The objection that state aid would mean state interference came only from anti-Erastian High Anglicans.) The 1888 majority report of the Cross Commission supported their cause and recognized the generally good quality of religious education in voluntary schools, but it united the Nonconformists in opposition. While Roman Catholics campaigned for local rate aid, Anglicans were divided about whether state or local aid was preferable. At the same time both denominations were losing well-qualified teachers trained in church training colleges[29] to better equipped state schools offering higher salaries, especially in urban areas (Chadwick, 1970, pp. 304–5). The Catholic teachers who moved out of Catholic schools were even threatened with excommunication; they formed their own association in 1892, but were almost defenceless against the sanctions the bishops could enforce.[30] The 1891 Education Act providing free elementary education merely created additional costs and exacerbated the widening gulf between voluntary and state provision.

When Sir John Gorst's 1896 Education Bill, proposing County Authorities and financial relief for denominational schools, threatened the religious compromise of 1870,[31] Arthur James Balfour intervened to scupper it, much to Queen Victoria's fury.[32] However, the 1897 Voluntary Schools Act, providing five shillings a head for voluntary schools, helped Balfour restore his reputation and gain the general support of the Church Party led by his cousin, Lord Cranborne (although the latter continued to push for total relief and security for the denominational school system). Faced with a crowded parliamentary timetable, 'a divided party, a muddled Church and an unreliable Board of Education', Balfour's difficulties were compounded in 1901; Archbishop Frederick Temple's 'irritability with rate-aiders', 'ill-temper and inertia' would 'produce no clear and constructive option for churchmen to follow', and 'the Education Department was in a state of absolute chaos' (Taylor, 1994, pp. 143–4). Nevertheless, Robert Morant[33] managed (by Christmas 1901) to persuade the Cabinet that rate aid was feasible; Evelyn Cecil's group in the Commons gradually negotiated the compromise that denominational schools should be given rate aid in return for some popular representation on the Board of Managers; and the Bishops Edward Talbot and Randall Davidson gained the Church's agreement at the Joint Convocation of York and

Canterbury (July 1901). This 'secret and effective alliance' encouraged Balfour to persevere.

By 1902 the position of voluntary church schools, guaranteed under the 1870 Act, had become untenable; they were educating half the nation, yet the state of most of the schools was appalling and the government really had no choice but to intervene. Once the initial surge of financial support for church schools following the 1870 Act had subsided, the 50 per cent capital grant permitted from the Education Department after 1870 had become plainly inadequate, and the notable success of the rival board schools, particularly in urban areas, highlighted the deficiencies still further. Balfour, introducing his Education Bill (devised by Morant) in the House of Commons in March 1902, commented that, while board schools were administered by school boards, voluntary schools were isolated and unconnected in their organization. Moreover they lacked resources.

> The fact remains that after all their great efforts on the part of the voluntary subscriber and after all the aid given from the National Exchequer, the voluntary schools are in many cases not adequately equipped and not as well fitted as they should be to carry out the great part which they are inevitably destined to play in our system of national education. (*Hansard*, 4th Series, cv, 854–5)

Balfour's Unionist Alliance categorically reaffirmed the government's commitment to the voluntary sector as a partner in the expanding national educational service, and it is instructive to observe that he allowed no room for manoeuvre to those who wished for the abolition of the dual system. Retaining the balance of denominational and non-denominational education, he insisted that government support was not to be merely financial in providing the 50 per cent capital grant. The 1902 Act ensured that the new local education authorities, supporting church schools with local rate aid, would appoint one third of the managers to voluntary schools, and His Majesty's Inspectors would have right of inspection to oversee standards in all schools; most importantly, all teachers were to be paid out of the public purse.

The consequences of such legislation brought into high profile the difficulties of government action in this delicate area. For the first time, local authorities were to have a direct say in the organization of the voluntary sector, a move accepted by both Anglicans and Roman Catholics as inevitable because of the impoverished condition of many church schools.[34] This change might have been considered by those opposed to a dual system as a move in the right direction, or at least as the half loaf which is better than no bread, since it meant that church schools were set on a path by which one day they might be wholly subsumed within the state system.[35] However, the cost to the ratepayer of supporting the voluntary sector, then 71 per cent of all schools, caused an outcry of such proportions that it nearly brought down the government.

The impassioned opposition is surprising in view of the fact that the State had been giving church schools central financial support for 70 years already. Yet the prospect of the common people's local rates being gathered and allocated to maintain denominational schools, from which on grounds of conscience their children were withdrawn, lit the blue touch-paper. The Protestant Nonconformists, led by the famous Baptist minister John Clifford (1836–1923) of Westbourne Park Chapel, rallied to the cry of 'Rome on the rates',[36] and his virulent pamphlets against the Bill sold in thousands. Protest meetings were held all over the country; sixteen special trains were needed to bring Dissenters to one in Yorkshire on 20 September 1902. Lord Rosebery presided over a rally at the Queen's Hall at which Lloyd George said of the Bill that 'it was originated by a wily Tory Cardinal, promoted by State clergy, who accepted Protestant pay for propagating Catholic doctrines' (Clegg, 1980, p. 166). With feelings running high and Liberal politicians bidding for the Protestant Nonconformist vote, it was not surprising that the parliamentary debate lasted fifty-seven days.[37]

After the legislation put forward by Balfour was passed in 1902, thousands of Nonconformists refused to pay their local rates, remaining adamant in their opposition regardless of personal cost; between May 1903 and December 1904, 38,000 summonses were issued and 80 objectors imprisoned. A fierce puritan austerity surfaced. Thus, on their election to power and in response to their constituents, the new Liberal government of 1906 introduced a bill to abolish the dual system and bring all state-funded schools under public control.

But now the bishops rallied to defend their cause. The nation's children were in danger of losing altogether their heritage of an education formed by the noble cadences and scriptural doctrine of the English Prayer Book. Charles Gore, the Tractarian bishop lately translated from Worcester to found the new diocese of Birmingham (1905), wrote in a letter:

> Loyalty to those who have gone before us and the sense of our great
> duty to the children of Church parents have impelled us to make
> great sacrifices that we might secure for such children instruction
> in the faith their parents hold. (Henson, 1939, p. 203)

Bishop Knox of Manchester, on the Evangelical side, told an audience of supporters:

> Your tea, your sugar, your beer and your incomes are to be taxed
> that the children of the Church may be robbed of their Church
> education and that your schools, built by your own free contribu-
> tions, may be useless for your own requirements. (Butler, 1982, p.
> 149)

After the furore of Nonconformist anger directed against the 1902
Act, and considering the skill with which Augustine Birrell, the new
President of the Board of Education and son of a Nonconformist
minister, presented the Nonconformist and Liberal government case
in 1906, it is surprising that the Liberal government's bill suffered
defeat.[38] Randall Davidson, by then Archbishop of Canterbury,
invariably spoke with great moderation on behalf of church schools
and clearly discerned the confusions of thought among their opponents. The support for the Liberal bill was an alliance of
incompatibles, partly atheist secularists imbibing the spirit of the
French Revolution and anxious to be rid of all religion as super-
stition, partly pious Nonconformists content with the Bible only or
even preferring to have no religion taught at all rather than to allow
the Prayer Book catechism to be taught in any school in receipt of
ratepayers' money. Even the young William Temple at the Oxford
Union (April 1906) argued against his archbishop, suggesting he
had 'an exaggerated conception of the importance of dogmas in the
education of little children'.

Augustine Birrell himself had great admiration for Roman Catholics, Jews and High Anglicans and did his 'best to secure their
position and entitle them to State aid' (Birrell, 1937, p. 189). He
wanted compromise, advocating the abolition of religious tests for
teachers and a state religious education confined to the Deist propo-
sitions of the fatherhood of God, the responsibility of man, and the
immortality of the soul, but excluding contentious matters of
revealed theology. The newly-established Catholic Education Council of 1906 reiterated the view of the Roman Catholic bishops that
parents had the right to religious instruction of their own denomination and that undenominational teaching was by definition

'Protestant'. Archbishop Davidson powerfully pointed to the absurd-
ity that a Liberal government should be denying parents the right to
obtain for their children instruction in their faith within the school
framework and, moreover, should be encouraging the appointment
of religious instruction teachers without any belief in what they were
talking about. He also urged[39] the injustice inherent in taking 14,000
schools by confiscation and demolishing their trusts by radical secularization, against which the sole safeguards offered by the
government were the 'pious hope' of the Education Minister Birrell
that nothing so drastic would happen on any great scale and that
denominational 'facilities' might be available if three quarters of the
parents required them.

The reasonableness with which Davidson argued the Church's
case persuaded the House of Lords, with the consequence that the
original issue of religious education became submerged in a greater
battle for power[40] between the Commons and the Lords; even the
King had to plead for compromise rather than conflict. The bill
finally fell when the Liberal government, having made considerable
concessions, refused to concede freedom to a qualified teacher to
give any religious instruction in a rate-supported school (which was
to mean any school other than an independent school) if that
instruction had content distinctive of 'denominational' Christianity.
As Norman suggested, 'a dangerous internal crisis for the Church
was avoided' (1977, p. 264).

Under Birrell's successors in the presidency of the Board of
Education, McKenna and the more effective Runciman, strenuous
efforts were made in 1908 to achieve a compromise described as a
'concordat'. Bishop Knox of Manchester, however, regarded it as
'the peace of death' (*Church Times*, 27 November) and declared
himself opposed to any compromise, counter to the diplomatic
negotiations skilfully (in Knox's view, too skilfully) conducted by
Davidson. Davidson came within an ace of persuading the Liberal
government to agree to allow 'denominational' teaching in every
elementary school in the country, and succeeded in winning the
concurrence of leading Nonconformists. But the bitter language of
1906 had fouled the nest; the Nonconformists became concerned at
the financial benefits offered to church schools and Anglicans and
Roman Catholics both feared that their own schools would become
isolated from the national system (*Hansard*, 4th Series, cxcvii, 1158,
1163.) There was evidence that the Board of Education
might impede denominational provision by regulations in 1907

which gave larger grants to undenominational schools and attempted to influence church training colleges. The emergence of further disagreements among the Anglican leaders (for example, in the Representative Church Council) enabled the government to withdraw a revised Bill which would have satisfied the Archbishop of Canterbury but not the firebrand Bishop of Manchester. 'No fewer than three Presidents of the Board of Education between 1906 and 1908 had to admit defeat in their endeavours to reach a religious settlement. The issue did not play a prominent part in educational politics again until the Butler Act was being shaped.'[41]

Cruickshank regarded Birrell's bill as 'unquestionably the great missed opportunity of the twentieth century' (1963, p. 103) to resolve the religious disputes in education, which continue to dog the footsteps of government ministers up to the present day. Nevertheless, the dual system was destined to survive right through the twentieth century.

NOTES

1 See W. D. Bayly (1820) *The State of the Poor and Working Classes*, p. 96. This is a view not dissimilar from those expressed by more recent Conservative government spokesmen (e.g. Kenneth Baker in *The Times*, 1 February 1988, 'In the moral dimension', and John Patten on 5 March 1993).

2 M. Jones (1938) *The Charity School Movement* (CUP); R. W. Unwin (1984) *Charity Schools and the Defence of Anglicanism*, University of York, Borthwick Paper 65, elucidates the work of James Talbott (author of *The Christian School-master*, 1707).

3 See S. C. Carpenter (1933) *Church and People 1789–1889* (London: SPCK).

4 Cf. also E. Halévy (1951) *History of the English People* V, p. 166: Anglican schools were built 'with the squire's money and taught with the parson's catechism'.

5 *Hansard*, xvii, 1378–81, 4 June 1839.

6 Similar concerns were expressed in the negotiations over Section 9 inspection for church schools in the 1993 Education (Schools) Act.

7 *Hansard*, xvii, 104–5.

8 Over half the Catholic children in England were unable to obtain a Catholic education, according to the *Tablet* (J. T. Ward and J. H. Treble (1969) 'Religion and education in 1843: Reaction to the Factory Education Bill', *Journal of Ecclesiastical History* xx, pp. 79–100).

9 J. Murphy (1971) *Church, State and Schools in Britain 1800–1970* (London, Routledge and Kegan Paul), p. 14. For half a century before 1611 Catholics had conducted a running battle against Protestant translations, especially the much-used Geneva Bible of which William Fulke composed a notable *Defence* (1583, reprinted 1843). Catholics were offended, e.g., when in Luke 1.30 'full of grace' became 'highly favoured', and when terms like 'priest' and 'sacrament' were avoided.

10 In 1844, the National Society raised £160,000 to provide more Anglican schools in industrial areas.

11 See *Reports of the Catholic Poor School Committee* 1849 (pp. 121–39) and 1850 (pp. 72–89), Appendix K.

12 He thought the clergy mistaken in transferring 'the charge of the teaching of the children of the Church from themselves to a department of Government – a Government which has no creed' (*Notes of My Life* (1878, 2nd edition), pp. 151ff). In chapter VII, he criticized the Church of England's failure to combat indifferentism.

13 This Code specified a single block grant to be paid to school managers, one third of which was to be dependent on the number of children in attendance, the rest on the performance of pupils in an annual examination in reading, writing and arithmetic; see N. Morris (1977) 'Public expenditure on education in the 1860s', *Oxford Review of Education* 3(1).

14 C. K. Francis Brown (1942) wrote, 'The Revised Code was a major disaster, both for the teachers and the children; it was an attempt, cynically indifferent to the welfare of all concerned, to save the tax-payer's pocket and the tax-payer acquiesced to it' (*The Churches' Part in Education 1833–1941* (London: National Society/SPCK), p. 125).

15 K. E. Kirk (1937) *The Story of the Woodard Schools* (London), p. 29.

16 Cf. 'Opinion' in the *Times Educational Supplement* (*TES*), 20 October 1995.

17 In addition, there was the real difficulty that it is hard to identify any statement of Christian faith which is not, in the last analysis, at least characteristic, and in some degree distinctive, of a particular ecclesial ethos. (E.g. the Lima *Baptism Eucharist and Ministry* (1982), though composed by Protestants, has been felt alarmingly Catholic by some.) None of the classical Christian creeds could be acceptable to a Unitarian.

18 *Hansard*, 3rd Series, ccii, 289.

19 Non-denominational elementary schooling was effectively advocated in the run-up to the 1870 Education Act, especially by the Education League founded in

Birmingham (a city with a powerful Methodist and Unitarian presence, and with a famous Congregationalist chapel at Carrs Lane). With substantial financial backing, the League held 200 public meetings and issued 250,000 publications. The radical Birmingham politician Joseph Chamberlain even suggested that Nonconformists should withdraw their support for the Liberal government which condoned sectarianism (C. W. Boyd (ed.) (1914) *Mr. Chamberlain's Speeches* 1 (London: Constable), pp. 13–14).

20 The Congregationalist said that 'plain people of low education and vulgar taste ... constitute ... nine parts in ten of most of our congregations' (1730); cited by Michael Watts (1978) *The Dissenters I* (OUP), p. 383.

21 In some Dissenting minds the doctrine of the Trinity was mere ecclesiastical tradition without foundation in Scripture alone, at least since Richard Bentley in 1715 had demonstrated 1 John 5.7–8 (the heavenly witnesses) to be a spurious interpolation.

22 Troublesome to liberals because of the sentence 'The Body and Blood of Christ are verily and indeed taken and received by the faithful in the Lord's supper'.

23 More than a century later, comparable ideas appear in William Temple's *Christianity and the Social Order* (1942): The explicit Christian teaching and worship of the school should be the focus of a school's own sense of community and its service to the wider community in which it is set' (London: Penguin, p. 93). In 1939 the more sceptical Herbert Hensley Henson wrote: 'The immemorial association of the clergy with the education of the people, and the dominance of religion in the scheme of sound education, have persisted in Anglican minds long after they have been abandoned by the State, the one as impracticable and the other as irrational' (1939, p. 192).

24 Among Anglicans there was disagreement. Contrast the position of Canon Gregory, treasurer of the National Society, who was elected to the London Board in 1873 and there used his influence to support denominational education and to restrict the expansion of Board Schools, with that of Dr Fraser, Bishop of Manchester, who was prepared to transfer his church schools to the State (Cruickshank, 1963, pp. 46–7). Walsham How (later Bishop of Wakefield) commented at the Church Congress in Southampton in 1870 that the Church should make the best of the Act; after all, 'the Church is not the nation; and this is a national measure' (quoted in Norman, 1977, p. 207).

25 W. O. Chadwick (1970) *The Victorian Church* vol. 2, p. 189.

26 Manning wrote to Gladstone from Rome: 'I fear we shall be compelled as in America to form our own schools' (E. S. Purcell (1973) *Life of Manning* vol. 2, p. 493). 'Let every sect, even the Huxleyites, have their grant if they fulfil the conditions' (J. Morley (1905) *Life of Gladstone* vol. 2, p. 308).

27 Cited in V. C. McClelland, 'Sensus Fidelium: the developing concept of Roman Catholic voluntary effort in education in England and Wales', in W. Tulasiewicz

and C. Brock (eds) (1988) *Christianity and Educational Provision in International Perspective* (London: Routledge and Kegan Paul), p. 67.

28 £5m in voluntary subscriptions enabled 1,726 applications for building grants to be approved in 1876.

29 In 1886 the Church of England colleges trained 67.5 per cent of teachers; Roman Catholic colleges 5.3 per cent; Wesleyan colleges 7 per cent; leaving only 19.8 per cent in undenominational colleges. At the same time 47.3 per cent of pupils attended secular board schools (Chadwick, 1970, p. 307).

30 See D. E. Selby, 'The Catholic teacher crisis 1885–1902', *The Durham and Newcastle Review* 37, Autumn 1976, pp. 33–47. In Northern Ireland, such episcopal sanction retained its power into the late twentieth century (cf. P. Chadwick (1994) *Schools of Reconciliation* (London: Cassell), p. 155).

31 Joseph Chamberlain wrote to the Duke of Devonshire (15 September 1895), 'These are the maddest proposals I have ever seen in my life ... They would repeal the Cowper-Temple clause and unite every Dissenter in the United Kingdom.'

32 A. Taylor (1994) 'Arthur Balfour and educational change: the myth revisited', *British Journal of Educational Studies* **xxxxii**(2), June 1994. The Queen wrote to Lord Salisbury: 'I deprecate in the highest degree a step which I consider may be disastrous for the Government' (20 June 1896); faced with the difficulties in the Boer War, 'a bold front' was needed. Taylor argued that this left Balfour (a Scottish Presbyterian, later to be prime minister 1902–5) with 'a profound loathing for education and its complexities and controversies'.

33 Taylor (*ibid.*, p. 145) describes Morant as 'an ambitious, ruthless political operator'.

34 Randall Davidson argued that the Act would help to redress the injustice of 'churchmen having to pay both for their voluntary schools and through local rates for the board schools (*Hansard*, 4th Series, cxv, 1220–1). The 1902 Act 'saved the voluntary system just as it approached breaking point; however it accepted the effective separation of religious and secular education' (S. G. Platten (1975) in *British Journal of Educational Studies* **23**(3)).

35 A fear earlier expressed by the Archbishop of Canterbury, Dr Benson, in 1893, since such state control might 'unchurch the Church schools' (*Guardian*, 31 May). This concern was more recently echoed by both Anglican and Roman Catholic spokesmen as a consequence of the legislation since 1988 and 1993.

36 M. Cruickshank (1963, p. 81) points out that, although Cardinal Vaughan as Archbishop of Westminster welcomed Balfour's proposals as a 'step in the right direction', it was actually the Anglicans with ten times more schools than the Roman Catholics who were to benefit most from the Bill.

37 R. A. Butler (1982) noted that 'Winston Churchill was stunned by the virulence of the debates, horrified to see that an educational dispute charged with religious issues could so split the nation that the Conservative Party lost the next election' (*The Art of Memory* (London: Hodder & Stoughton), p. 148). After this, it can be no cause for surprise that Churchill was hesitant about a new Education Bill in the war years of 1940–44.

38 Birrell recalled: 'Never have I drawn my breath in so irreligious and ignorant an atmosphere as that of the House of Commons when debating religion'. (A. Birrell (1937) *Things Past Redress* (London: Faber), p. 188). Spinks argued (1952) that the Nonconformists' bitterness led to the Liberal government's determination to disestablish the Anglican Church in Wales in 1912 (*Religion in Britain since 1900* (London: Dakers), p. 94).

39 *Hansard*, 4th Series, clxii, 934.

40 G. K. A. Bell (1952, 3rd edition) *Randall Davidson* (OUP), p. 524. The battle was exacerbated by Balfour, now in opposition, who 'blocked all the roads that might have led to a settlement' (A. Birrell, 1937, p. 191).

41 P. Gordon, R. Aldrich and D. Dean (eds) (1991) *Education and Policy in England in the Twentieth Century* (London: Woburn Press), p. 20.

2

THE 1944 EDUCATION ACT

THE CONTEXT

One cannot consider the parliamentary debates of 1906–8 without wondering what created the profound change of climate under which agreement was possible in 1944. How were feelings so modified that the government would come to welcome the role of church schools in the national scheme of education,[1] and accept religious education as an essential element in the nation's investment for the future? Perhaps even more surprising was that, in the last quarter of the twentieth century, the fundamentals of the 1944 legislation remained the basis of state educational policy in England and Wales, reasserted by the 1988 Education Reform Act. What had contributed to the dissipation of earlier bitterness and anger?

The achievement of Archbishop Davidson in 1908 in gaining calm understanding and concurrence from Protestant Nonconformist leaders may be taken to show that in a different atmosphere agreement was possible. Perhaps by 1908 some of the more moderate Nonconformists had come to realize that, if they were not very careful, they were going to get what they had been asking for, and that it looked uncomfortably like a 'sell-out' to the militant secularists. The Anglicans had also appeared more accommodating during the 1918 Fisher Bill which, apart from planning to expand secondary and higher education opportunities,[2] hoped to remove the divisiveness of the dual system; but again, vociferous opposition throughout 1920 from Roman Catholics and Nonconformists forced the government to drop the proposals. The 1929 Labour government's progressive plans for 'secondary education for all' similarly foundered because of 'the vested interests of the Church of England and the Roman Catholics' (Barber, 1994, p. 2).

Following the Hadow reorganization,[3] the 1936 Education Act had allowed local authorities to contribute 50–75 per cent of the capital costs for new church secondary schools and had created a category of 'Special Agreement' schools whereby all teachers could be deemed 'reserved' and therefore appointed by denominational governors.[4] Nevertheless, the position of church schools was far from secured; the financial implications of secondary school expansion proved increasingly unrealistic and the raising of the school leaving age would mean restructuring their categories of 'infants' and 'seniors' schools. The 1941 'White Memorandum' even threatened to remove the 'single-school' areas, affecting large numbers of Anglican schools.

Then during the Second World War the threat of Nazism to the survival of Britain and the general crisis of humanity helped to concentrate the mind of the nation on its values, to which its Christian past was far from irrelevant. What were people fighting to preserve? The patriotic answer 'Britain' presupposed something further, namely the kind of freedom and mutual respect which the English religious tradition had a hand in forming. Accordingly in 1944 public discussion of educational policy in the future could not plausibly marginalize religious values. For many, no doubt, Christianity was the folk religion of social custom, a part of the British heritage. Secularism and materialism seemed an inadequate basis for the values and virtues required to deal with such external threats.[5] Many people in Britain felt that Christianity had been a major contributor to the liberal legal and political institutions of democracy as they understood it. At least for the Church of England mind, a centralized autocracy and dictatorship seemed repellent.

The White Paper of 1943 recorded the fact that a serious respect for the values which could be inculcated by good religious education was widespread in British society:

> There has been a very general wish, not confined to representatives of the Churches, that religious education should be given a more defined place in the life and work of the schools, springing from a desire to revive the spiritual and personal values in our society in our national tradition. (Educational Reconstruction, Cmd 6458, 1943 III, p. 36)

Similar views were expressed in *The Times* leader of 17 February 1940:

> More than ever before it has become clear that the healthy life of a

nation must be based on spiritual principles ... Christianity ... is not a philosophy but a historic religion which must dwindle unless the facts on which it is founded are taught, and such teaching made the centre of our educational system ... Education with religion omitted is not really education at all.[6]

THE ANGLICAN PERSPECTIVE

These sentiments were not altogether dissimilar from those being expressed by some Anglican church leaders of the time. In 1939 the ever-candid Herbert Hensley Henson had written:

> With characteristic lack of logic, the English people have hitherto refused to adopt the naked secularisation of the national system which democratic principle appears to require ... total absence of moral and religious teaching from the school curriculum is not thought by many eminent educational authorities consistent with the requirements of efficient education. (Henson, 1939, p. 197)

Never himself an enthusiast for the dual system, Henson was confident that if all education was entrusted to state schools, Christian teaching within the constraints of the Cowper-Temple clause would be effective in providing the religious education needed, with the advantage that denominational squabbles might be relegated to the lumber room of past history, and coherence in society would be increased.

However, William Temple, who became Archbishop of Canterbury in 1942,[7] was a forceful advocate of church schools (85 per cent of which were Anglican), while at the same time aware of the broader perspective demanded by a national system of education. He was conscious of the extent to which liberal democracy was dependent on Christianity; just as the Nazis had used education to develop a sense of common purpose, so Temple realized that the British schools should

> foster individual development on the one hand and world fellowship on the other ... There is only one candidate for this double function: it is Christianity. We must then take steps to ensure that the corporate life of the schools is Christian. (Temple, 1942, p. 93)[8]

The degree of consensus between national and church spokesmen had provided sufficient incentive for negotiations to begin in 1941

under Temple's predecessor at Canterbury, Cosmo Gordon Lang,
when an Anglican/Free Church deputation had put 'five points' on
religious education to Butler.[9] The Anglicans had two particular
problems, the on-going issue of the 'single-school' areas and the
implications of any rise in the school leaving age,[10] but discussions
were accelerated by more immediate practical considerations. There
was no avoiding the fact that the condition of voluntary school
buildings had reached crisis point. When R. A. Butler called Archbishop Temple to the Board of Education on 5 June 1942, he
presented him and the Bishop of Oxford with a horrifying catalogue
of statistics, showing that 399 out of 700 condemned school buildings, on the blacklist prepared some twenty years previously, were
Anglican schools. More than 90 per cent of voluntary school buildings antedated the 1902 Education Act, and yet the church
authorities could scarcely afford to repair or maintain more than a
few of them. William Temple took little convincing that such a
situation was untenable. But he had the unenviable task of persuading other weighty figures. As he wrote to Canon Tissington-Tatlow, 'I
was doing a rather elaborate egg-dance, and some of the eggs are
such as it is most important not to break, because the smell would be
awful' (Iremonger, 1948, p. 572).

Yet in 1943, when the White Paper on Educational Reconstruction
was published, Temple boldly told his Diocesan Conference (on 25
October) that it presented 'a glorious opportunity'; he acknowledged that, in single-school areas where all children had to attend
their local Anglican school, the Nonconformists had a grievance that
seemed justifiable; the government had recognized Anglican financial constraints and was generously offering 50 per cent of the cost
needed to bring voluntary schools up to standard. Temple was also
able to take the wider view:

> Above all, let us not give the impression that our concern as church
> people is only with the adjustment of the dual system: we ought as
> Christians to be concerned about the whole of educational pro-
> gress. I am quite sure that the raising of the school leaving age will
> of itself do more to make permanent the religious influence of the
> schools than anything that can be done with directly denomina-
> tional purpose. (*Ibid.*, p. 573)

This broader perspective expressed an optimism not shared by all
Anglicans. Some were determined that the Churches should retain
control of all their denominational schools, believing that a school's

religious ethos is more effective than any religious lesson; at the Church Assembly in 1942, Temple had a difficult task convincing the meeting to ratify the agreement negotiated with R. A. Butler which allowed LEAs to run church voluntary-controlled schools. Lord Selborne (1887–1971), who combined cabinet office with a prominent role in the Church Assembly, wrote at the time to Butler: 'After that debate I don't think Temple could possibly carry the Church in conceding anything else.'

The Nonconformists also had to be persuaded, though the issues were for them wholly different. They stood by the Cowper-Temple clause on non-denominational religious instruction in all state schools, insisting that its acceptance at primary level must be extended to all secondary schools. Their main grievance, however, remained the single-school areas, where the Church of England school was the only educational institution available to their children and, despite many meetings between the Churches over which Temple presided, no solution could be found. At the same time this disagreement was not enough to scupper the bill, an indication that co-operation and unity were a higher priority than traditional hostilities. The advantages to be gained by the expansion of state education and the guarantees on religious worship and instruction were too great to lose. As Temple wrote to the then Moderator of the Free Church Council, Dr R. D. Whitehorn of Westminster College, Cambridge, it was important that no heated controversy should 'lead to the withdrawal of the Bill, partly because the main reforms in the Bill are so urgently needed, partly because it would vastly increase the prospect of a purely secular solution' (*ibid.*, p. 576).

The Church negotiators were not the only people who had to 'watch their backs'. R. A. Butler's interest in bringing about reasonable educational reforms with a safeguard for the Church's proper concerns was not an enthusiasm shared by his Prime Minister. Indeed Winston Churchill, too well remembering the débâcle of 1902, vetoed a new Education Bill in 1941, and insisted that 'we cannot have party politics in wartime'. Nevertheless Butler persisted.[11] In *The Art of Memory*[12] he recalled that late one night, before the bill was actually published, Churchill summoned Butler to his office and introduced him to Lord Selborne and Lord Salisbury with the dry comment: 'I have asked you to meet your enemies in religious teaching'. To Churchill's surprise, the two lords – both pillars of the Church of England's laity – expressed their satisfaction that Butler had done all he could for the Church.

THE ROMAN CATHOLIC PERSPECTIVE

The Roman Catholics, however, were far from happy with the Bill's proposals.[13] The idea that the local authority would take control and fully maintain church schools with certain safeguards for denominational religious education was unacceptable. The alternative of 'aided' status where the Church retained control but only received a 50 per cent state grant for capital maintenance also caused anxiety, for the Church could not afford to keep up all its schools on this basis. Unlike the Anglicans, for whom the sense of boundary between church membership and citizenship could easily become blurred, the Roman Catholics were determined to adhere to Pius XI's principle of Catholic schools for all Catholic children, set out in the 1929 encyclical *Divini Illius Magistri.* Their rejection of the 'controlled' option may be traced back to this encyclical, which proclaimed:

> The mere fact that religious teaching is imparted in a school does not make it satisfy the rights of the Church and the family, nor render it fit to be attended by Catholic pupils. For this, the whole of the training and the teaching, the whole organisation of the school, teachers, curriculum, school books on all subjects, must be so impregnated with the Christian spirit under the guidance and motherly vigilance of the Church that religion comes to provide the foundation and culminating perfection of the whole training.

This was a list of requirements that could only be met in the independent sector or, assuming proper safeguards, in grant aided schools.[14] The Catholic 'atmosphere' was deemed more important than the school buildings.

When we remember that the negotiations for the 1944 legislation took place twenty years before the Second Vatican Council, at a time when the tone of that great assembly was quite unimaginable, it is perhaps not surprising to find a defensive and ghetto-like mentality prevailing. Certainly the feeling of 'minority interest' was found not only among Roman Catholics but among those who observed them from without. It is of interest that Bishop Hensley Henson, who was in favour of entrusting Anglican schools to the State, could write in 1939:

> Neither Roman Catholics nor Jews can be brought into any general system of general teaching, for both are minorities so largely alien in race and creed as to be properly accorded distinctive treatment ... denominationalism must remain a feature of national education. Roman Catholic and Jewish schools are genuinely denomin-

ational institutions, for they are only provided where there is a definite denominational demand to be satisfied, and their sharply distinctive character renders them unattractive to the general body of English people. (Henson, 1939, p. 201)

If such sentiments feel irretrievably dated, that is clear evidence of the reality of the ecumenical progress made possible by Vatican II. Henson was adamant that Roman Catholics, as

a highly specialised minority who have set a fence about themselves
... cannot rightly or prudently be allowed to prohibit a recognition in the State schools of the fundamental agreement with respect to Christian faith and morals which happily exists among the people. (*Ibid.*, p. 202)

R. A. Butler felt much the same, and had reason to be concerned that a vociferous minority could fatally rock a very fragile boat. In an Advent pastoral letter, the then Bishop of Hexham and Newcastle wrote: 'We shall have our Catholic schools where our Catholic children shall be educated in a Catholic atmosphere by Catholic teachers approved by a Catholic authority. We cannot surrender our schools.' And in May 1942 the Roman Catholic Archbishop of Liverpool, Dr Downey, said: 'We shall continue to struggle for our denominational schools even though we have to fight alone.'

However, it was not until September 1942 that Butler met the first formal Catholic delegation: 'It may be that the delay by this stage owed as much to design on Rab's part as to any procrastination on the part of the Cardinal-Archbishop' (Howard, 1987, p. 124). Cardinal Hinsley, Archbishop of Westminster,[15] argued for 100 per cent state funding for all Catholic schools (as in Scotland) and, in November 1942, wrote to *The Times* arguing that political parties which claimed to respect freedom of conscience and minority interests were honour-bound to accommodate the views of his Church.[16] The Roman Catholics owned 12 per cent of the voluntary schools and educated 8 per cent of the school population, but they well knew that they would have a difficult task in bringing their 6 per cent 'black-listed' schools up to the expected standard and in providing sufficient new schools to meet the growing demand.

Butler sensed that there was a weakness in their position: 'The only chink in their armour was that some of them feared that, if they became too defiant, I might exclude them completely from the public system' (1982, p. 153). At a difficult meeting[17] at Ushaw College, Durham, the Roman Catholic bishops insisted that the grant aid be raised to 75 or 80 per cent.[18] Butler realized that such concessions would alienate the Protestant Nonconformists and risk parliamentary defeat. He found the Roman Catholics difficult to deal with. The largely shared assumptions in support of educational reform between Anglicans and Nonconformists created a predisposition to an amicable atmosphere. This could not be presumed in negotiation with the Roman Catholics, a minority group whose long memory of persecution in England had given them a feeling of being embattled with their backs to the wall, but also an instinctive hope that one day, provided they were sufficiently uncompromising, they would see the Protestants off altogether. As Butler recalled, 'The Roman Catholics still wanted to act independently. There was no question of an alliance between them and the Church of England' (1971, p. 101).

Compromise with a secular government's plans for a common system of religious education was in Roman Catholic eyes suspect from the start, and this feeling that they must be seen to be combative affected the style of the negotiation. 'The pursuit of a separate Catholic school system and the emphasis on religious endogamy was a major mechanism by which the Catholic community maintained its group identity'.[19] Of Dr Downey it was reported to Butler that he was 'ambitious not only for celestial but also for terrestrial renown. He spoke quite fairly in private but appeared, as an Irishman, to enjoy a public fight' (*ibid.*, p. 105); Worlock described him as 'the soporous but reluctant interim leader of the hierarchy after Cardinal Hinsley's death' (1995, p. 21). Butler felt nettled and frustrated that, having successfully dealt with bitterly opposed religious groups in India and Palestine, he should be experiencing such difficulty in England: 'What hope there is lies in getting hold of them personally and assuring them of the sincerity and sympathy of one's approach' (1971, p. 102). His diaries reveal his sense of failure at not finding 'one man of dignity and reliability with whom one can perpetually be in touch on a personal basis' (Howard, 1987, p. 130). He considered that it was better to present the Roman Catholic leaders with a virtual *fait accompli* rather than go through the unrealistic pretence of negotiation (*ibid.*, p. 125).

The Roman Catholics did not wish to be drawn into any consensus, and had difficulty in making their position comprehensible. Barber even considered that it 'seemed to be part of the Catholics' tactics to be nebulous' (1994, p. 47). Whereas in the 1880s Anglicans and Roman Catholics had found themselves united against the Nonconformists, this time the Catholics were isolated. John Heenan, later himself to become Archbishop of Westminster, wrote in 1943:

> The English hostility to Catholic education is the result less of fear than of ignorance. Cardinal Hinsley's task was made the more difficult by reason of the well-known broadmindedness of the Church of England which, for several years, had been in the habit of handing over its schools in large towns, almost on demand, to the local authority ... The Cardinal found it difficult to persuade the authorities and the public that the Catholic attitude towards education is not fanatical. (1944, p. 132)

Responding to the White Paper in 1943, the hierarchy insisted, 'at no stage have we agreed to the financial conditions now made public ... Our people will stand united and determined in what to them is a matter of life and death' (*Education*, 3 September). Against such a background it was a remarkable gesture when Cardinal Bernard Griffin, the new Archbishop of Westminster appointed in December 1943 following Hinsley's death in March, attended the second reading of the bill on 19 January 1944 and the next day presented Butler with the eight-volume set of the *Lives of the Saints* by Alban Butler and Herbert Thurston, a work of considerable scholarship and a standard source for reference. Griffin himself had the unenviable task of trying to unite a Catholic hierarchy doubly split, north and south, Irish and English, while the government clearly preferred to deal with Roman Catholic members of the hereditary peerage such as Viscount FitzAlan (Worlock, 1995).

Nevertheless, the Roman Catholics did not feel in 1944 that they were being treated quite fairly and sensibly.[20] They were obviously right in forecasting the inadequacy of the 50 per cent grant to voluntary schools, and later the government had to concede an increase to 75 per cent in 1959, to 80 per cent in 1967, and to 85 per cent in 1975, 'giving what Catholics called, neither contemptuously nor ungraciously, instalments of justice'.[21] But at the time of the bill, such concessions would almost certainly have wrecked the only chance of 'settling the religious question' which, since 1870 and indeed earlier, had created so much bitterness.

THE FINAL SETTLEMENT

The Butler Act finally approved a national system of free primary, secondary and further education to be administered through the local authority and supported by the rates and central government grants. The school leaving age was to be raised to fifteen from 1947 onwards, and sixteen as soon as practicable (this was achieved only in 1970).[22] The dual system was to continue but to be modified by offering a choice of 'controlled' or 'aided' status to all voluntary schools. 'Controlled' meant that denominational instruction was guaranteed a specific place in the curriculum if requested by parents and would be taught by a 'reserved' teacher; otherwise religious education would be taught according to the local authority's agreed syllabus. The local authority would retain a two-thirds majority on the school's management committee and meet all the maintenance and improvement costs of the school building and plant, although the Church was guaranteed two places on the committee and would still own the site. By contrast, 'aided' status meant that the Church retained overall control, but would only receive a 50 per cent grant towards improvement expenditure, while the local authority met all the running costs. Because of the huge sums required for 'aided' status, the government evidently hoped and confidently expected most schools to choose the 'controlled' option.[23] Although Butler had to compromise his ambition to establish a single national system, he felt that the agreement he achieved on one publicly funded system was at least a substantial move in the right direction.

For the Anglicans the choice between 'controlled' or 'aided' status was a realistic one. Where financial resources permitted, aided schools could be set up.[24] But controlled schools also seemed to be a viable option, since denominational instruction was safeguarded; as Cruickshank commented, 'their character depended essentially on the vigour of the local clergyman, the loyalties of the teachers and the extent of Anglican influence over new appointments' (1963, p. 175). Even where local authorities had control of church schools, Anglicans were confident that the State would do nothing to undermine the rights of the national Church. Geoffrey Fisher, appointed Archbishop of Canterbury after the sudden death of William Temple in 1944, clearly preferred the 'aided' option for Anglican schools; he felt the Roman Catholics' demands for 100 per cent funding would 'at one blow destroy the settlement in Butler's Education Act' and 'reawaken all the old ecclesiastical squabbles'. He 'took a more realistic approach, namely that if the Church were to ask for 100 per cent for denominational schools, they might go altogether' (Carpenter, 1991, p. 431).[25]

The 1944 provision for religious education was particularly significant in that it was consistent with the Archbishop's 'five points' first put to Butler in 1941. The school day was to begin with a collective act of worship and, for the first time, every maintained school had to provide religious instruction according to a local agreed syllabus,[26] although parents' rights of withdrawal were safeguarded even in voluntary schools. The subject was to have equal status in the curriculum with other subjects and be taught at any time of the day. It was also open to inspection. Butler had been encouraged by the successful agreed syllabuses, such as that of Cambridgeshire (1924), locally negotiated between the wars. Addressing the World Conference of Faiths in June 1943, he emphasized that

> these are not intended to be a form of State religion but are the beginnings of the teaching in what I may call the literacy of faith ... This subject has given rise to more dissension than any other ... I beseech and implore leaders of religious life to approach the question of the future of Church schools and teaching in schools, so that it does not result in disagreement and faithlessness instead of faith.

The agreed syllabuses created a structure for religious education that required professional handling and, where LEAs took it seriously, by and large it stood the test of time, resulting in flexible and imaginative schemes of work.[27] The Protestant Nonconformists, led by Mr Garvie (Congregationalist) and Dr Scott Lidgett (Methodist), who had both been involved in the controversy of 1902, were undeviating in regarding the provision for undenominational instruction as a precondition of their agreement to co-operate. On the other side, the National Union of Teachers wished to be assured that no religious tests for teachers were going to be required, having had their proposal for a nationally agreed RE syllabus rejected by Temple and Butler.

Throughout the negotiations Butler was accompanied by his Parliamentary Secretary in the coalition government, James Chuter Ede, a socialist and Nonconformist whose early career had been as a teacher in Surrey elementary schools; his advice to Butler proved invaluable and invariably judicious. Said to have had 'a dour countenance which belied both his integrity and his true sense of humour',[28] Ede was old enough to remember Fisher's 1918 attempts at a religious settlement and the speed with which those hopes had been dashed and 'vividly recalled the three separate efforts ... to untangle the anomalies of the dual system' under Ramsay

MacDonald (Howard, 1987, p. 114).[29] He recognized that parents wanted children to have a 'grounding in the principles of the Christian faith as it ought to be practised in this country' (*Hansard,* 10 March 1944, 2425). Chuter Ede described the operation as a 'knife-edge with precipices on either side' (Butler, 1982, p. 160), but Butler recognized that 'it was when William Temple kissed Cowper-Temple that my settlement was found' (Cruickshank, 1963, p. vii).[30] Butler's and Ede's 'great success was to persuade both sides, by long and skilful diplomacy, to acquiesce' (Wallace, 1981, p. 289).

The fact that religious education was the subject of relatively few headlines and leading articles in the press during the early post-war period should not be taken as a reliable indicator of either change or the absence of it in county or church schools. The 1944 legislation was not without its problems, as Sutherland observed:

> The sophistication of the Act is political, ecclesiastical and economic. The lack of sophistication is theological and intellectual . . .
> The Butler Act held out the mistaken hope that the problems of theology and religion created by the extension of education could be solved by compulsory school worship and religious instruction for forty minutes each week. (Sutherland, 1986, pp. 38–9)

Certainly rumours of government intentions to repeal the clauses on compulsory religious education in the 1944 Act were enough to trigger cries of protest (e.g. *The Times* leader, 31 October 1984). Apprehension about upsetting the delicate balance may have ensured that controversy was minimized; nevertheless, the advance in secularization in the country[31] altered the context of the debate in the post-war period.

The Anglicans welcomed the government's proposals and at the 1948 Lambeth Conference the provisions for worship and religious instruction were commended. The Conference report also recognized the need for continued co-operation between Church and State in the furtherance of Christian education (No. 11 Report), a view shared by Archbishop Fisher (Carpenter, 1991, p. 432).

Once more, however, the Roman Catholics were far from happy with the compromise. While they were keen 'to promote educational progress within the national system', they were determined to retain control of their schools at all costs. In 1941 Cardinal Hinsley wrote:

> I dread the possibility of the Government assuming the mission committed by our Lord Jesus Christ to his apostles . . . If we consent to a united statement of doctrine, the Board of Education may well

say: 'The Dual System is unworkable and Catholic schools must go; we know now the minimum of religious teaching required by Christians and all schools must be content with that'. We have built up our schools at the cost of immense sacrifice amid our poverty. Now we must and will uphold them in their full religious character. Consequently we fear that any hint of our readiness to compromise on our religious principles would give the secularists in the government a handle for the abolition of our schools.[32] (Heenan, 1944, p. 148)

Ironically, Catholic intransigence led to just such a threat from the Nonconformists and the National Union of Teachers in 1943. The Catholics' distrust was not only of the State but also of majority Protestantism, which was regarded as essentially compromising with the secular spirit. In Roman Catholic eyes Protestants diluted the faith, lacking definitive statements on Marian dogma or the divine presence in the sacraments and a living teaching authority in the Roman primacy.

This standpoint explains Hinsley's sharp negations: 'Denominationalism is a bogus slogan. The undenominational teaching in the provided schools is Protestant and the Agreed Syllabuses are Protestant and so denominational' (*ibid.*, p. 130). Therefore the Roman Catholics had no choice but to opt for 'aided schools' where the distinctive 'sacred atmosphere' could pervade 'the hearts of teachers and scholars alike' (p. 141) and Catholic religious education be safeguarded. As Hastings noted, the Act 'raised them educationally without submerging them religiously' (1986, p. 422).

Relief that a general consensus had been achieved in relation to the problem of church schools and religious education meant that these thorny issues no longer preoccupied the minds of legislators and educationists in the next few years after 1945. They were rightly more concerned with the implementation of free secondary education for all children; with raising the school leaving age to fifteen and then sixteen; and with the introduction of the Certificate of Secondary Education (CSE) national examinations and 'comprehensivization' (cf. Circular 10/65). Interest in specifically religious questions was limited to raising the percentage grant for capital expenditure in voluntary-aided schools to more realistic levels[33] and testing the legality of progressive religious education agreed syllabuses.[34]

The Churches' preoccupations were, for the Anglicans, managing the large number of small (mainly rural) schools[35] and, for the

Roman Catholics, building sufficient new urban schools for their rising population.[36] Both had difficulty meeting the requirements of new building regulations (e.g. for assembly halls and specialist workshops).[37] Yet a more coherent and realistic Roman Catholic education policy was developing under the leadership of Bishop Beck of Salford, recognizing, for example, the need for the Catholic community to contribute to their schools' upkeep (*TES*, 15 July 1957). Anglicans also were prepared to allow Free Church representatives on to school governing bodies in single-school areas. By 1959, the Church of England had reduced its share of schools by 10 per cent and Roman Catholic schools had increased by about 25 per cent to meet the needs of their rising pupil numbers; this left 13 per cent of the nation's children being educated in Anglican schools and 8 per cent in Catholic schools (Cruickshank, 1963, p. 174).

The main denominations also continued to invest in teacher training colleges to provide staff for church or county schools, considering that this investment would lead to effective Christian influence in all schools. Between 1947 and 1969 the number of students in church colleges more than trebled from 6000 to 19,000, alongside the government's post-war 'emergency training' expansion of the local authority colleges. The Churches wanted to offer something distinctively Christian, and not just in training for religious education. Bishop Bell, then Chairman of Governors at Bishop Otter College in Chichester, wrote in the college magazine in June 1946:

> its distinctive atmosphere is most clearly seen in its possession of a chapel, with a Church of England chaplain as its minister, ready at all times to help all members of the college, irrespective of creed, by teaching or counsel or fellowship.[38]

However, following the 1972 White Paper proposals in *A Framework for Expansion*, the James Report *Teacher Education and Training* and DES Circular 7/73, the 51 church colleges were faced with major reorganization as the government sought to rationalize provision and link teacher training into higher education validation structures. By 1985 only 22 of them remained; of those, only 9 of the 12 Anglican institutions remained free-standing and many others had merged, often into ecumenical partnerships.

CONCLUSION

We have seen in this chapter that the debates involving Church and State in education up to 1944 focused primarily on the appropriateness of specific denominational teaching in schools funded by the tax-payer. The difficulties in defining a non-denominational religious education for state-controlled schools resulted in serious political upheaval and created a legacy of distrust in Church/State relations. This sense of unease was exacerbated by the tensions arising from the Churches' demands for just and equitable funding for their own schools, many of which predated any secular provision.

Yet the compromise of the 'dual system' tied both Church and State into a vital partnership in educating the nation's children. Neither side could easily walk away from the other, even when the pressure exerted by individual factions among denominational groups and political parties threatened to tear it apart. The government found it needed to concede financial support, particularly as aided schools developed after 1944: 'it had been deliberately intended that conviction and self-sacrifice rather than past benevolence should be the criteria of their existence. In the event, the strain had exceeded all war-time estimates and had necessitated a measure of alleviation' (Cruickshank, 1963, p. 177).

We have seen how the Churches' negotiating position was often undermined by denominational rivalries throughout this period. While the secularist desire to eliminate religious education from all schools might be resisted, the opportunities afforded by the post-1988 legislation to strengthen RE's infrastructure still risk being undermined by a lack of consensus among its proponents. As we move into the twenty-first century, it becomes of the first importance to ask whether the ecclesial bodies in England, which constitute the great majority of practising Christians, can or cannot come closer together in a common approach to their church schools and religious education, putting behind them the antagonisms and defensiveness of the past and creating a formidable alliance in education which a future government dare not ignore.

NOTES

1 C. K. Francis Brown noted that the Anglican Church had a 'magnificent record . . .
of clerical effort and self-denial for the sake of the elementary education of their
country's children' (1942, p. 126).

2 The 1918 Fisher Education Act raised the school leaving age to the term when a
child became fourteen.

3 The 1926 Hadow Report on *The Education of the Adolescent* recommended a three-
tier structure for post-primary education to at least age fifteen (grammar, modern
and junior technical) to replace the all-age elementary schools.

4 Lowndes described this as 'the first modest fissure since 1902 in the outworn
"dual system" ' (1969, 2nd edition) *The Silent Social Revolution* (Oxford: OUP),
p. 220.

5 For further analysis of this debate, see K. Robbins (1985) 'Britain, 1940 and
Christian Civilization', in *History, Society and the Churches*, eds D. Beales and G. Best
(CUP). Such views were not dissimilar from those expressed in the 1987–8
debates, e.g. Baroness Cox: 'All we are trying to do is ensure that our children have
the opportunity to become familiar with the Christian heritage of our country'
(*Hansard*, 16 May 1988, House of Lords 13).

6 This article, entitled 'Religion and National Life', had also revealed that over half
the grown-up children evacuated from English towns had no idea whose birth was
celebrated on Christmas Day. John Heenan, in his biography of Cardinal Hinsley,
commented that the Cardinal was very disturbed by the article, which strengthened his resolve to defend Roman Catholic schools (1944, pp. 215–16).

7 Churchill was not over-impressed with the possible choices for archbishop. He was
said to have described Temple as 'a half crown in a penny bazaar'.

8 Temple's Christian understanding of democracy was of equality before God and
the law, the very Christian notion of the consensus of the faithful imparting and
recognizing authority in the community's leaders, in whose election they had a
say.

9 Butler's Parliamentary Secretary, the Nonconformist James Chuter Ede, recorded
in his diaries (15 August) that Butler had even asked him on the day of the
meeting, 'What is an elementary school?'

10 If it were raised from fourteen, creating compulsory secondary education for all,
the Anglican all-age elementary school would have to end at eleven and the
Churches would have difficulty offering secondary provision.

11 'Having viewed the milk and honey from the top of Pisgah, I was damned if I was
going to die in the land of Moab. Basing myself on long experience of Churchill

over the India Bill, I decided to disregard what he said and go straight ahead' (1971, *The Art of the Possible* (London: Hamish Hamilton), p. 95). The political gamble paid off and Butler managed to steer his Bill through.

12 1982, p. 163.

13 The negotiations between the Churches and the government over the White Paper and the Education Bill 1943–4 were described by John Davies in 'L'Art du possible', in *Recusant History* (Catholic Record Office), October 1994.

14 It is interesting to note that Roman Catholic schools have an additional dimension: while some come under diocesan authority, others (both independent and grant-aided) fall under the jurisdiction of particular religious orders, and many of these long predate the 'dual system'.

15 Derek Worlock, then Private Secretary to the Archbishop of Westminster and later himself to be Archbishop of Liverpool, described Arthur Hinsley as 'a great old Yorkshireman ... whose thundering war-time broadcasts had made him a national hero' (*Briefing* Education Special, June 1995, p. 20).

16 R. A. Butler recalled how Churchill cut this letter out, stuck it on cardboard and sent it round to him saying 'There you are, fixed, old cock' (1982, p. 159).

17 R. A. Butler recalls that 'the Roman Catholic bishops made no attempt to control their supporters, believing that their anxieties justified them in encouraging a fuss' (1971, p. 107).

18 The same request was made later by William Temple in the House of Lords on 4 August 1943, which threatened to forge a new alliance between Anglicans and Roman Catholics, leaving the Free Churches resentful and isolated.

19 T. McLaughlin, J. O'Keefe and B. O'Keeffe (1996) *The Contemporary Catholic School: context, identity and diversity* (London: Falmer), p. 5.

20 'We shall never accept the Bill as it now stands', they declared on 4 January. Such entrenched opposition was mitigated in February after Butler offered long-term loans to improve school buildings: the government estimated Catholic liabilities as almost £10m. Worlock thought 'that under protest they did accept that the new provision should not be fought beyond the brink' (Worlock, 1995, p. 23).

21 Cardinal Heenan's autobiography (1971) *Not the Whole Truth* (Hodder & Stoughton), p. 265.

22 Temple had called for the raising of the school leaving age to sixteen as long ago as 1924, in his opening speech to the Anglican Conference on Politics, Education and Citizenship (COPEC).

23 'For the plan to succeed Anglican schools would have to opt for controlled status in large numbers' (Butler, 1971, p. 101). Chuter Ede, Butler's Parliamentary

Private Secretary, thought that only some 500 out of 9000 would elect for 'aided' status (K. Jefferys (1987) *Diary of Chuter Ede*, 16 September 1942).

24 To the surprise of both Butler and Temple, over 3000 of the 9000 Anglican schools opted for aided status, particularly in Lancashire and London: the Bishop of Blackburn, Wilfred Askwith, insisted that church schools could only retain their distinctiveness by aided status. By 1959, 4500 Anglican schools nationally had controlled status, about three-fifths of the total number. As recently as 1983, the diocese of Southwark took legal action against a vicar who, as chairman of governors of a small aided Anglican secondary school, negotiated with Lambeth LEA to become 'controlled' in order to expand the pupil roll and ensure the school's future viability.

25 Interestingly, the English Dominicans were the only Catholics to share his caution: 'Catholics will do well to console or fortify themselves by considering the disadvantages which would have accompanied the 100 per cent if we got it. The buildings would not belong to us ... Also every denomination that could get enough parents to sign a requisition would be able to get a school' (Lowndes, 1969, p. 247).

26 Butler had early on dropped a proposal to remove the Cowper-Temple clause from the Bill (1971, p. 99), but this 1870 clause had only guaranteed non-denominational religious instruction in local authorities who chose to provide it (although most did). Temple recognized that the bill 'writes religion into national education in a way which has never been done before' (*Hansard*, 5th Series, cxxxii, 37, 6 June 1944).

27 The agreed syllabus framework was even strengthened by more recent legislation in 1988 and 1993 and, after extensive consultation with representatives of the Churches and other faiths, nationally agreed RE 'model syllabuses' were published in July 1994.

28 Worlock, 1995, p. 22.

29 Chuter Ede (1882–1965) was given his first ministerial post by Butler; he became famous as Home Secretary (1945–51) when capital punishment was being debated, and was made a life peer a few months before his death (see Chuter Ede's diaries 1941–45, K. Jefferys (ed.), 1987).

30 Butler was asked by Temple if he was starting a 'state religion' based on the agreed syllabuses, just as Birrell had been accused of starting a new creed of 'Birreligion' through his 1906 Bill.

31 Deplored by Archbishop Fisher: 'We are becoming not better but worse educated ... out of it all comes nothing of faith and practice worth living by' (Carpenter, 1991, p. 439).

32 Such views have more recently had a remarkable echo in Cardinal Hume's opposition to the 1988 Act, whose 'opting out' proposals threaten the 'very provision of Catholic voluntary education' (*The Times*, 13 January 1988).

33 Following the 1959 negotiations, Archbishop Fisher congratulated Bishop Stopford, Chairman of the Anglican Board of Education: 'You have delivered the Churches and the Political Parties from a miserable and unedifying renewal of conflict' (letter quoted in R. Holtby (1986) 'Duality: the National Society 1934–1986', in J. Yates (ed.) *Faith in the Future* (London: National Society), p. 32).

34 E.g. when the inclusion of Marxism and Humanism in Birmingham's 1976 syllabus handbook caused public outcry.

35 A government report in 1953 (Cmnd 9155) reported that over 1000 uneconomic village schools had closed in the previous decade, the majority of which were Anglican; Butler called it 'the slaughter of the innocents'. In 1959 another revealed that almost 4000 Anglican schools had fewer than 100 pupils (Cmnd 1088); the average size of Anglican schools was 111 (mainly rural), of Roman Catholic schools 261 (mainly urban) and of county schools 283 (Cruickshank, 1963, p. 175).

36 By the mid 1960s only 60 per cent of Catholic pupils had access to a Catholic school. In 1963 the Catholic Education Council sent a memorandum to the Minister of Education expressing concern about overcrowded classes and shortage of Catholic teachers. In January 1965 Bishop Beck (Chairman of the Council) reiterated the claim for 100 per cent government funding (to meet the costs of comprehensive reorganization) and again in 1976 when the direct grant was abolished (one third of RC schools were direct grant and could not afford independent status). At their peak in 1974, Catholic schools were educating about half a million primary-age children and well over 350,000 secondary pupils.

37 By 1954 church school building programmes were barely underway, leaving over 200,000 senior pupils still in all-age schools; Circular 283 applied pressure by requiring managers to complete reorganization within a fixed time. But the 1958 White Paper recognized that the Churches would need more financial support and the 1959 Act raised the grant to 75 per cent for both new and existing aided secondary schools. Even then, some Anglicans sided with the Nonconformists in objecting to funding for new Roman Catholic schools (letter to *The Times*, 23 January 1959).

38 Quoted in G. P. Macgregor (1981) *Bishop Otter College and Policy for Teacher Education 1839–1980* (London: Pembridge Press), p. 178.

3

THE PARTNERSHIP BETWEEN CHURCH
AND STATE IN EDUCATION SINCE 1944

INTRODUCTION

The English school is unique in operating within a fine balance between political, church, community, parental and professional interests. The school is 'maintained' through that balance and its effectiveness might be measured by the way in which the contribution of each interest is accredited and valued. (Waddington 1984, p. 14)

The concept of 'partnership' formed the basis of R. A. Butler's 1944 proposals for a viable maintained system of primary and secondary education, ensuring educational opportunities for all classes and conditions of society and guaranteeing the universalist vision of 'One Nation' working together for a better future. The national system, locally administered, provided for consultation with teachers and parents as essential partners in the enterprise and with the Churches, other voluntary bodies and key organizations, in the effective implementation of the dual system.

The Ministry of Education would be the benevolent provider, grant maker and co-ordinator. The Local Education Authority would plan and provide, offering a framework of development, and itself delegating much to the head and staff of individual schools, through the intermediary agency of managing and governing bodies. Teachers accountable to the LEAs became accountable for the quality of the teaching and ethos of the school to individual parents and the children themselves. The role of parents as the primary educators was to be acknowledged by a close relationship between home and school; parents were accredited, if non-professional, partners ... The Churches would now play their part, exert an influence and, it was hoped, assist in growth and consolidation. (*Ibid.*, p. 13)

How far can it be said that the balancing act between the partners has been successful? Between 1944 and 1988, relationships were at times uneasy, if not strained, but the tensions were not felt to be destructive. However, the legislation, particularly from 1988, raised important questions about the future role of each partner in the education service and, in considering the involvement of both Anglican and Roman Catholic Churches in education, some analysis of the consequent changes is necessary and appropriate. This chapter traces a tentative but noticeable convergence of view about the purpose of church schools between Anglican and Roman Catholic authorities, which may have further consequences for fostering ecumenical co-operation, while being in some part the fruit of a greater mutual confidence already achieved.

Since 1944, church schools have had close links with arms of central government, particularly since the DES, now DFEE,[1] was responsible for 85 per cent of their capital funding. At the same time they were maintained by their local education authorities (LEAs) on whom they were largely dependent for professional support. In addition, they were part of their diocesan community, attracting the interest of the bishop and his diocesan officers. Such complex and interwoven relationships with their partners in the education service have always created both difficulties and constructive opportunities for Anglican and Roman Catholic church schools. As Archdeacon Mayfield commented in 1963, 'A partnership, in terms undreamed of only twenty-five years ago, has been set up between Church and State; it penetrates the whole field of education' (p. 172).

Yet the Education Acts of 1980, 1986, 1988, 1992, 1993, 1994 and 1996 involved changes which were far more than peripheral or cosmetic, not only to the content of the curriculum but also to the accountability and management structures within the education service.

Margaret Thatcher's 1979 government had removed the obligation on local authorities (under Circular 10/65) to replace grammar with comprehensive schools and had introduced the Assisted Places scheme to enable talented children from poorer backgrounds to attend private schools. Keith Joseph had been made Secretary of State for Education in September 1981, with a brief to undermine the 'anti-enterprise culture' of the DES (Thatcher, 1993, p. 151). He advocated new curriculum guidelines and changes in teacher training, creating the Council for the Accreditation of Teacher Education in 1984;[2] but, despite the Prime Minister's encouragement for them, he recognized the political inexpediency of introducing education vouchers (*ibid.*, p. 591), particularly during a period of considerable teacher unrest.[3] In the May 1986 Cabinet reshuffle, Joseph's mantle fell on Kenneth Baker,[4] who recalled Thatcher's words: 'there are lots of problems which I want you to sort out' (Baker, 1993, p. 161).

Following Mrs Thatcher's 1987 election victory, the Conservative government's legislative programme gathered momentum,[5] (chiefly developed by Brian Griffiths, head of her Policy Unit and based on the principles of 'standards' and 'choice', giving much greater autonomy to school governors in the management of their schools, whether county, voluntary-aided or controlled. They could admit as many pupils as they wished (up to the limit of their 1979 'standard number' approved by the DES) without being restricted by LEA policy. They had control of their own budgets – although the choices between expenditure on additional staffing, computers, or classroom redecoration were no less difficult for them than they used to be for LEAs. They were even able to 'opt out' entirely from local authority control with the endorsement of parental ballot and draw on 100 per cent central government funding by adopting 'grant-maintained' status (GMS).[6]

Schools like the new City Technology Colleges (CTCs)

> were the first challenge to the LEA's monopoly of free education . . .
> Although the Roman Catholic Church frowned upon CTCs, we
> found they were quite willing to realise the capital values of closed
> schools by considering their sale to the CTC Trust. (Baker, 1993,
> pp. 181, 185).

In 1989, the Anglican diocesan board in Southwark agreed to sponsor the first Church of England City Technology College in the Surrey Docklands redevelopment, despite the public outcry that the Church was being tainted by involvement in an élitist policy, providing facilities to which not all pupils were entitled (*Observer*, 29 January; *Church Times*, 3/10 March 1989). Later 'technology schools' were encouraged to introduce specializations, admitting up to 10 per cent of pupils with aptitude in, for example, technology, languages or music. Baker commented that CTCs 'incorporated many of the changes I wanted to introduce into the whole system – parental choice, per capita funding, local managerial control and independence' (*ibid.*, p. 187).

With so many policy initiatives, it was not surprising that the detailed implications were not fully worked out[7] – which was even admitted by Thatcher (1993, p. 579) – and the longer term effects of such major changes only gradually became clearer.

However, in marked contrast to these policies for increasing local school autonomy and parental choice, there was one area of education which the government reclaimed for itself, namely, control of the curriculum and pupil assessment. The development of the National Curriculum, which prescribed programmes of study and attainment targets for pupils from the ages of 5 to 16, established centralized control over what was to be taught in the nation's schools and how it was to be monitored.[8] Only one subject, religious education, had to be taught according to a locally agreed syllabus, a framework already established by the 1944 Education Act, in which the Churches retained an active and lively interest.[9]

The government's declared intention in these legislative changes was to make radical alterations in the balance of power between central and local government. Thatcher intended to 'curb what were often the corrupt and wasteful activities of local government' (Thatcher, 1993, p. 39). Peter Hennessy argued that 'to cope with Mrs Thatcher in full trajectory did require a very quick, very tough and very high-level form of counterballistics of which few were capable'; as Ian Gilmour recalled, 'Her belief that dialogue was a waste of time rather than a means of arriving at an agreed course of action was part of her rejection of consensus politics'.[10] Thatcher herself recalled the culture shock in a 'self-righteously Socialist' DES more accustomed to a consultative style (Thatcher, 1995, pp. 165–6). She thought that, once most schools had chosen GMS, LEAs would be left 'with a monitoring and advisory role – perhaps in the long term not even that' (Thatcher, 1993, p. 597).

Intended primarily as a political strategy to reduce local control, this policy had, however, unforeseen repercussions for another 'forgotten' partner in the education service, namely the Churches.[11] As Bishop Michael Adie later regretted, '"partnership" seems to have slipped out of the Government vocabulary' (Adie, 1990a). The government was strangely disconcerted and even taken aback by the cries of dissatisfaction from both Anglicans and Roman Catholics, which drew attention to the fundamental changes in the partnership between Church and State in relation to church schools brought about by the new legislation. Just as Kenneth Baker appeared reluctant to be drawn into the issue of religious education in the proposals for the National Curriculum, so also it seemed that he had neither

anti pated nor fully considered the 'knock-on' effects for the rela-
between the Churches and central government: 'I am
d that the Churches should criticise this extension of choice',
he commented in *The Times* (1 February 1988).

However, a confidential written report following a Carlton Club
seminar on 31 January 1991, which was highly influential in Conservative educational policy-making, explicitly criticized the
excessive influence of the Churches' diocesan education committees. John Patten as Secretary of State later tried to dismiss this
opinion as 'unrepresentative' (*Church Times*, 30 October 1992), but
seminar participants included the then Chairman of the Conservative Party, the Parliamentary Under-Secretary of State for Education
and the Chairman of the Education Select Committee.

Nevertheless, as both Anglican and Roman Catholic authorities
struggled to assess the likely implications and consequences of the
legislation, they found themselves increasingly arguing from the
same general standpoint, particularly over the issues of 'grant-
maintained' status and religious education. This ecumenical alliance
created a determined and potent lobby, notably in the House of
Lords which, in the debates on the 1988 bill, found itself in the
position of being almost the only effective critical opposition. The
government found it disadvantageous to 'cross swords' with so many
among whom it might have expected on other matters to find friends
but who, with a substantial majority, proved a formidable opponent.
The shared concern for the Church's involvement in education also
highlighted the extent to which the Churches were developing an
increasingly common perspective on the value and purpose of
church schools, offering marked contrast to the divided factions that
had dogged the debates of 1902 and 1944. The antagonisms, far
from being born of distrust between separated Churches, seemed on
this occasion to be between Church and State. Accordingly, the
following chapter attempts to explore the network of relationships
affecting church schools and their partners in both Church and
State, tracing the development in these relationships and the changes brought about by recent legislation, in particular the policy of
grant-maintained status.

PARTNERSHIP WITH CENTRAL GOVERNMENT

The Department of Education and Science had traditionally left to
the teachers the responsibility for school organization, classroom

practice and curriculum content, while it provided central funding for salaries through the local authority and inspectorial support through Her Majesty's Inspectorate. Such delegation of responsibility came under fire in the late 1970s and 1980s for a number of reasons: criticism was voiced by industry that schools were not turning out skilled young people for the labour market,[12] by the Treasury that there seemed to be little accountability despite the vast expenditure on education, by the media that standards of morality and discipline were deteriorating in schools and therefore in society, and by government officials who felt that the 'secret garden' of the curriculum should be opened up to closer public scrutiny. The Great Debate, launched by James Callaghan's Ruskin College speech in 1976, heralded a major shift in the structure of accountability in education.

The 1977 recommendations of the Taylor Report (*A New Partnership for Our Schools*), incorporated into the 1980 Act, extended representation on school governing bodies to include teachers and parents, and also allocated a place for a representative from industry or further education; in the process, however, it removed the right of the Churches to appoint two-thirds of the governing body in an aided school. The Labour government had previously promised the Churches that it would not allow the Taylor Committee to consider aspects of voluntary-aided schools' governance which would affect their voluntary character (Sallis, 1977). In 1979 the Churches lobbied to ensure that foundation governors still retained overall control in aided schools after the 1980 Act, with the result that, unlike county schools where two parents are elected, in aided schools one of the two parent governors is appointed by the foundation trustees.[13] The 1986 Education (No. 2) Act further revised the instruments of government of controlled schools, even allowing them the option of (re)gaining aided status, and required all governors to hold an annual meeting to report to parents.

The establishment of the Assessment of Performance Unit in 1984 began to provide the DES with valuable statistical data to monitor standards across the country. The curriculum debate progressed from HMI's identification of nine 'areas of experience' (*Curriculum 11–16*, 1977), through the DES's more subject-specific core curriculum proposals (*The School Curriculum*, 1981) to the National Curriculum of three core and seven foundation subjects, plus RE, enshrined in the 1988 Education Reform Act.[14] Meanwhile the teacher-dominated Schools Council, whose curriculum materials

erally well respected by classroom practitioners, was
in 1984 by the more centrally accountable Curriculum
ent Council, whose role was then overtaken by the govern-
‑‑‑‑‑‑‑‑ational Curriculum Council (NCC). Meanwhile a new body,
the Schools Examination and Assessment Council (SEAC), was created to control the public examination system. Baker had been
sensitive to the argument that the government was centralizing: 'by
creating two bodies, we were trying to draw upon wider voices outside
the DES ... There was a lot of intellectual cohabitation between the
department and the education system' (*TES*, 31 May 1996).

However, under his later successor Kenneth Clarke, the respected
educationists and chairmen Duncan Graham of NCC and Philip
Halsey of SEAC were summarily removed in July 1991 and replaced
respectively by an executive from British Petroleum, David Pascall,
and Brian Griffiths of Thatcher's Policy Unit, both members of the
Anglican congregation at St James's Church, Muswell Hill – perhaps
the Churches had more influence than they realized. *The Times*
leader noted these as 'political appointments which bypass the
educational establishment ... [The Secretary of State] is seeking to
rectify an unbalanced set of relationships ... in the only way this
government knows how, which is to accrete more power to the
centre' (19 July 1991). By 1994, both the NCC and SEAC were
subsumed into the School Curriculum and Assessment Authority
under Sir Ron Dearing, then the chairman of the Post Office.

As pupil rolls fell in the late 1970s, teacher training provision was
also rationalized, resulting in the closure of smaller colleges, many of
which were church foundations with particular interest in providing
staff for church schools; the DES no longer felt it needed to take into
account the denominational factor in teacher education (cf. Catholic Education Council Report, 1983). By the 1980s, areas for
in-service training were centrally specified through the education
support grant allocated to local authorities and the long established
role of Her Majesty's Inspectorate was in 1992 absorbed into a more
market-oriented inspectoral framework run by OFSTED (the Office
for Standards in Education).

The unquestionable shift towards greater central direction and
control had a marked effect on the balance of the 1944 partnership,
increasing the influence of central government over a wide range of
issues that had hitherto been the domain of professional teacher
organizations and local education committees. Appointed as Thatcher's Secretary of State for Education when John MacGregor was

removed after 'listening too much to the teachers', Kenneth Clarke claimed he was not a centralizer but admitted that he would need more power 'to control quality, raise standards and direct overall policy ... Like Mrs Thatcher, he was prepared to grant local autonomy only so long as he could retain (and centralize) power in his own hands'.[15] Fletcher acknowledged that 'Education is no longer a partnership of providers. What is evident now is an attempt to have local education authorities controlled by ministers, central bureaucrats, quangos[16] and consumer choice' (1994, p. 73).

While this shift to the centre is easily discernible at one level,[17] at another the picture is not so clear. Mrs Thatcher's government appeared keen to take control of the curriculum and assessment but less happy to keep hold of the purse strings, thereby seeming to reverse previous roles.[18] Whereas previously schools had very limited control over their budgets, from 1990 under the Local Management of Schools (LMS) they had a considerable say in the allocation of their resources. Sceptics might argue that the government could then redirect any blame to schools rather than itself for the underfunding of education, but its failure to fund the teachers' salary increase recommended by an independent Review Body in 1994 brought governors and parents on to the streets in protest.[19]

The expectation that schools would raise their own supplementary funds was encouraged,[20] implicitly by the inclusion, for example, of 'Gifts received' in the annual governors' report to parents (required from 1986 onwards), and explicitly by the introduction of the 'Technology Schools Initiative' in 1994 (whereby government agreed to 'matched' funding if £100,000 was raised by local commercial sponsorship for a particular school). The Southwark diocesan board published new guidelines on sponsorship for its schools in March 1996, but the controversial announcement in May 1996 that British American Tobacco was to sponsor an Anglican voluntary-aided comprehensive in that diocese prompted its MP and Liberal Democrat health spokesman, Simon Hughes (himself an Anglican), to comment: 'It is as near to prostitution as you can get in the management of secondary schools' (*TES*, 24 May 1996). Meanwhile, in 1995, when the government announced its 'Private Finance Initiative', the Anglican Board of Education's Schools' Officer (speaking at the Anglican Secondary Heads' Conference in September) recalled the DFE's surprise when he pointed out that aided schools had been providing private finance for years through their voluntary contributions. The government's move towards greater

control through the National Curriculum might seemingly be coun-
terbalanced by its insistence on the delegation of financial
resources.

Where did these changes in central policy leave church schools?
Throughout the debates on the Education Bill in 1988, the government seemed to hold up the voluntary sector as a model for the
county schools of the future. Three characteristics were highlighted
by Alastair Burt, the Secretary of State's Parliamentary Private Secretary, at a conference in November 1987 organized by the Culham
College Institute: namely, a degree of independence from local
authorities, some financial responsibility for its own affairs, and the
ability to respond to parental choice. He continued:

> The government's proposals should be very acceptable to you. The
> grant-maintained school will be, as the Church school, a free
> school. It will have independence from the local authority and a
> large measure of control over the handling of its own affairs ... We
> believe it is precisely because independence, responsibility, and
> choice have been at the heart of the *raison d'être* of Church schools
> that they have had a popular existence in the state system. If this
> independence is important for your schools and if it provides a
> useful option for your existing schools, why then should it not be
> extended? (Culham College Institute (1987) *The Way Ahead?*)

The resounding criticisms from both Anglican and Roman Catholic
educationists concerning the legislation clearly dismayed and seemingly mystified government officials, who expressed surprise that
church schools should be so hostile to the extension of their 'privileges' to all schools.[21] Yet such criticism emanated not from anxiety at
the extension of 'privilege' but from concern in the Church that the
established partnership of Church and State in education, strongly
defended since 1944, was now being undermined. The unequivocal
reduction of local authority influence on curricular policies, funding
priorities and the management of school rolls could not pass without
protest from church authorities who had long worked closely, if not
invariably easily, with local government.[22] Particularly for those
Anglicans who had traditionally placed emphasis on the role of
church schools as part of the local community, such developments
were generally unwelcome. An educational philosophy which
seemed to encourage 'survival of the fittest' at the expense of others,
and to view parents as consumers rather than partners, was profoundly disturbing to many who envisaged the Christian presence in
education as one of reconciliation and service in the community and

did not see market forces as providing the overarching motive to create a happy and prosperous society.[23]

If the Anglican authorities welcomed the diversity created by church schools in 'warning the nation off a monolithic, politically directed education system' (Waddington, 1984, p. 27), they did not bargain for a diversity that could lead to 'isolated, isolationist fragmented units' outside any clear diocesan framework (cf. Geoffrey Duncan at the Culham Conference, November 1987). Baker recalled,

> When it came to the Church of England, the person I dealt with was Graham Leonard, the Bishop of London. I enjoyed our relationship since we are both High Anglicans, though at times the advice Graham received was, I thought, neither High nor particularly Anglican. The Church of England, like the Catholic Church, was opposed to grant-maintained schools, though its arguments were not quite so classy. (Baker, 1993, p. 218)

The Roman Catholic bishops argued that schools had

> enjoyed the right to determine the complete school curriculum in the light of their understanding that the educational process should serve and nurture the whole person. The proposed Bill takes away that right ... In practice this means that the Secretary of State and his advisers have the last word on what shall be taught in Catholic schools, even if this conflicts with the ideals and practices of Catholic education. (Bishops' Conference of England and Wales, 1987, p. 11)

The bishops failed in their attempt to persuade the government to allow their schools exemption from the National Curriculum (similar to that for CTCs and independent schools). Their complaints about religious education being marginalized rather than at the 'core of the core curriculum' also fell on deaf ears. As James Arthur concluded, 'Voluntary-aided schools have simply had their right to determine their own curriculum removed in favour of central control'.[24]

However, it was the issues of pupil admissions and trustees' control which most exercised the Roman Catholic hierarchy. The 1986 Education (No. 2) Act had already required governors of aided schools to consult their LEAs over admissions policies, but the 1988 Act proposals went further. Under the government's policy of increasing parental choice by allowing schools to admit pupils up to their 1979 'standard number', a Catholic school could lose the right to limit entry to non-Catholic pupils in order to preserve its religious ethos; if a parent appealed unsuccessfully to the LEA, the matter could be referred to the Secretary of State, whose ultimate jurisdiction might not be in sympathy with the philosophy and practice of Catholic education.

The issue of trustees' control was even more contentious. The bishop as trustee of his diocesan schools (although not those run by religious orders) appointed foundation governors as episcopal representatives to have 'oversight' of the schools' Catholic character. In the negotiations for the 1988 Education Reform Act, Cardinal Hume argued unsuccessfully that the trustees should have the right to veto a Catholic school's proposal to adopt 'grant-maintained status' if it was considered to be disadvantageous to other Catholic schools in the area (*The Times*, 13 January 1988). There was also understandable concern that the trustees (even if opposed to GMS) would remain liable for any debts or loans outstanding once a church school 'opted out', or for compensation due to the Secretary of State for any capital grants if the grant-maintained (GM) school subsequently closed. Nevertheless, under the Act, the trustees retained the right to appoint the majority of governors to denominational GM schools, even if they had no guarantee of the latter's compliance with the bishop's wishes. The Catholic Education Service (CES) expressed its concern that 'the trustees are required by law to nominate the foundation governors of a proposed grant-maintained school which is currently a voluntary school, even though they object to the proposed change of status' (CES, 1989, p. iii).

Cardinal Hume strongly objected to GMS, as it undermined the relationship between the bishop and his flock by removing his apostolic authority (received from St Peter) to have the final say on the control of Catholic schools. Kenneth Baker recalled in his memoirs:

> I was conscious that I was not dealing merely with a local authority, or merely a trade union, or even the British Cabinet, but with one of the great and enduring institutions of Western civilization ... [Hume] conveys a sense of holiness, kindliness and courtesy, and it is not easy to argue with such a saintly man. But within that scarlet and purple apparition was the sinewy force of a prelate concerned with temporal as well as spiritual power ... The Cardinal in effect was arguing that all Catholic schools should be excluded from the provisions of the Government's legislation. The Church should prevail over the State ... In the Anglican tradition I argued for the

supremacy of Parliament, for at the end of the day the issue was who should determine the law relating to the education of English children in England ... I much enjoyed our long deliberate talks, and found the Cardinal the most formidable of my opponents, since he reflected the settled authority of centuries. (1993, pp. 217–18)

Bishop David Konstant of Leeds, Chairman of the CES, considered by 1993 that 'the Dual System of Education has been quite radically altered'; the CES continued to draw attention to 'what were properly perceived as a number of potentially damaging suggestions' which 'could have a deleterious effect upon that very partnership between Church and State which had so successfully stood the test of time' (CES, 1993, p. 3). In a personal letter to his diocesan governors and headteachers, Konstant noted:

It has always been the policy of the Catholic Church in this country to cooperate with the education policies of the Government ... One of my deepest concerns is for the sense of partnership between all the Catholic schools of our diocese and for good relationships with the Authorities whether they be LEA or Central Government. I would not want the issue of Grant Maintained Status to cause division within a school or the local community.

Church schools also had some reason to be sceptical about central government enthusiasm for their status. As voluntary-aided schools, they were dependent upon 85 per cent funding from the DES for capital expenditure projects, which in recent years the Department had been slow to allocate. Back in May 1987 a joint letter to the Secretary of State from the Anglican Diocese of London and the Roman Catholic Diocese of Westminster had expressed serious concern about the substandard conditions experienced by many church schools in London, whose building schemes (merely to bring them up to DES minimum standards) were still to be programmed by the DES. The letter continued:

It is disturbing to find the general level of capital expenditure on County schools appears to be considerably ahead of that on voluntary aided. LEAs have more than one source of funds, whereas voluntary-aided schools, except for a very few with wealthy foundations, are entirely dependent upon central government grant. We hope that it will be possible for the imbalance to be redressed.

The government's policy advocating grant-maintained status as a way of opting out from local authority control seemed an attractive option for church school governors attempting to raise their 15 per cent liability (in some cases amounting to over £1m), when the government was offering to fund 100 per cent of capital expenditure for grant-maintained schools. As one Catholic head wrote to the *TES* (8 February 1991), the bishops did not have to take responsibility for educating children in substandard accommodation: 'the only way forward is to join the GM queue'.

To what extent such funding would be actually forthcoming was unclear, particularly following the public expenditure reductions in the 1990s. Faced with surplus places in local county schools, the Under-Secretary for Education, Michael Fallon, incensed Roman Catholics in February 1992 by refusing to fund buildings for over-crowded Catholic primary schools;[25] his suggestion that the Catholic children could be accommodated in county schools brought accusations from church leaders that he was attempting to end the 'dual system'. The day after an emergency meeting with the Anglican and Roman Catholic bishops Michael Adie and David Konstant, the then Secretary of State, Kenneth Clarke, announced his Popular Schools Initiative, whereby money would be available from April 1993 for oversubscribed schools to expand; the decision had 'nothing to do with the election; I respect the right of people to have a denominational education', Clarke commented (*TES*, 14 February 1992). However, following the government's re-election in April 1992 and Clarke's transfer to the Home Office, the plan was quietly dropped on Treasury insistence, the day after the publication of the White Paper *Choice and Diversity* under Clarke's successor, John Patten.

Kenneth Clarke, having been booed at the North of England Education Conference (Leeds 1991) for dismissing criticism of favourable funding for GM schools as 'paranoid nonsense', later conceded that if they had 'gained an advantage, they have gained it as a result of their courage' (*Guardian*, 19 February 1991). By June 1993, Local Schools Information (a lobbying group opposed to GMS) had calculated that 260 GM schools had benefited from 'double-funding', by receiving extra grants for services that LEAs had already delegated to their schools. In February 1994, the Commons Public Accounts Committee criticized education ministers for making unnecessary payments of £13.6m to GM schools, but its plea that these be removed within two years was rejected; a more gradual four-year transition period was eventually conceded. The Muslims, however, joined the Churches in protesting at such inequity: 'It's not acceptable and it's not Islamic to disadvantage the majority for the benefit of the privileged minority' (*TES*, 1 July 1994).

When John Patten announced appointments to his new Funding Agency for Schools (FAS), a 'quango' to have oversight of the development of GM schools, both Roman Catholic and Anglican leaders were furious that their recommendations for church representatives had been wholly ignored in favour of others known to have pro-GMS views; Michael Adie accused the government of breaking its statutory duty to consult both Churches fully (*TES*, 25 March 1994).[26] In June 1994 the FAS, threatened with legal action by the London Borough of Hammersmith and Fulham, admitted overfunding the Oratory School by £400,000 due to 'clerical error' (*Independent*, 10 June); this Roman Catholic school had earlier created controversy in 1990 when the head's salary of £50,000 became the highest among the country's state schools. Gillian Shephard, who succeeded John Patten as Education Secretary in 1994, acknowledged at a conference of GM heads in December 1994 that 'despite very tight constraints on spending generally ... we have preserved favourable treatment for the GM sector in the allocation of capital provision'. The Director of the Catholic Education Service insisted that all schools should be treated equitably, regardless of their status, and Bishop Brewer of Lancaster regretted the government's 'two-tier system' (*Catholic Herald*, 9 December 1994). By 1996, the pressure on public expenditure in the run-up to the general election led to the FAS having to withdraw the annual round for GM capital bids and encourage more private-sector borrowing. One Roman Catholic GM head lamented:

> One of our strongest reasons for going GM was the fact that local parishes were struggling to find the 15 per cent of building costs required by us as a voluntary aided school. GM status was supposed to free us from all that. Now it seems we must find 66 per cent. (*TES*, 9 February 1996)

Certainly diocesan authorities expressed anxiety about the effect of 'opting out' on the future of church schools, both in relation to diocesan policies and also on the extent to which 100 per cent DFEE funding (through the FAS) would give total control to central government. The London diocesan director of education, addressing the Allington Conference of headteachers in May 1991, recalled that Sir George Young MP had asked ministers why Conservative policy was to encourage GM rather than extend voluntary-aided status; the government's response was that 'we have got beyond that point'. The DFE originally denied that they had any records of the previous status of church schools that became GM, until MP Andrew Smith's parliamentary question (11 May 1994) required officers to retrieve the data. The director of the Grant-Maintained Schools Trust, interviewed on 25 May 1994, was adamant that a church school's previous status was irrelevant: 'we wouldn't differentiate at all between aided, controlled or county once they're GM', a view confirmed by the chief executive of the FAS in November 1996. Thus the distinctive status of church schools seemed to be being subsumed into an alternative secular institutional category.

One Southwark officer, commenting on GMS, had noted: 'The greatest danger is that it could lead to the dismantling of the voluntary sector' (*Education*, 25 January 1991). This view was taken up by headteacher Dennis Richards at the Anglican secondary heads' conference in 1993:

> I remain dismayed that the system created by the 1944 Act, which has served the Churches well, is being dismantled before our eyes. I am not convinced that in the future voluntary-aided and grant-maintained schools will have the same interests and objectives. (*Education*, 1 October 1993)

In the same report, Geoffrey Duncan of the Anglican Board of Education regretted that 'failure to back our belief in Church schools with our own money might be the loose brick which could bring us down' by 'weakening the case for Church schools under an unsympathetic Government'.

Yet Bishop Adie,[27] not wishing to alienate those Anglican schools that had already 'opted out' of unsympathetic LEAs, recognized that 'there cannot be an overall policy. We can point out the factors which governors and parents must consider, but they will make their own decisions in the light of local circumstances' (*ibid.*). Another Anglican in Southwark suggested that GMS might be the only viable option since so many governors and dioceses could not meet their 15 per cent commitments; 'opting out' should be co-ordinated by the diocese[28] (*Education*, 4 October 1991). Some Roman Catholics facing the same predicament also advocated GMS (*TES*, 22 January 1993) and one Anglican GM school participated in the DFE's controversial 1994 GM advertising campaign.[29] Both Churches found themselves divided on the issue.

In 1994 tensions were further exacerbated by a report in the

Church Times (29 April 1994) that a future Labour government would not return aided schools that had 'opted out' to their previous status, but only allow them to become 'controlled', thus tying them even more closely to the very local authorities they had attempted to escape from by going 'grant-maintained'. Ann Taylor, then Shadow Education Secretary, had written to the Churches the previous autumn; a future Labour minister

> will undoubtedly wish to restore the important partnership between central government, local government and the Churches which underpinned the 1994 Act. However it would be unrealistic ... to attempt simply to put the clock back to 1944. It cannot be assumed that church schools that have felt the need to give up their voluntary-aided status in return for 100 per cent state funding would have, or would even wish to have, voluntary-aided status restored. (*Church Times*, 29 April 1994)

Roman Catholic leaders like Bishop Konstant were most agitated that the Church trustees' control of their schools, for which they had made such great sacrifices throughout the twentieth century, could be undermined in this way: 'there is the clearest possible signal that schools which become grant-maintained risk being lost to the Church' (*ibid.*). Anglican officers too were anxious that 'aided' status should be reinstated to their GM schools, but one diocese's advice to its schools noted that

> whatever the substance behind such statements, Governing bodies should recognise that becoming GM involves a risk which might in the future seriously affect the freedom of a Church School to implement its Trust Deed in the way it had customarily done.

Nevertheless, there was by now a groundswell of resentment among some Anglican aided schools that had eschewed the financial advantages of 'opting-out' on the principle of remaining in partnership with their county school colleagues; they felt that those who had 'taken the money and run' should not so easily be allowed to opt back in. Their very public disagreement, involving both Anglicans and Roman Catholics (e.g. correspondence in *Education*, 2 September to 21 October 1994), worried Geoffrey Duncan of the Anglican Board of Education, who desired to keep his church school 'family' together.

The proposals for blocking the return to aided status were finally dropped when the newly appointed Labour leader, Tony Blair, revealed that his own son would be attending the Oratory School, one of the most advantaged GM Catholic schools in London run by trustees who would not tolerate any dependence on the LEA or even the Cardinal. When the Labour Party's policy paper, *Diversity and Excellence*, was published in October 1995 it attempted to step carefully between the 'Scylla' of GM schools adamantly wishing to retain their newly-won autonomy, and the 'Charybdis' of LEA church and county schools demanding that they be compensated for the publicly acknowledged injustices of GM funding. David Blunkett's suggestion, as Shadow Secretary of State, that there should be three choices for schools, 'foundation', 'aided' or 'community' status, with equality of funding and no selection on ability, was seen by many as a political compromise which satisfied neither side. Again the Churches were not consulted prior to its publication.[30] Interviewed in September 1995, the former Labour minister Roy Hattersley, while adamant that GM schools should be returned to their LEAs, stated that he had no objection to church schools as long as their admissions policies were non-selective.[31]

In September 1995 the Churches were taken by surprise yet again when John Major unexpectedly announced the possibility of a new 'fast-track' to grant-maintained status for church schools.[32] The consultation paper was hastily drafted and schools were given only one month to respond.[33] Concerned to boost his flagging policy (of all state schools, only 16 primary and 7 secondary had become GM in January 1995 compared with 77 and 127 respectively in September 1993), and encouraged by Sir Robert Balchin (chairman of the Grant Maintained Schools Trust,[34] who considered lobbying by opponents of GM to be excessively obstructive in the ballot process),[35] the Prime Minister suggested that church schools, whose ethos was already more independent from local authorities than county schools, should be permitted to 'opt out' without having to consult parents through a ballot. The scheme applied only to voluntary-aided schools, not controlled schools.

The Churches were outraged. The Anglican and Roman Catholic bishops of Ripon and Leeds respectively, as education spokesmen for their Churches, protested that a government whose policies had always seemed to advocate increased parental choice, were suddenly and arbitrarily removing that very choice from church school parents. The overwhelming majority of around 2000 responses to the consultation, most of them from church schools, were highly critical. A survey of Anglican voluntary secondary school heads in the autumn of 1995 revealed that 87 per cent objected to the divisiveness of GMS,

79 per cent felt solidarity with their county school colleagues, 57 per cent wished to retain their independence from central government and 54 per cent even thought GMS was incompatible with their Christian ethos (*Education*, 22/29 December 1995).

Geoffrey Duncan, speaking at a DFEE conference for Anglican schools interested in 'Going GM' (October 1995), explained the dilemma: church school governing bodies needed to work in partnership with their parents and their communities – a distinctive route to GMS could be disadvantageous or lead them to be criticized for a 'privilege' they had not sought; he also noted that the proposal had 'grave implications for the dual system we have known for fifty years' (*Church Times*, 9 November 1995). In their response on 17 November, the Roman Catholic Bishops' Conference similarly noted the proposals as 'discriminatory and divisive'; while recognizing the government's 'continuing support for Church schools', it deeply regretted the way the proposals isolated the Churches 'from their partners in education'. Even the chairman of the Conservative Education Association expressed reservations that a large GM sector would result in the nationalization of schools and would erode choice:

> Conservatives cannot spend sixteen years telling parents that they believe in parental choice and then disenfranchise parents because most of them will not choose what some ministers want them to. Many parents value the support of their local education authority, and in much of the country they are right to. (*Church Times*, 22 December 1995)

Both the DFEE and FAS had privately expressed caution about the proposals.[36] The government, weakened by two highly publicized MP defections and denying rumours of a split between the Prime Minister and the Secretary of State on the issue (e.g. *The Times* leader, 18 December 1995),[37] eventually announced on 10 January 1996 that it would not after all be proceeding with the 'fast-track' scheme 'for the time being'; however, it remained 'fully committed to extending the benefits of self-government to all schools'.

There can be little doubt that any remaining confidence the Churches had in the partnership with the State had been badly damaged. The Churches had worked tirelessly during the 1988 and 1993 legislation to safeguard their interests, but it had seemed an uphill struggle constantly to persuade ministers that their views should be respected. Since 1988 they had found themselves increasingly on the defensive, often first hearing about plans which affected church schools from the media, again and again having to react to government initiatives rather than developing their own, and finding themselves seemingly a mere 'pawn' in Conservative party policy-making. In 1993 (*Church Times*, 16 July) Bishop Adie claimed the Churches' negotiations over the bill as 'no mean achievement'; they would have more flexibility with the assets from closed church schools, more influence in turning around any 'failing' schools, and small Anglican schools would be allowed to 'cluster'; with the demise of statutory LEA Education Committees, the Churches would retain representation on their LEAs. He seemed to be putting on a 'brave face' in the light of central government's apparent undermining of local democratic accountability. By the end of the twentieth century, it was difficult still to claim any meaningful sense of partnership with central government.

PARTNERSHIP WITH THE LOCAL EDUCATION AUTHORITY

It may seem surprising that the Churches should wish to defend their partnership with local authorities. Over the years, the relationship had been severely strained by such pressures as falling pupil rolls, 16+ reorganization, admissions procedures, staff redeployment and buildings maintenance. The dependence of church schools on the LEAs was considerable, especially in the Anglican sector where, out of its 21.3 per cent stake in maintained schools, 12.5 per cent were 'controlled' while only 8.8 per cent were 'aided'. Roman Catholic schools, on the other hand, were entirely 'aided' and constituted 9.8 per cent of the whole system; 'special agreement' schools counted as 'aided'.[38]

In these 'voluntary controlled' schools, the foundation governors were in a minority and depended to some degree on the goodwill of the LEA governors – which was not always forthcoming, despite the legal but obsolescent safeguards of withdrawal classes and reserved teachers – to maintain the association with the Anglican parish community. Specific denominational teaching within the school's general religious education programme and compulsory Anglican worship were prohibited by the 1944 legislation. There was therefore a real incentive on the part of both LEA and Church to encourage an atmosphere of mutual trust and partnership. This delicate balance was acknowledged in *A Future in Partnership*.

There is often a generosity of spirit on governing bodies which deliberately seeks to make sense, in informal ways, of the historical link with the Church of England. There is a corresponding degree of trust that the Church will not overstep the bounds of informal relationships and begin to manufacture 'right' out of any well-developed and long-standing practices that have developed informally. (Waddington, 1984, p. 98)

'Voluntary-aided' schools, on the other hand, had far greater autonomy and were free to establish their own syllabus for religious education, advised by diocesan officers, and to engage in denominational church services. In return for their 15 per cent liability for capital costs, the governors had the right to develop their own policies and priorities, which might differ from those of the LEA. Specific examples included aided governors retaining their Sixth Form provision when the LEA decided to reorganize its secondary schools as 11–16 institutions feeding into Sixth Form colleges (for example, Surrey 1975); aided schools considering religious affiliation to be a high priority in staff selection, although local 'equal opportunities' policies explicitly excluded such considerations (for example, Ealing 1986); aided governors being reluctant to reduce their annual pupil intake if heavily oversubscribed, so that all local schools would share the burden of falling rolls and in order to prevent school closures (for example, ILEA in the 1980s).

Managing an education service which included voluntary schools was not easy for an LEA preoccupied with its own concerns, and with its professional officers battling to manage educational policy in an increasingly party-political area and cope with the pressures brought about by corporate management interests.[39]Nevertheless, insensitivity could also be indicative of a reluctance on the part of the LEA to accept the Churches as full partners in the enterprise of education, despite the involvement of diocesan representatives on local education committees. For example, there was an outcry in Sheffield in February 1991 when the LEA, without consultation, announced reorganization plans to close five Anglican schools and merge another with a county school; no Catholic schools were included in the review. Reservations were publicly expressed by left-wing educationists about the divisive nature of church schools in a community, if governors encouraged 'hidden selection' of pupils through social, racial, or ability bias.[40] By contrast, right-wing councils might tacitly condone those voluntary schools which exercised pupil selection according to ability, if it coincided with their own implicit policy to reintroduce grammar schools against local opposition. As the National Society's Green Paper pointed out: 'It is increasingly difficult to separate political expediency from educational viability, for the clamour of the former too often drowns the quieter deliberative voice of the latter' (Waddington, 1984, p. 76).

Discretionary school transport to denominational schools was often jeopardized by LEA spending cuts.[41] Local authorities were required to provide free transport if a child's nearest school was beyond walking distance (taken to be three miles). Even in 1944 R. A. Butler had been concerned that this issue might threaten the settlement with the Churches. Since then, most LEAs have offered discretionary buspasses to children wishing to attend denominational schools and in 1980 Roman Catholic peers helped defeat a proposal to remove that obligation. Because of the effect particularly on the larger number of Roman Catholic secondary schools (the majority of Anglican schools being neighbourhood primaries), Cardinal Hume found himself in the High Court in 1992 in a test case against Hertfordshire's attempt to cease the arrangement. In 1995, Conservative-controlled Brent indicated that it would not pay for a Catholic child to travel past an LEA school with spare places; the deputy director of the Catholic Education Service was confident that the DFE would 'have no choice but to direct Brent to abolish this tendentious policy' (*TES*, 24 March 1995), but the government refused to intervene in a matter it pragmatically considered to be LEA responsibility. Again, denominational interests took second place to economic priorities.

Some might have argued at this point that the quicker church schools disentangled themselves from local authority interference the better. But this assumed that there was no real advantage to them in building up an effective working relationship with the LEA. Many church schools acknowledged their reliance on local authorities to ensure satisfactory educational provision for their own children, setting aside for a moment any responsibility for the community as a whole. LEA officers usually provided support in a number of ways related to staffing, buildings and the curriculum. Local authorities paid the salaries of staff appointed by the governors and provided the professional advice necessary in the event of redeployment or dismissal proceedings, acting as an independent arbiter where there was conflict within the staff of a school.[42] Too often school governors faced crises related to buildings, such as asbestos, fire, or vandalism, when LEA support was essential in effecting repairs or replacements or even providing alternative temporary accommodation. In addition, LEA professional curriculum advisers offered in-service training and guidance in implementing new curricular policies (e.g. records of achievement for school leavers) initiated by local or central government.

For reasons like these, Anglican diocesan authorities have generally been keen advocates of the partnership with LEAs. Not surprisingly, the Anglican Board of Education (with such a high proportion of voluntary controlled schools reflecting LEA majority interest) has tended to be more vocal than the Roman Catholic authorities in defending it. In 1985 the Board of Education's report to the General Synod emphasized

> the importance of working even more closely with local authority partners, particularly in the areas of admissions policies and staffing for Church schools. There will also be a need for close consultation over issues involved in reorganisation[43] ... and the fuller use of the potential of Controlled status. (National Society, 1985, p. 33)

The Rev. Bob Kenway wrote to the *Church Times*:

> While many governors might be strongly critical of their LEAs, I am sure that there are many like me who do not want to see them withering on the vine and are fearful of the consequences if they do. Equally I know many governors are concerned by the parallel trend in which diocesan boards are increasingly seeing themselves as substitutes for LEAs. (23 July 1993)

He went on to argue that church leaders should be asking 'whether the reforms themselves may not be leading to some fundamental inequalities in the provision of education in this country'.

The most public declaration of support for the Inner London Education Authority (ILEA) came from Dr Graham Leonard, the Bishop of London, when the government was determined to abolish it along with the Greater London Council[44] in 1985. With so many church schools in London, the Bishop was concerned that the break-up of the ILEA would leave a fragmented and weakened support network for its schools. He rallied support in the House of Lords and defeated the government's proposals; however, Thatcher's determination to destroy the ILEA and the power of local government meant the reprieve was only temporary.[45]

Roman Catholic headteachers and diocesan officers also expressed their support for the partnership with the LEA. One headteacher writing in the *Tablet* (20 February 1988) commented that, although it has been difficult dealing with the 'complex and seemingly cumbersome bureaucracies, which seem to have been designed to ensure equity, uniformity and rectitude in the use of public money', 'all schools rely heavily on their LEA for administrative support, resources, and advice'; the opportunities afforded by financial delegation should be sufficient to overcome such difficulties without having to opt out and dissolve 'a partnership which, in the main, has served many voluntary schools well in the past'.

Especially in the Roman Catholic communities where church schools often serve socially deprived areas, the isolation inherent in independence from local authorities could also undermine the efforts of diocesan planners 'to serve the best interests of all the Catholic pupils of an area' (Cardinal Basil Hume in the *The Times*, 13 January 1988). One Catholic diocese, where only 3 out of 218 schools had opted out by 1995, replied to the government's 'GM fast-track' consultation:

> In the main there is a very good working relationship between the voluntary sector in this diocese and the various maintaining local authorities ... The sign of partnership afforded by the presence of local authority representative governors is something we value.

This view was endorsed by the Director of the Catholic Education Service:

> One of the reasons for rejecting the 'fast-track' proposals was that they would have isolated Church schools from others in the maintained sector, those controlled by local authorities. The latter's powers have been considerably weakened by legislation over the past decade, but we have retained our generally good relationships with them ... The LEA associations have emphasised the value of our partnership with increasing warmth as their own powers have diminished. (*Tablet*, 18 May 1996)

Geoffrey Duncan (interviewed in June 1996) agreed, recalling that Graham Lane of the Association of Metropolitan Authorities previously used to describe church schools disparagingly as 'independent schools on the rates', but since GMS, Lane had been more supportive, impressed by the professionalism of church educationists throughout the post-1988 period. Even Sir Malcolm Thornton, the former Conservative chairman of the House of Commons Select Committee on Education, speaking in 1996, regretted having voted for many of the 1980s reforms that stripped LEAs of their powers of planning and co-ordination (*Education*, 8 March 1996).

Nevertheless, in spite of its many distinguished advocates, the relationship between church schools and their local authorities already looks very different from 1944. The framework of four decades has undergone radical change in the light of the 1986 and 1988 Education Acts and subsequent legislation. The provisions of the Education (No. 2) Act (1986) significantly minimized the differences between county and voluntary schools, in particular with regard to the power of governors and the school's LEA accountability,[46] and to some extent signposted the phasing out of the dual system.[47] Important modifications in the maintained sector might have seemed unremarkable in the light of central government's declared policy of replicating the voluntary school model for the county school system and creating greater autonomy for county schools in relation to their local authorities. However, the effect was to reduce considerably the distinctiveness of voluntary status. The additional requirements of the 1988 Education Reform Act, ensuring that LEAs handed over much of their budgetary control to individual school governing bodies under 'Local Management of Schools', reduced that distinction still further, and the creation of the grant-maintained sector raised the serious question whether or not the Churches were getting value for money by holding on to voluntary-aided status and their LEA partnerships.

PARTNERSHIP WITH THE DIOCESE

The diocesan dimension, referred to throughout this chapter, now comes under discussion. At the 1987 Culham Conference on church schools, Vincent Strudwick, then Anglican Director of Education for the Oxford diocese, outlined the role he saw the Church playing within the educational partnership of Church and State. Because aided governing bodies have considerable autonomy even in relation to the diocese, the responsibility of a diocesan board is to offer advice rather than prescription, based on relevant information and experience; the provision of the 1988 Act for grant-maintained status and open enrolment had serious repercussions for diocesan planning: 'Opting out will destroy a key role of the partnership that is there to ensure that one person's choice is not made to the detriment of the other' (Culham College Institute, 1987).

This Anglican viewpoint was shared by the General Synod's Board of Education Schools Officer, Geoffrey Duncan. Speaking at the same conference, he welcomed the importance of diversity in the education system, but admitted to feeling concerned that grant-maintained status could give scope for aided church school governors 'to forget that they are part of the diocesan family, part of the national Church family, part of a much wider maintained system of education'. However, balancing this consideration against the arguments from market forces and self-interest must be difficult for governors whose school is under threat of reorganization or closure. 'We could be in the process of changing the dual system virtually beyond recognition' (*Church Times*, 2 October 1987).

Similar concerns were expressed by the Cardinal Archbishop of Westminster, Basil Hume, whose criticism of the government's proposals (as noted above) had been widely publicized (e.g. *The Times*, 13 January 1988). He emphasized that 'no Catholic school can stand in isolation from others in a given area', and suggested that diocesan policies backed by the bishop's authority should be the prior consideration for governors. Such remarks may in part reflect difficulties within the Westminster diocese, where diocesan proposals for Catholic Sixth Form Colleges were opposed by the governors of Cardinal Vaughan Memorial School, who wished to retain its Sixth Form and whose grant-maintained status in April 1990 provided escape from the imposition of diocesan policies. The chairman of the Parents' Action Group put it this way:

> Some of the parents are in a terrible dilemma because they have never before been disobedient to the Church. But they believe that the interests of their children must come first. We don't want to fight against the Church but we must protect our school. (*The Times*, 14 November 1988)

It is interesting that the diocese's concern for the 'common good' of the Roman Catholic community was not mentioned; the dilemma was polarized into 'obedience' versus 'the children's interests'.[48] Traditionally, the bishop's authority, communicated through the school's trustees, had been widely respected, but the new factors brought in by the 1988 Act radically altered this long-established relationship. The government refused to concede to the Cardinal's request that the diocesan trustees' consent should be given before a Catholic school sought to become grant-maintained.

The Cardinal went on to express two reservations about admissions procedures for diocesan Catholic schools. First, the Catholic character of a school could be threatened by the modification of its admissions policy if, under GMS, it chose to be more selective on pupils' ability or social background, thereby excluding other Catholic children. Secondly, the procedures for open enrolment up to the 1979 'standard pupil numbers' could mean taking in a higher proportion of non-Catholic children, with governors obliged to admit applicants without regard to the balance necessary to preserve the Catholic character of the school; a limit of 15 per cent non-Catholic admissions to Catholic schools was normally recommended by the church authorities.[49] It is of interest to note the common concern among both Anglicans and Roman Catholics for the nature of the ethos and character of a Christian school. The more 'domestic' view reflected in the Cardinal's comments is clearly in line with the Vatican's insistence, reaffirmed in the recent revision of canon law, on Catholic education for all Catholic children.

Nevertheless, this debate also brought out a more 'general' view among some Roman Catholic advocates of government policy:

> If there are empty places and no Catholic applicants, should not the Bishops welcome the opportunity to meet the duty incumbent on the Church 'to announce the mystery of salvation to all men' (*Gravissimum Educationis*)? This might be the only chance non-Catholic children will ever have of being introduced to the Catholic faith. (Sheila Lawlor, deputy director of the Centre for Policy Studies, *Tablet*, 20 February 1988)

Such a view needs to be seen in context, for Dr Lawlor went on to criticize the hierarchy's use of its authority in not allowing sufficient diversity: 'The governors may, in championing the cause of their individual school, come into dispute with the diocese intent on sacrificing the interests of one school to those of the wider Catholic community.' Her priority was unequivocally the principle of freedom of parental choice, over and above the responsibility for the diocesan community as a whole. This priority was shared by another Roman Catholic, Piers Paul Read, in a letter to the *The Times* (14 January 1988), who sought support for his view by reference to the Second Vatican Council:

> The Cardinal's views appear at odds with the teaching of the Second Vatican Council which, in its Declaration on Christian Education, gave to parents, not to bishops, the primary responsibility for the education of their children and called for 'the fullest liberty in their choice of school'. There are in fact many Catholic

parents who, far from agreeing with the Cardinal's objections, look to Mr Baker's Bill to free their schools from interference by the bureaucracies of their bishop's diocesan educational services.[50]

This notion was, hardly surprisingly, contradicted by a statement from the Catholic Bishops' Conference circulated to every diocese and parish in England and Wales in February 1988. The bishops argued that the government's proposals favoured the interests of a minority of parents at the expense of the majority, a principle 'difficult to reconcile with Catholic ideals'. It would be difficult for Catholic schools to remain faithful to the Church's tradition of caring especially for the poor and deprived and might open the way for a small group of transient, unrepresentative parents 'looking for only short-term gains, or acting from social or racial motives harmful to the interests of the Catholic or wider local community' to bring about a fundamental change in a Catholic school.[51] This statement, supported unequivocally by the Pope[52] at a Vatican meeting on 29 February, was of particular importance since it indicated an evident concern for the 'general' as opposed to the 'domestic' purpose of church schools, and in principle was not dissimilar to the views of the Church of England's Board of Education expressed in *A Future in Partnership* (Waddington, 1984, p. 63). As one Anglican diocese advised its schools in February 1994,

> For Christians, there are not only political and pragmatic con-
> siderations but also an ethical dimension to the decision to apply
> for Grant Maintained school status that cannot be ignored. For
> example, the preferential funding which GM schools receive, in the
> form of transitional grant and more favourable capital allocations,
> can be seen as being at the expense of neighbouring schools, and of
> other schools generally who share the national cake. (Blackburn
> Diocesan Board of Education, 1994)

This ethical dimension was reiterated by the director of the Catholic Education Service interviewed in 1995: 'tossing aside the community for individual gain is immoral and unChristian'.

There can be little doubt that parental choice has always played an important part in the *raison d'être* of voluntary schools and in the justification for their existence within the maintained sector. It is somewhat ironic that this should now be used to draw church schools away from their diocesan links, when church policies appear to hold back a particular school's development or attempt to support weaker schools and less privileged children in the Christian community. Mgr

Nichols of the Bishops' Conference warned that, although the Catholic authorities were partners with the State in the dual system, 'it is for the Church to propose and for the State to accept or reject but not to arbitrate between dissenting voices within the Church' (CES, 1989, p. 37). Trustees and governors have found themselves at loggerheads in defending their interests in Catholic schools, for example when the former intervened to prevent governors appointing as head a divorcee who had remarried in a registry office, which the trustees considered would undermine the 'Catholic character' of the school. In 1989, two legal cases (*ILEA v. Brunyate* and *R. v. Westminster Roman Catholic Diocese trustees, ex parte Andrews*) judged that 'trustees cannot remove a governor where this would usurp the governors' independent function under legislation'. The Catholic Director of Education in the Archdiocese of Southwark, Christopher Storr, warned: 'the day cannot be far off when a trustee, acting in accordance with the requirement of his trust deed, finds himself at odds with the governor acting in accordance with the articles of government of his school' (*Tablet*, 10 February 1996).

An additional note of caution was sounded by church education officers prior to the 1992 general election, about the vulnerability of church schools in the future if they are 100 per cent dependent on central government. In a letter to heads and governors of Catholic schools in April 1991, Storr suggested that 'opting out' was 'politically inopportune' and 'morally questionable', since there was no guarantee that a different government would allow schools to return to the maintained sector. 'That could be a gift on a plate to some future administration that wants to get rid of Church schools', warned Anglican spokesman Geoffrey Duncan. His colleague, Canon Strudwick, was explicit:

> I ask whether the proposals will strengthen the effectiveness of the partnership to enable the better education of all children in an area or will it destroy the partnership as an effective force, making all the partners to a greater or lesser degree pawns of central government policy and practice? (*The Way Ahead?*, November 1987)

In ensuring a degree of independence and freedom for church schools to operate within the nation's education service, that diocesan link may be critical in the future, whichever party is in power.

There was yet another dimension to the debate on grant-maintained status. Under sections 87 and 89 of the 1988 Act, the governing body of a grant-maintained school can change its religious character, provided the trustees agree and the Secretary of State approves. The implications of this were clarified by J. D. C. Harte,[53] who suggested that governors and parents might wish their opted-out school to reflect the religious views of a particular Christian or non-Christian group; objections to the establishment of Muslim schools on the grounds that they encouraged racial segregation or gender discrimination could be overruled by the pressure of parental choice. Certainly where a county school is 90 per cent Sikh (Ealing) or an Anglican school is 99 per cent Muslim (Bradford), there would seem to be a powerful argument for becoming grant-maintained. It might come about that through parental pressure a church school could simply become Muslim or even cease to have a religious affiliation altogether and adopt a secular ethos.

The pressure by the evangelical Christian Schools Campaign for their independent schools to receive government funding, supported by influential figures such as Baronesses Cox[54] and Blatch, gathered momentum in the 1990s, and their right to GM status, along with that of Muslim schools, was written into the 1993 legislation. The bid submitted to the DFEE by an evangelical Christian school (Oakhill in Bristol) to become GM was, however, rejected in September 1995 on the ground that there were surplus places in nearby schools. The head Ruth Deakin protested that 'the goal posts have changed', since throughout debates on the 1993 Act 'politicians were suggesting that parental demand and "denominational need" for new religious school places would be considered more important than the need to remove surplus places' (*TES*, 22 September 1995). By 1996, plans had been drawn up for a new GM Catholic secondary school in Oxfordshire and a GM Jewish school in Leeds, where parents would have to raise 15 per cent of the initial costs; as neither the diocese nor the LEA could finance the new school, GMS was the only alternative. Proposals for the John Loughborough School, run by the Seventh Day Adventists in Tottenham, to receive 25 per cent funding from the FAS prompted front-page headlines ('Sect school on brink of getting state cash', *TES*, 18 October 1996).

The Cardinal's fears about loss of diocesan jurisdiction over Catholic schools and his bishops' concern that 'total financial dependence on central government will have serious implications for the ability of our schools to retain their distinctive Catholic curriculum and ethos'[55] had similar echoes in the Anglican Church. The Bishop of London (then Graham Leonard) commented:

'Creeping privatisation of the education system is no more acceptable than would be the outright handing over of all schools to commercial enterprise' (*Education*, 9 October 1987).

The General Synod attempted to require a church school's governing body to consult its diocesan Board of Education and 'have regard to that advice' if it was considering opting out or altering the religious character of the school. Such proposals indicated that the Anglican Board of Education was as much prepared as the Roman Catholics to defend its interest against central government or local pressure groups. Indeed, the Diocesan Boards of Education Measure of 1991 required every diocese to appoint a diocesan director and gave the boards powers of direction over their church school governing bodies, additional to the appointment of foundation governors.

The Churches were frustrated at the lack of clarification of government policy in relation to the future of LEAs.[56] Under the 1992 Further and Higher Education Act, Sixth Form Colleges, a number of which were Anglican and Roman Catholic, were removed from LEA control and incorporated into the planning remit of the Further Education Funding Council, another government 'quango' on which the Churches had no statutory role, although some representation. This legislation also removed the distinction between polytechnics and universities, leaving church colleges of higher education out on a limb, needing to reassess their position in relation to the new university sector and the accreditation of their degree courses.

The 1993 Education Act[57] then set up administrative structures for grant-maintained schools, anticipating large numbers of schools 'opting-out', driven by the principles of parental choice[58] and market forces. It required governing bodies to discuss GMS annually, reporting their decision to parents, and removed the original requirement for a second parental ballot; however, it still allowed no return from GM to LEA status,[59] even if parents wished it. It rescinded the obligation on LEAs to retain an education committee on which Anglicans and Catholics with denominational schools in the area had representation.[60] The Churches were reluctant to see a 'two-tier system' with their LEA partners 'withering on the vine' or church schools 'floating away' from their diocese. The Anglican Schools Officer noted that the concept of partnership

> presents some problems at regional level, not least at times of local authority reorganisation when it may be unclear with whom and

how the church is in partnership. Further with some schools relating directly to a national agency rather than a local authority, partnership becomes potentially more complicated for dioceses. (D. W. Lankshear, 1996)

The Churches were disappointed at the prospect that John Patten (as a Roman Catholic) should be instrumental in the demise of the dual system which, over the years, had ensured the success of so many church schools.

An alternative, perhaps surprising, view was advocated by Frank Field, a Labour MP of strong Anglican allegiance, who saw grant-maintained status, far from undermining the Christian ethos of a school, as a vital chance to safeguard or even restore the role of Christianity in a predominantly secular society. Critical of William Temple's capitulation to the State in 1944, he insisted that 'The Government's opting out proposals offer the Church what might be its last chance to re-establish its position in our educational system' (Field, 1989). Mr Field argued that Christian grant-maintained schools could create a strong federation, sharing expertise and resources and emerging as a significant force in English education, less vulnerable to political pressure than at present (an anti-Erastian view consistent with his Anglo-Catholic tradition). One Anglican priest and governor of a large Church of England grant-maintained comprehensive school agreed: 'The truth is that our "churchness" has been strengthened by opting out' (*TES*, 8 May 1992).

The Schools Minister, Lady Blatch, wrote to both the Archbishop of Canterbury and Cardinal Hume as the 1993 legislation moved to royal assent:

> The Government place [*sic*] the highest importance on the preservation of a flourishing body of church schools. The Church has been, and remains, a major provider and stakeholder in the education system of the country ... Each diocese sees its schools as a family, and rightly so. But a step towards greater independence is a matter for congratulation in any family and achieving self-governing status is just that kind of step – a sign of confidence and success. Self-governing schools[61] do not leave your flock. They retain their foundation governors and their religious ethos and values, and they continue to look to the diocese for all the support it has always offered. (*Church Times*, 30 July 1993)

Nevertheless, the Catholic Bishop Brewer argued that the schools in his diocese, none of which had opted out, were 'a family; we stick together' (*Catholic Herald*, 9 December 1994).

By late 1994 the DFE had decided to extend to church schools their special conferences for interested heads and governors about 'Going GM'.[62] Anglican and Roman Catholic headteachers of GM schools spoke enthusiastically from the platform, even if several delegates interviewed felt that many of the advantages advocated had, since 1990, become available to voluntary and LEA schools through local financial delegation. One governor of a GM Catholic school (Swindon RC Conference, 27 January 1995) recalled his original anxiety that he would be disobeying his diocesan bishop and the Church if the school opted for GMS; although he was made aware of the bishop's disapproval, he felt relieved when the bishop said he would not prevent the school going GM.[63] At the same conference, Robin Squire, who succeeded Lady Blatch as Schools Minister in 1994, suggested that the government 'officially' had no plans for all schools to become GM, but were 'utterly sold on the advantages'. Reflecting that 8 per cent of Roman Catholic but only 4 per cent of Anglican schools had opted out, he quipped to his mainly Catholic audience, 'Methinks the Protestants do protest too much.' At the 'Going GM' conferences for Anglican schools, Geoffrey Duncan emphasized that, although the Church was concerned if GMS undermined local democracy, whatever decision governors made, the schools would remain part of their 'diocesan family'.

In June 1995, John Gay of the Culham Institute published a significant survey on the future of Anglican Diocesan Boards of Education (DBE). It noted that, as LEA services had declined and the new unitary authorities were being established under the Local Government Commission, church schools were increasingly looking to their DBE for support and advice, particularly in relation to inspections. Endorsing the need to resist financial cutbacks in the light of the £8m lost by the Church Commissioners' property speculation in 1994, DBEs should be prepared to adopt a more market-oriented culture and seize opportunities for supporting church schools, whose influence on their 850,000 pupils was considerable.[64] The DBE representation on local education committees and Standing Advisory Committees on Religious Education (SACREs), and their effective liaison with LEA and DFE officers, 'apart from the bishops in the House of Lords, represents the last major area of national secular life where the church continues to have a statutory role' (p. 27).

CONCLUSION

The 'grant-maintained' debate focused attention yet again on the *raison d'être* of the contemporary church school and it was paradoxical to find opinions from such opposite ends of the political spectrum forcefully arguing in favour of 'opting out' for church schools. Is a grant-maintained church school, as Sheila Lawlor pointed out, a Christian community in which parental choice should take precedence over diocesan authority or is it, as Frank Field suggested, a Christian enclave upholding values threatened by secular society? Or is a Christian school one which places a higher priority on its role within the wider Christian community across a diocese or LEA, as advocated by many Roman Catholic and Anglican diocesan authorities? With important principles at stake, such tensions were unlikely to be easily or quickly resolved, even by government 'diktat'.

These debates raised serious questions about the future of the partnership between Church and State in education, which had seldom been under such pressure since 1944. The alarming prospect of the head of the Roman Catholic Church in England and Wales being taken to court[65] was without precedent in recent years, and the Anglican Church's relationship with Parliament was hardly less uncomfortable after the Commons' rejection of the Synod's proposal to allow divorced persons to be ordained. Headlines (for example, *TES*, 13 September 1995) about episcopal threats to defeat policies advocated by the Prime Minister on GM status did not help relationships. It appeared that 'the Church is no longer automatically invited as a valued partner to negotiate about government proposals which aim at changing existing education law'.[66]

There also seemed to be a real danger that the political ethos enhancing the primacy of 'self-interest' was having an influence on church schools to the detriment of a sense of responsibility towards the diocesan community as a whole.[67] This seemed likely to result in greater emphasis being placed on the 'domestic' role for Christian education, tending to create more 'ghetto-ized' institutions. James Arthur noted that

> many Catholic schools are increasingly marked by a high degree of formal control emphasising selection and competition ... This is a highly secular approach ... which conflicts with the Church's view of education, which is that it be provided not to gain power or as a

means for material prosperity and success, but rather to serve others. (1995b, p. 452)

As individual schools face the reality of financial management and market economics, 'survival of the fittest' becomes the name of the game. The Anglican priest Bob Kenway wrote to the *Church Times*:

> I do not believe that competition between schools will lead neces-
> sarily to the higher educational standards envisaged by the
> government, and it is beginning to create a climate of mistrust
> between schools locally . . . The free-market philosophy which has
> been applied to so many of our institutions . . . is having pernicious
> social effects. (30 July, 1993)

Meanwhile, the position of diocesan authorities and even LEAs has moved away from the role of partner to one more like that of a consultant or adviser; this shift has changed the way in which they can influence schools or implement policy. Recent Education Acts have placed responsibility and control firmly in the hands of individual school governing bodies, parents and headteachers, who can have different priorities for their church school from those of their diocesan officers or even their bishop. Where such differences exist between the school and its trustees, tensions may be unavoidable. As the government intended, the balance of power in church schools has irrevocably changed. The 'dual system' of Church and State involvement in education, strengthened by R. A. Butler in 1944, looks radically different by the end of the twentieth century.

NOTES

1 The Department of Education and Science changed its name to the Department For Education (DFE) in 1992 and in 1995 to the Department for Education and Employment (DFEE).

2 See John Fletcher (1994) 'Research, education policy and the management of change', *Oxford Review of Education* **20**(1), pp. 68–70). Some of the effects of these changes on church teacher training colleges have already been noted in the previous chapter.

3 On the announcement of Joseph's continuation in post after the 1983 election, *Report* described him as 'Quirky, coolly provocative, sublimely unconscious of the problems of teacher morale, academically abstruse yet instinctively populist' (June 1983).

4 'I was not as intellectually distinguished as Keith, but I was a doer', Baker recalled. Michael Barber considered Baker (Secretary of State for Education 1986–9) a

rare political talent, compared 'with his three predecessors – Williams, Carlisle and Joseph – who achieved remarkably little – and his three successors – Clarke, MacGregor and Patten – who stumbled and fell' ('Why are you still smiling Kenneth?' *TES*, 31 May 1996). Nigel Lawson admired Baker's political skill but felt that it was 'hard to imagine we would get from Kenneth the fundamental thinking about educational reform that I was sure was needed' (1992, *A View from No. 11* (London: Bantam Press), p. 601).

5 Interestingly, Kenneth Harris's 1988 biography, *Thatcher* (London: Weidenfeld & Nicolson), had only 5 references to education, whereas her 1993 autobiography (*The Downing Street Years*) contained 45. The 1979 manifesto had three inches on education, that in 1983 nine inches, and that in 1987 about ten pages.

6 Thatcher and Baker had differing views on GMS, the latter planning to implement it in a limited way, while the former hoped that all schools would eventually become 'independent state schools'.

7 Denis Lawton described Baker as 'an exemplar of Tory confusion on education', a 'pluralist' in 1979, a 'privatizer' by 1988 (1994, *The Tory Mind on Education 1979–1984* (London: Falmer), p. 67).

8 See B. Simon and C. Chitty (1993) *S.O.S. Save Our Schools* (London: Lawrence & Wishart), chapter 4.

9 Bishop Graham Leonard of London led the debates on RE in the House of Lords in 1988. Leonard's successor as Chairman of the General Synod's Board of Education, Michael Adie, described the local Standing Advisory Committees on RE (SACREs) as 'crucial to the future of RE under current policy' (*Education*, 22 January 1993).

10 Hennessy's Gresham Lecture: 'A tigress surrounded by hamsters' (20 February 1996). I. Gilmour (1992) *Dancing with Dogma* (London: Simon & Schuster), p. 4.

11 Nearly 25 per cent of primary schools eligible to 'opt out' were Anglican, yet the Church first heard of the government's announcement through the media.

12 A cry reiterated by the Confederation of British Industry (CBI) in 1994 (*Thinking Ahead*) and in 1995 (*Realising the Vision: a skills passport*).

13 'The provision of new instruments and articles of government for Anglican schools took many years following this act, not least because of the complexity created by the need to ensure that the tradition of parochial involvement in the governing bodies was continued to the satisfaction of every parish' (D. W. Lankshear (1996) 'From Research to Policy 1980–1996: the case of the Church of England school', paper given to the International Symposium of Church School Studies, Durham, 3 July).

14 John Fletcher traces the increase in the DES's control of the curriculum in 'Policy-making in DES/DFE via consensus and contention', *Oxford Review of Education* 21(2), June 1995.

15 M. Balen (1994) *Kenneth Clarke* (London: Fourth Estate), pp. 215, 225. Simon Jenkins charted the centralization of power under Thatcher in *Accountable to None: the Tory nationalisation of Britain* (1996, London: Penguin).

16 'Quango' was the name given to new 'quasi-autonomous non-governmental organizations' which had the power to steer and implement government policy. This 'new magistracy' increased the capacity of the centre to drive policy (cf. J. Stewart (1992) 'Accountability to the Public', paper to the European Policy Forum). Sir Geoffrey Holland, who resigned as Permanent Secretary at the DFE under John Patten, considered that quangos led to 'fudging and avoiding accountability' ('Alas Sir Humphrey, I knew him well', 3 May 1995, Royal Society of Arts lecture).

17 Duncan Graham, having been sacked from the NCC, lamented the demise of Her Majesty's Inspectorate and the bureaucratic interference and obstruction by government; all members of the National Curriculum subject groups were personally interviewed by the Secretary of State (D. Graham with D. Tytler (1993) *A Lesson for Us All: the making of the National Curriculum* (London: Routledge).

18 An Anglican headteacher of a grant-maintained comprehensive reported in November 1992 that he had observed the Secretary of State at a heads' conference advocating the virtues of parental choice, paradoxically flanked by two large conference posters on 'curriculum and assessment', areas where, he noted, 'choice' seemed no longer to exist.

19 This renewed alliance suggested a fresh partnership was 'being forged, but this time on the terms of the teachers' unions and active parents, offended at the divisiveness implicit in league-tables, as well as overwork' (J. Fletcher, 1995, pp. 141–2).

20 In 1987, Thatcher sugggested at a press conference that GM schools might 'raise additional sums', much to Baker's concern: 'I was intensely annoyed that our flagship was now receiving inaccurate directions from the bridge ... there was as usual no apology' (Baker, 1993, pp. 194–5).

21 'Privileged position' is explicitly condemned by the Vatican in *The Catholic School* (1977, Rome), para. 58. Hostility from LEAs and teacher associations led Thatcher to set up the Grant-Maintained Schools Trust, led by Robert Balchin, to promote GMS (Thatcher, 1993, p. 593).

22 Cf. Bishop Michael Adie (*Education*, 14 December 1990 and House of Lords debate, 12 May 1992, *Hansard*, 279) and Cardinal Basil Hume (reported in *Education*, 27 September 1991).

23 The economics editor of the *Observer*, William Keegan, later commented in the *Tablet* (22 July 1995) that John Major, as Thatcher's successor, had not modified the 'Thatcherite' beliefs in pushing market philosophies to their absolute limits: 'Where there is no concept of society, there is no concept of decency and fair play.'

24 J. Arthur (1995b) 'Government education policy and Catholic voluntary-aided schools 1979–94', *Oxford Review of Education* 21(4), p. 452.

25 It was estimated that 27 Roman Catholic schools' bids for capital improvement between 1988 and 1992 were rejected because of spare places in neighbouring LEA schools (*TES*, 7 February 1992).

26 Back in 1993, he had confidently written in the *Church Times* (16 July): 'In nearly every respect, the Government has amended the bill to take account of our comments. So the Secretary of State has a statutory duty to consult the Churches when appointing people to the FAS.' He had reason in retrospect to think he had been 'taken for a ride'.

27 Duncan recalled Adie's effectiveness as the Anglican Church's spokesman on education: Adie never revealed his personal politics and tried to be 'positive yet not uncritical' of government policy, but he 'became increasingly furious with the way policy was developing' and 'by the end he was running rings round Emily Blatch in the Lords' (interview, June 1996).

28 John Patten (appointed as Secretary of State for Education in April 1992) had indicated that he was 'not in favour of mass opt-outs' (*TES*, 8 May 1992), but 'clusters' of small schools were later permitted to go GM under the 1993 Act after the Churches expressed concern for their smaller rural primary schools.

29 Complaints to the Advertising Standards Authority in 1994 that the DFE had spent £200,000 on party-political publicity about the benefits of GMS were not upheld, but the government quietly dropped the campaign.

30 Geoffrey Duncan, interviewed in 1996, regretted this lack of consultation with the Churches. One diocesan director of education considered the document 'confused ... in its understanding of the law' as a result (*Church Times*, 14 June 1996).

31 This issue hit the headlines in January 1996 when Harriet Harman (then Shadow Health Minister) decided to send her second son to an Anglican selective grammar school, her other boy being already enrolled at the Oratory School: 'it is strange to seek a Catholic school for the eldest and a Protestant one for the second unless one is really ecumenical', commented one editor wryly (*Education*, 26 January 1996).

32 Some commentators suggested that even the Secretary of State, Mrs Shephard, was not previously consulted (*Guardian*, 16 September) and a DFEE officer admitted privately to being taken aback by this sudden shift in policy.

33 'At least it came out in term time' commented a church school head rather cynically, recalling the original National Curriculum proposals being published on the day after schools closed for the summer in 1987. DFEE spokesmen justified the short period for consultation in order to meet Parliamentary deadlines but, after protests, it was extended by a week.

34 This quango was privately described by even a supporter of GMS as 'heavily politically motivated; it was given too much power and no accountability'. Balchin, interviewed in June 1996, denied that the fast-track was his idea, claiming that it came from the head of the London Oratory School.

35 One GM head interviewed in 1996 likened Balchin's GM heads' conferences to 'revivalist meetings'. Another inner-city GM church school head thought the male-dominated, middle-class atmosphere was reminiscent of the 'the Tory Party at prayer'.

36 A senior DFEE officer even sought advice as to 'how to get the Secretary of State off the hook' from one diocesan representative in autumn 1995. The latter later argued privately that the GM initiative had been sadly hijacked by the 'political Right' and could therefore be vulnerable following a change of government.

37 These rumours of a split continued into 1996 over Major's plans for grammar schools in every town and the extension of vouchers from nurseries to post-16 provision (*The Times* leader, 14 June 1996).

38 Figures from DES Statistical Tables, January 1988. One Catholic school was apparently given 'controlled' status by administrative error, although several were designated as 'special agreement'.

39 Cf. Robert McCloy (Director of Education for the Royal Borough of Kingston-upon-Thames) in *Crosscurrent*, October 1982 (The National Society).

40 E.g. at the Socialist Education Association conference (March 1990), a county headteacher commented that, in admissions, voluntary schools 'are the most un-Christian schools in our neighbourhood' (*Education*, 23 March 1990). *The Fourth R* (Durham Report 1970) warned Church schools against 'ghetto-like' huddles (para. 47).

41 See S. Thornthwaite (1990) 'School transport – the need to change', *British Journal of Educational Studies* **38**(2). In 1991 the Audit Commission (*Home to School Transport: a system at the crossroads*, HMSO) recommended the withdrawal of this discretion on economic grounds.

42 Cf. Tony Smith, then Chief Inspector for the ILEA, at the Culham Conference in November 1987, entitled *The Way Ahead?*

43 In Ealing, the co-operation between the London Diocesan Board and the local authority in 1981 resulted in the successful establishment of a new Anglican

secondary comprehensive school which is now oversubscribed and well respected in its local community. The mutual trust built up by a close relationship between Church and LEA was critical in manoeuvring through the rapids of local party politics.

44 The GLC was then run by Ken Livingstone, a radical Labour left-winger, who infuriated the Conservatives by parading the unemployment figures on a banner across the façade of County Hall directly opposite the Houses of Parliament.

45 The ILEA was finally abolished under Baker's 1988 Act. One diocesan director, unsympathetic to the teachers' union influence on LEAs, felt that the abolition of the ILEA was 'the most significant milestone; in a hundred years' time, that will be more important than the National Curriculum reforms'. He reflected in an interview (June 1996) that the ILEA was only one of the issues on which the Church had seemed confused and ambivalent since 1870.

46 County school governors took control of their staff appointments and premises, like voluntary schools hitherto, and voluntary-aided governing bodies were obliged to report to their LEA on 'the discharge of their functions as the authority may require'. Certainly the marked change in regulations concerning temporary pupil exclusions, for example, meant that the right exercised by voluntary schools governors to suspend or exclude a pupil for more than five days in a term was subject to LEA veto.

47 Yet an employment appeal tribunal on 2 November 1994 ruled that 'the provision of education in a voluntary-aided school was a service provided by the governing body, not by the state. The governing body was not under the control of the state ... The governing body of a voluntary-aided school existed within a state, providing a public service but it was not an emanation of the state' (*The Times*, Law Report, 9 November 1994).

48 This and other challenges by schools to the diocesan bishops' authority are discussed in James Arthur's 1992 D.Phil. thesis, *Policy and Practice of Catholic Education in England and Wales Since the Second Vatican Council* (Oxford), pp. 122–130; he reflects that the Cardinal's inability to influence, let alone control, the foundation trustees on Catholic school governing bodies and the lack of support for his position from Catholic MPs (p. 94) are indicative of the decline in episcopal authority and the increase in the power of the laity since Vatican II (p. 209).

49 See *The Month*, May 1985, pp. 157–8. Leslie Francis (*Tablet*, 15 February 1986) warned that closing schools might be a more honest policy than admitting non-Catholic children without taking proper account of their needs. James Arthur recognized that 'changes in the educational perceptions and practices of the Catholic community have reduced the ability of the Church to implement the official principles and diocesan guidelines of Catholic education' ('Admissions to Catholic schools: principles and practice', *British Journal of Religious Education* 17(1), Autumn 1994).

50 For further discussion, see J. Arthur, 'Parental involvement in Catholic schools: a case of increasing conflict', *British Journal of Educational Studies* **xxxxii**(2), June 1994.

51 In 1989 the Catholic Education Service (CES) issued a guide to *The Education Reform Act and Catholic Schools* offering 'limited comment' on GMS since it was 'likely to be a minority interest'. On the government's argument that Catholic parents should have the same rights as county school parents, it rather patronizingly criticized this 'dubious assumption that parents first naturally coalesce, secondly spontaneously adopt an attitude which is genuinely their own'.

52 Kenneth Baker's autobiography recalls: 'I was amazed that the Holy Father had taken such a close interest in my Education Bill' (Baker, 1993, p. 217).

53 Lecturer in Law at Newcastle University, in a paper in the *Ecclesiastical Law Journal* of 5 July 1989.

54 Her Private Members' Bill was withdrawn for lack of support on 4 March 1991, but the issue was addressed explicitly in the 1992 White Paper.

55 *TES*, 8 May 1992. The government was adamant that diocesan authorities should not obstruct Catholic schools from opting out. The most the Secretary of State was willing to concede (under pressure) was that he would take into account the trustees' views when Catholic schools sought GM status.

56 See Bishop Michael Adie, *Education*, 29 January 1993; *TES*, 12 February 1993. Conservative MP Bob Dunn (Education Minister 1983–8), interviewed on BBC1, described LEAs as the 'dead hand' on education and thought that their residual role as 'service providers' could be privatized ('On the record', 28 April 1996).

57 This started as the longest-ever Education Bill: it was also the first in which the Roman Catholic Church had been mentioned 'positively' since the Reformation and the RC diocesan authority was specifically defined (*Catholic Herald*, 5 November 1993).

58 Bishop Leonard sensed that GMS was likely to result in reduced parental choice as schools became more selective in admissions (B. Simon (1988) *Bending the Rules: the Baker reform of education* (London: Lawrence & Wishart), p. 79). This situation indeed arose, e.g. in the London Borough of Hillingdon in 1994, when most secondary schools were oversubscribed, but the FAS refused to intervene: 'Parents will have to make what choices they can' (*TES*, 23 September). DFEE figures showed appeals lodged for county and controlled primary schools rose from 7308 in 1988–9 to 18,423 in 1993–4; the comparable rise for secondary schools was 10,732 to 16,316.

59 In 1994, the Bennett Memorial Diocesan School in Kent held a favourable parental ballot for GMS, but during the consultation stage with the DFE, the

Secretary of State insisted that its admission policy be altered to allow prospective pupils to take the 11+ examination still operating across the LEA; the governors tried unsuccessfully to retreat from opting out.

60 The Churches nevertheless insisted that they should have representation on any LEA committees where educational policy was being discussed.

61 Although the term 'grant-maintained' was the legal description for schools that had opted out of LEA control, the government increasingly used the term 'self-governing' in its publicity on GMS.

62 In 1994, the DFEE's 37 regional 'Going GM' conferences had attracted representatives from about 12 per cent of schools at a cost to the government of £114 per delegate. Between Easter and Christmas, only 10 secondary schools had opted out. One Anglican head privately likened the conferences to 'evangelical meetings where people seem to need to convince themselves they are right or alternatively preaching at a 6.30 p.m. evensong for the already converted'!

63 The director of the Catholic Education Service, interviewed in 1995, clarified the bishop's position: he could use Canon Law and remove the school's 'Catholic' status, but 'the scandal would be great'.

64 According to the 1988 National Society Report, *Children in the Way*, 17.5 per cent of the nation's children attended Anglican primary schools, compared with only 10 per cent involved in church-related activities.

65 The Court of Appeal refused the Cardinal's application for judicial review when his removal and replacement of two trustees from the governors of the Cardinal Vaughan School in Westminster was deemed illegal (*The Times*, Law Report, 18 August 1989).

66 J. Arthur (1995b), p. 454.

67 Cardinal Hume's address to the National Conference of Priests (5 September 1989) and Archbishop Carey's speech to Anglican headteachers (19 September 1991) warned against such self-interest.

4

RELIGIOUS EDUCATION AND COLLECTIVE WORSHIP: THE DEBATE SINCE 1944

Religious education (RE) and its influence on the relationship between Church and State has been no less significant in recent years than it was in the period up to Butler's 1944 Education Act. Having successfully negotiated a framework based on the Cowper-Temple clause to establish 'religious instruction' as a compulsory subject in the school curriculum, permitting the teaching of Christianity and a daily act of collective worship in every state school, the post-war government felt confident that herein lay the basis for a morally stable society rooted in its common Christian heritage. In the light of the experience of two world wars, secularist opposition attracted little support, the only serious objections to RE coming from those who considered compulsion unnecessary for what was in reality accepted practice.[1] Edward Norman commented in 1977 that 'the successful operation of the 1944 Act has removed education as one of the potential causes of friction at the centre of the relations of Church and State' (1977, p. 453). Few had any premonition of the upheavals yet to come.

POST-WAR DEVELOPMENTS

The content of RE in the 1950s, in accordance with each locally agreed syllabus, was undenominational[2] but confessional in approach, consisting primarily of Bible stories and church history. Few pupils studied the subject to public examination level and there was a serious shortage of teachers qualified in the subject,[3] a picture still regrettably familiar many years later. With a syllabus based on memorizing Bible knowledge rather than related to the pupils' experience, it was perhaps not surprising that a 1961 survey concluded that 'the standard of religious knowledge in the schools today . . . . is clearly very poor'.[4]

Collective worship hardly fared better. The traditional hymn and a prayer[5] to accompany the school's sports results at morning assembly was the common pattern in most schools, county or denominational. Assembly was often used to set the tone for the day, either encouraging pupil achievement or reprimanding miscreants. However, as schools expanded, particularly at secondary level, the logistics of assembling large numbers of pupils together in one place became increasing difficult[6] and people began to question the effectiveness of the exercise.[7] As school teaching was gradually seen more as a profession than a vocation, so teachers seemed more focused on their subject disciplines and less willing to assume responsibility for collective worship, although they might encourage their own form tutor group to present a school assembly; worship planning was normally left to the headteacher or the head of RE. In Anglican and Roman Catholic aided schools, however, all staff were often still expected to participate in and lead worship as part of their contracts.

By the 1960s, as the Durham Report on Religious Education noted (1970, paras 35–7), economic prosperity had encouraged more materialistic values and 'the shadow of the Bomb' led to 'an increased sense of purposelessness and cynicism', where 'religion was seen as neither true nor false but merely irrelevant' (para. 37). The 'New Theology' (e.g. John Robinson's 1964 *Honest to God*) had created the impression that not only Christian doctrine but also Christian ethics were in the melting-pot; questions were more important than answers. The continuing developments in biblical criticism, alongside those in science and technology, had changed the context for religious education in schools. Harold Loukes[8] therefore advocated a more 'problem-centred' discussion approach to classroom RE and Ronald Goldman's influential research[9] suggested that adult concepts of God as presented in the Bible were generally inappropriate for primary age children (a view reflected in a minority report of the 1967 Plowden Committee). Nevertheless, the commissioned Reports of Crowther (1959), Newsom[10] (1963) and Plowden (1967) all emphasized the importance of religious education in schools for helping pupils in the search for a faith by which to live; and the importance given to religious questions by secondary pupils was attested by the Alves Report[11] in 1968.

The 1970 Durham Report summed up the issues: 'the teaching

given in religious education must be based on sound scholarship, intellectual integrity and a concern for the enrichment of experience' (para. 116). 'It seeks neither to impose nor to indoctrinate' (para. 114). 'Some experience of worship is essential on educational grounds ... religious education without worship is like geography without field studies' (para. 117). 'To take Christianity as a base for religious education does not at all preclude the pupils learning something of the beliefs of other religions' (para. 123). 'It is clear that religious education must continue to make an important contribution to the moral education of pupils' (para. 171).

This encouragement to a more pupil-centred, 'implicit' approach, aiming to relate Christian teaching to a more questioning contemporary society, led to criticism that RE in secondary schools seemed to be primarily about 'drugs, sex and rock-'n'-roll'. The left-wing political influences of the 1970s, reflected in resource materials for RE such as the *Probe* booklets published by SCM (e.g. 'Community Relations', 'Revolution')[12] or Ian Birnie's *Focus on Christianity* series (e.g. 'Christianity and Politics' and 'The Church in the Third World', published by Edward Arnold), made 'liberation' rather than 'domestication'[13] the prime rationale for education; and RE's 'open' approach corresponded to the mood of the times. Even overtly Christian publishers could produce a series entitled *Christianity on Trial* (1973, 1974, Lion Publishing), encouraging pupils to question the truth of Christianity and the existence of God, with the options clearly presented; similar resources were being published for the expanding market of social studies or civics. The Schools Council suggested in Working Paper 36 that

> Religious education seeks to promote awareness of religious issues, and of the contribution of religion to human culture in general; it seeks to promote understanding of religious beliefs and practices; it also aims to awaken recognition of the challenge and practical consequences of religious belief. (Schools Council, 1971)

An increasingly pluralistic British society, resulting from the growth of immigration in the 1950s and 1960s, also raised issues about the understanding of non-Christian faiths (particularly Hinduism and Islam); Birmingham even attempted to include the secular 'life-stances' of Humanism and Marxism in its 1975 agreed syllabus until a successful legal challenge. 'The purpose of religious education was now to bring about an understanding of a variety of belief systems, rather than commitment to one'.[14] 'Many religious educators saw their contribution to multicultural education in terms of aiming to change negative attitudes towards religions and cultures of Britain's new citizens through knowledge and understanding, sometimes enhanced by personal acquaintance' (Jackson, 1995, p. 274).

This more 'explicit' and 'phenomenological' approach, characteristic of the late 1970s and early 1980s, encouraged education 'about religion' rather than 'into Christianity'. However, it led to a rather superficial 'Cook's Tour' of religions or even a comparative religion approach[15] squeezed into very limited curriculum time. By the late 1980s, this sociological and cultural focus was balanced by a more empathetic understanding of people's beliefs and an exploration of the spiritual dimension to human experience,[16] an approach clearly reflected in the 1988 debates on religious education.

RE AND THE 1988 EDUCATION REFORM ACT

As we have noted previously, Parliament had relatively little interest in the development of RE during the post-war period, assuming that its place in the curriculum was guaranteed by law and its content was the responsibility of locally agreed syllabuses. The legally-specified structure of the agreed syllabus conference within each LEA, guaranteeing representation for the different Churches, consisted of four committees: (1) Christian denominations other than Church of England; (2) the Church of England; (3) the teachers' associations; and (4) the LEA. However, by the 1980s this framework was being widely reinterpreted to meet local requirements, particularly by including representatives of non-Christian faiths on Committee 1.[17] Similarly, there was general acknowledgement that the daily act of collective worship in county schools was more often met in the breach than the observance. Consistent appeals from educationists[18] and headteachers[19] that the 1944 Act's requirements were unworkable, since large numbers of children had no concept of religious (let alone Christian) worship and most schools did not have sufficient space to assemble all pupils, still failed to stir the government into action. Ministers were far too interested in improving the quality of attainment in schools, the content of the secular curriculum and the standards of assessment, to be willing to concern themselves with a subject whose controversies had undermined government reforms in the past.

Under Margaret Thatcher, education policy was deemed a high

priority. Following her third election victory in 1987, she instructed her Secretary of State for Education, Kenneth Baker, to draw up proposals for a radical rethink of the nation's curriculum to ensure that children would be better equipped for the late twentieth century in their understanding of science and technology. She was particularly keen that 'a basic syllabus for English, Mathematics and Science with single tests to show what pupils knew' should be established (Thatcher, 1993, p. 593), but the Great Education Reform Bill (colloquially known to teachers as Baker's GERBILL) proposed a National Curriculum of not only those three core subjects, but also seven foundation subjects (History, Geography, Modern Languages, Art, Music, Technology and Physical Education).[20] Reflecting back in 1993, Thatcher observed:

> Ken Baker paid too much attention to the DES, the HMI and progressive educational theorists in his appointments and early decisions; and once the bureaucratic momentum had begun it was difficult to stop. John MacGregor, under constant pressure from me, did what he could ... Yet the whole system was very different from that which I originally envisaged. (*Ibid.*, p. 597)

Even when Kenneth Clarke[21] took over the education portfolio from MacGregor, after Geoffrey Howe resigned in autumn 1990 and precipitated Thatcher's downfall, he had difficulty managing the demands of the various National Curriculum working groups. In the famous dispute over the history syllabus, he suggested that events over the previous twenty years could not be classed as history; Thatcher had already considered the working group's findings 'too skewed to social, religious, cultural and aesthetic matters rather than political events'; she wanted 'a clear chronological framework – which means knowing dates' (Thatcher, 1993, pp. 595–6).[22] It was not until Sir Ron Dearing was appointed to simplify the requirements in 1994 that acrimonious debate began to subside.

In the midst of all these changes, religious education was expected to continue much as before under the 1944 framework. Its name was now legally amended from 'instruction' to 'education', but its 'Cinderella' status was enhanced only by additional procedures whereby parents could make official complaints if they were dissatisfied with the RE provision in their county school. The government clearly believed that affirming 'the special contribution' RE made to the education of all pupils (cf. HMSO (1985) *Better Schools*) was sufficient endorsement for the subject in the curriculum. Baker considered that as the Butler Act had been 'essentially a religious settlement', his own Bill did not need 'the powers and responsibilities of the Churches at the forefront' (Baker, 1993, p. 209).

The Churches thought differently, sensing that in the wholly changed environment created by the National Curriculum framework, there was little chance that RE would survive in any recognizable form. During the arguments about the implementation of a National Curriculum, outlined by the DES in July 1987, the Anglican and Roman Catholic Church spokesmen again became embroiled in a conflict with central government. Interestingly, once again the two main Churches found themselves on the same side, making common cause to defend the position of religious education in the curriculum. How did this public alliance come about? It could be argued that their concern was unimportant if not irrelevant, since their own 'aided' schools were unaffected by such proposals; religious education continued to be determined by governors and diocesan boards/commissions, while 'controlled' schools continued to follow their locally-agreed syllabuses.

Nevertheless, there were two main reasons for the Churches' intervention in the national debate. First, from a 'domestic' point of view, church schools were likely to find themselves having to reduce the amount of time allocated to RE in order to meet the demands and attainment targets of the other subjects in the National Curriculum, thereby undermining one of the main reasons why parents sent their children to church schools.[23] Secondly, from a more 'general' viewpoint, the Churches felt obliged to stand up to what they felt bound to consider a serious threat to the spiritual dimension of education in the nation's schools as a whole.

There can be little doubt that the government's original proposals were dominated by a secularist viewpoint, indicative of an increasingly utilitarian and materialistic approach to education in which market economics would become the overriding ethos of schools. Dr Graham Leonard, the Bishop of London, commented in an open letter to Kenneth Baker in September 1987: 'The main point we want to raise concerns the overall vision of education which inspires the government's plans.' Cardinal Hume's article in *The Times* (13 January 1988), entitled 'No room for Religion', stated:

> I come reluctantly to the conclusion that in its obsession with technology and economic prosperity, society is in danger of losing its vision and its soul. Certainly this bill as it stands offers us an

educational system and curriculum at the heart of which is spiritual emptiness.

The Catholic Bishops' Conference issued a statement in February:

> Catholics believe that Religious Education is not one subject among many but the foundation of the entire educational process . . . [RE] is not simply a body of knowledge co-terminous with Religious Studies, not merely to be 'fitted in' after time and resources have been allotted to the ten Core and Foundation subjects prescribed in the Bill. Rather, it stamps the Catholic school in every aspect of its operations with its distinctively Catholic character.

The government seemed to take notice of these criticisms, possibly because they themselves had not fully appreciated the predominantly secularizing nature of the DES proposals; or possibly because they realized that, to allow the bill to pass smoothly into law, they would need the support of the church representatives in the House of Lords. The legacy of being a national Church may still have had advantages. Yet at the same time, Baker was anxious to avoid his radical curriculum proposals becoming enmeshed in controversies over religious education, which past history had shown to be capable of bringing down the government of the day: 'I want to hold the principle established in the 1944 Act that the nature and content of RE should be locally determined. I am against central prescription in this sensitive area' (*The Times*, 1 February 1988).

This view, however, did not appear to take into account the fact that, under the 1944 Act, the Secretary of State retained ultimate legal responsibility for both the content and implementation of the agreed syllabus arrangements for RE; it was his duty to intervene if a local authority could not accept or agree on the syllabus of the statutory conference.[24]

As the debate intensified, Baker came under increasing pressure.[25] The Bishop of London, backed by the Catholic Education Council and the Free Church Federal Council, put forward specific new suggestions which on 17 March 1988 were eventually accepted and incorporated into the proposals before Parliament. Dr Leonard made four main points:

(i) RE should be firmly placed in the 'basic' curriculum of every maintained school.

(ii) The agreed syllabus procedure should be strengthened.

(iii) RE should be included under the provisions of the new complaints procedure.

(iv) All LEAs should have a duty to constitute a Standing Advisory
Council on RE.[26]

Baroness Hooper informed the House of Lords that 'with the help of
the churches ... we have reached agreement on ... additional
safeguards for the position of religious education in our schools'
(*Hansard*, 18 April, 1213). As Bishop Leonard later commented in
the House of Lords:

> In our judgement it was essential to reaffirm positively the position
> of the 1944 Act with regard to religious education, both because of
> its intrinsic importance and because, if left where it was, religious
> education would have become virtually neglected. (*Hansard*, 3 May
> 1988)

This view was supported in a letter to the *The Times* signed by nine
Anglican bishops (including the future Archbishop of Canterbury,
George Carey), endorsing the Christian elements of RE: interestingly, Leonard was in ignorance of the letter prior to publication.
Nevertheless, Bishop Leonard recalled (interview, June 1992) that
Baker never appreciated the difference of approach between Anglicans and Roman Catholics – the former being primarily concerned
for the community and the latter for nurturing their own children in
faith. Bishop Leonard found himself in the dilemma that if he were
to be sympathetic to the Roman Catholic approach, 'he would open
the door to the traditionalists' such as Baroness Cox, who was calling
for 'predominantly Christian' RE to be taught separately (*Hansard*, 3
May, 502), which would imply that RE was about 'teaching faith'
rather than 'teaching about faith'.[27] The Catholic Education Council
described the issue of 'predominantly Christian' as 'over-simple in
view of the complex religious position of the country' (CES, 1989, p.
7), but the controversial issue of 'predominance' was to re-emerge in
the DFE Circular 1/94.

There can be little doubt that the last-minute amendments proposed by Baroness Cox and Lord Thorneycroft on 4 and 12 May
1988,[28] insisting on specific reference to Christianity in RE and
school worship respectively, created considerable anxiety among the
bishops and other peers.[29] Bishop Leonard (interview, June 1992)
recalled one anxious moment when he feared he might find himself
having to vote against a pro-Christian amendment (*Hansard*, 1347).
After midnight on 12 May, some peers (whom Leonard dubbed 'the
Tribe') encouraged Lord Thorneycroft to put his amendment to the
vote. However, Lord Belstead reassured the Bishop of London,

having made sure that only the seventeen supporters of the amendment would be voting, that it would fall without him having to vote against it, since Standing Order No. 55 required a minimum of thirty peers to vote. At 8.30 a.m. the following morning, Kenneth Baker telephoned Bishop Leonard to discuss what to do next.

On the one hand such clauses would strengthen the Christian elements in the Act; but at the same time they ran the risk of alienating the sizeable community of Britain's non-Christian citizens, who could then undermine the inclusion of the spiritual aspects of the curriculum for all pupils by exercising their rights of withdrawal from school RE and worship altogether.[30] In an attempt to save the situation, the Bishop of London engaged in rapid consultation with other national religious and educational representatives to produce an agreed formula, viz. that each agreed syllabus should 'reflect the fact that the religious traditions in Great Britain are in the main Christian, whilst taking account of the teaching and practices of the other principal religions represented in Great Britain.'[31] Baker feared that Cox's supporters[32] would demand not 'collective' but 'separate' worship, thus allowing other faiths the right to their own religious education and worship within school hours: 'it was touch and go right up to the Third Reading in the House of Lords on 7 July' (Baker, 1993, p. 209). But by then Baroness Cox was pleased to have explicit reference to Christianity, while the bishop was relieved to have strengthened the place of RE without jeopardizing the established practice of multi-faith RE in many county schools.[33]

What both were agreed upon was the need to ensure that RE, including Christianity, took its place alongside other subjects in the National Curriculum. Their views were shared by Cardinal Hume, who also expressed the hope that Roman Catholics would be able to play a fuller part in determining religious education than in the past (*The Times*, 22 June 1988), implicitly recognizing that his Church's combative isolationism might now seem disadvantageous. Bishop Leonard recalled: 'I didn't talk much to Hume on education; although a charming person, he held himself aloof. We went as far as we could together. The Catholics seemed not to be speaking with one voice' (interview, June 1992).[34]

Yet the Churches, if united in common cause, could prove a formidable power-base. For instance later on 3 February 1992 the bishops, supported by Conservative backbenchers in the House of Lords, defeated the government by insisting that RE and worship should be retained in Sixth Form Colleges granted independence from LEA control. Although Anglicans had only one controlled Sixth Form College, they rallied to the cause of the Roman Catholics who had many.

When the Education Reform Bill finally passed into law in July 1988, both the government and the Churches seemed generally satisfied with the proposals. Baker acknowledged that 'the religious aspects of education had certainly been strengthened' (Baker, 1993, p. 209). Events had shown that the majority of people in our democracy were not ready to support a wholly secular upbringing for the nation's children[35] and that the Churches, when united in defending their Christian heritage, were far from being a toothless partner in the Church/State relationship.

THE AFTERMATH OF THE 1988 ACT

As the practical implications of the 1988 Education Reform Act became clearer, the Evangelical lobby grew increasingly concerned.[36] Agreed syllabuses on which the legislation depended were far from being 'mainly Christian' in content. Some in fact did not even mention God or Jesus Christ. One well publicized test case, brought by a parent (Mrs Denise Bell), resulted in Kenneth Clarke's ruling in April 1991 that the Ealing LEA agreed syllabus was unacceptable. Another test case in September 1992 (supported by the Parental Alliance for Choice) focused on Christian collective worship at a Manchester primary school. On 25 December 1992, a *TES* survey reported that 83 per cent of secondary schools did not hold daily acts of worship for all pupils and the HMI Report on the National Curriculum (January 1993) noted that collective worship was generally unsatisfactory in both primary and secondary schools. A booklet by Colin Hart entitled *From Acts to Action*, published by the Christian Institute, Tyneside, and launched at the House of Lords on 14 June 1991, encouraged parents to use the new complaints procedure. The Anglican General Synod Schools Officer, David Lankshear, while welcoming this booklet as 'helpful', regretted 'its confrontational style with schools and local authorities' (*Church Times*, 21 June). The partnership model with LEAs seemed all but gone.

In a statement on 20 June 1992 Baroness Blatch, then Minister of State for Education, regretted that two out of three local authorities had yet to redraft their syllabuses in line with the 1988 Act.[37] It can therefore have been a matter for no surprise that in the 1993 legislation LEAs which had not yet revised their syllabuses were required to set up an agreed syllabus conference by April 1995 and the requirements were tightened to emphasize that 'Christianity is the main cultural and religious heritage of our children.'[38] Nevertheless, as Bishop Leonard had foreseen, the Muslim Education Forum, deeply aggrieved at what they saw as these 'discriminating' proposals, launched a campaign for equal rights on 22 February 1993.

Meanwhile, assessment regulations were also moving forward.[39] Brian Griffiths, by autumn 1991 chairman of the Schools Examination and Assessment Council, himself a committed Evangelical, wanted to ensure that the study of Christianity was safeguarded in GCSE Religious Studies syllabuses. Nowhere were the consequences of the policy more apparent than in Roman Catholic schools: with 58 per cent of RE examination candidates entered from Catholic institutions, the RE traditionalists in the Archdiocese of Birmingham were able in 1992 to go further and insist that pupils should be offered an exclusively Roman Catholic option which took no account of any other Church. Other Catholic RE teachers, who wanted to encourage more ecumenical understanding by including a study of at least one other Christian denomination, regretted this more 'sectarian' emphasis.

On 29 June 1992, addressing a national conference on 'RE – the way ahead?' organized by Culham and St Gabriel's Trust, the Archbishop of York urged the government to reconsider the exclusion of RE from the National Curriculum. Dr Habgood highlighted the pressure on curriculum time and the shortage of qualified RE teachers.[40] He noted the move to bring agreed syllabuses into line with a national framework and attainment targets and argued that, with the demise of LEA influence, RE should no longer be marginalized in local agreements: 'the argument for local control is ... incompatible with stronger syllabus direction from the centre'.

The fact that the Archbishop's statement was widely welcomed by the Churches and government ministers indicated how far the debate had shifted since 1944. The Churches were united in wishing to prevent RE in their schools being squeezed by National Curriculum requirements. At the same conference Baroness Blatch herself suggested that there was room for further discussion with government. The chairman of the National Curriculum Council (NCC), David Pascall, in a speech to RE advisers and inspectors on 10 July 1992, recognized the Archbishop's concerns but reiterated the government's view that local bodies should take their legal obligations seriously, supported by guidance from the NCC. However, the government's declared commitment to the principle that schools should use their local RE syllabus had already been called into question by its own 1992 White Paper proposal allowing GM schools to use the agreed syllabus (if revised since 1988) of any LEA in the country (1993 Education Act, sections 138, 142).

The need for general curriculum rationalization was recognized by government. For example, back in January 1991 Kenneth Clarke had gone even further than the National Curriculum Council's new guidelines that foundation Key Stage 4 subjects like History and Geography might be combined for the GCSE examination; he had announced that only the three core subjects would be compulsory for 14–16-year-olds, to make space for more vocational courses. The present writer recalls her interview with Baroness Young back in 1987 when these 'quart into pint pot' problems were categorically denied to exist.

Meanwhile, the government issued a White Paper entitled *Choice and Diversity* (July 1992), with a section on 'moral and spiritual development' thought to have been written by the then Secretary of State himself, John Patten. In its response, issued as a press release, the Anglican Board of Education wrote,

> The contribution of RE to providing a moral framework needs also to take account of the fact that ethical responses to situations often differ from one member of a faith group to another ... We regret that the White Paper does not address the question of the supply of well-trained teachers ... We continue to press that the Government should recognise RE as a shortage subject.

On 5 March 1993, Patten finally announced a change in policy: he wished to explore, in consultation with the Churches and other faith groups, the possibility of a national framework for RE. Pascall even asked the Anglican Board of Education to draw up a framework for a 'model' agreed syllabus; Alan Brown, the Board's RE Officer, had some reservations about one denomination advising other faith groups but sensed that such a framework might be the only way the government could be persuaded to specify a minimum percentage of curriculum time for RE and what percentage of that time should be allocated to Christianity (SACRE conference, 5 January 1993). The need for the model syllabus framework was reinforced by evidence from the HMI Report on the introduction of the National Curricu-

lum (January 1993); this again noted that RE had inadequate
curriculum time and resources and that 30 per cent of non-
examination RE teaching for pupils in Years 10 and 11 in secondary
schools was deemed 'unsatisfactory'.[41]

DFE CIRCULAR 1/94

On 31 January 1994, the DFE published its long-awaited Circular
1/94 on *Religious Education and Collective Worship*, described by Patten
as a potential 'turning point in the spiritual life of this country' (*TES*,
4 February). It regretted, as 'a matter of deep concern', that RE and
collective worship 'do not take place with the frequency required or
to the standard which pupils deserve' (p. 9) and clarified the aims of
RE in schools:

> to develop pupils' knowledge, understanding and awareness of
> Christianity, as the predominant religion in Great Britain, and the
> other principal religions represented in the country; to encourage
> respect for those holding different beliefs, and to help promote
> pupils' spiritual, moral, cultural and mental development.

Reiterating the 1988 Act that RE should be 'in the main Christian',
the DFE emphasized that pupils should 'gain a thorough knowledge
of Christianity, reflecting the Christian heritage of this country' (p.
10). Similarly on collective worship (which in line with the Act was to
be 'wholly or mainly of a broadly Christian character'), it wished to
go beyond 'simple passive attendance' and 'encourage participation
and response, whether through active involvement in the presentation of worship or through listening to and joining in the worship
offered' (pp. 20–1); Christian collective worship should accord
special status to Jesus Christ, although schools could still seek a
'determination' from their local SACRE for alternative worship
arrangements (for example, if the majority of pupils were of a non-
Christian faith tradition).

The Circular caused an outcry among educational professionals.
Why should pupils have a 'thorough knowledge' of Christianity but
only 'knowledge' of other religions? How could schools ensure
'active involvement' in Christian worship if most pupils in a school
are Muslim (National Association of Headteachers (NAHT), *Bulletin*,
February 1994)? Why were circulars 'being used to promulgate
Ministers' personal predilections' (Association of Teachers and Lec-
turers)? Why was Christianity to 'predominate' , when this did not
appear in the 1988 Act (*TES*, 4 February)? The General Secretary of

ne National Association of Schoolmasters and Union of Women Teachers (NASUWT) protested that

> The Government is beginning to verge on the totalitarian and insufferable in insisting upon particular forms of collective acts of worship ... Ramming Christianity down all pupils' throats will not change society's values which have been so undermined by the sleaze and sordid commercialization associated with this Government. (*Education*, 4 February)

Professor John Hull even expounded what he saw as the government's own 'theology': Christianity has to be seen as distinct from other religions:

> in its integrity it is to be pure, as heritage it is to be typical of the nation, and in predominating it is to be powerful ... There is a Christianity which interprets itself in competitive market forces, extending separation and competition even into the place of worship. (Hockerill Lecture, November 1993)

The *TES* ran two leader articles reflecting on the debate. The first on RE (21 January 1994) regretted that

> the battle for religious education is fought without regard to practicalities, or evidence come to that. Instead Christianity has become a key element in that shapeless longing for the past now travelling as a Back to Basics policy. It has not gone unnoticed that the simpler, safer past full of Christian folk is probably also white. In short, RE has been presented as a matter of symbol, aspiration and self-definition from which many old-fashioned liberals, let alone minority faiths, feel excluded ... If the Christian right insists on pretending that this is a struggle for the soul of the nation, then at least Government ministers should stop giving them credence.

The second article (18 February) concerned school worship. The Anglican Bishop of Ripon, David Young, appointed as Bishop Adie's successor at the Board of Education, had publicly expressed doubts about the compulsory nature of acts of worship in schools, despite his predecessor's efforts at all-party compromise in the 1988 legislation.[42] Other Christians had even sensed 'sacrilege in the attempt to force children to participate in worship of a God that can be broadly, but not distinctively, Christian' (Trevor Cooling's letter, *TES*, 18 February 1994). The *TES* leader-writer felt that headteachers had not really tried to implement the law on daily collective worship:

> In an increasingly hedonistic society, personal values and beliefs have become a great liberal taboo. Many are more at ease with their

sexuality than their spirituality. Certainly, schools have become less inclined to address moral and spiritual truths, let alone assert them.

One deputy head, Andrew Evans, commented:

> It is perhaps because for too long society has apologised for religious faith, for being uncertain or unconcerned about basic moral principles, that we are witnessing the growing tide of dispossessed, dispassionate and disappointed young people in our society. Daily worship will not provide a panacea to cure all of society's ills, but it might just provide an opportunity for hope. (Evans, 1994)

The seriousness of the problem was brought home by the Office for Standards in Education (OFSTED) report on *Religious Education and Collective Worship 1992–1993* (1994), which provided evidence gleaned from inspections over the previous academic year confirming RE's low status and the shortage of specialist teachers. There was no RE provision in 20 per cent of primary schools and 75 per cent of secondary schools were not meeting the legal requirements at Key Stage 4. While primary school collective worship often encouraged social and moral development, the spiritual dimension was neglected and few secondary schools attempted to meet worship requirements. Resources and in-service training were generally limited and non-specialist teachers were unable to raise standards to an acceptable level. However, the report noted that in voluntary-aided schools 'RE and collective worship generally enjoy a higher status and are of better quality'. A year later, in its report on 735 inspections in 1993–4, OFSTED was unable to point to any improvement; unsatisfactory resourcing resulted from 'the low priority given to religious education in recent years'.

The pressure was mounting on the DFE to identify RE as a 'shortage subject', despite the fact that statistics indicated sufficient RE teachers were being trained. John Patten suggested that taxpayers' money was being spent 'training RE teachers who then vanish' (*TES*, 4 February 1994). An Early Day motion brought the issue to the House of Commons (13 April) and the Gates Report[43] argued that the DFE had failed to address the long-established hidden shortages; the Department was over-reliant on 'reported' vacancies, which ignored the lack of qualified specialists, the above-average class sizes, the demands of new agreed syllabuses and the poor time allocation (below Sir Ron Dearing's recommended 5 per cent). In addition, according to the DES 1988 staffing survey, 20 per cent of RE specialists were in church secondary schools, catering for only 10 per cent of secondary school pupils; county school RE shortages were therefore even more serious. Gates suggested that the DFE's reluctance to admit to the problem was less likely to be caused by 'conspiracy' or 'wilful negligence' than by political pressures to avoid additional costs.

A NATIONAL FRAMEWORK FOR RE

While the implications of Circular 1/94 were being further debated, the draft model RE syllabuses from the new Schools Curriculum and Assessment Authority (SCAA)[44] had been published in January 1994. After five years' intensive lobbying, the government's change of heart over a national framework for RE was widely welcomed by the Churches and educationists. The new SCAA chairman, Sir Ron Dearing, already entrusted with the task of reviewing and simplifying the demands of the National Curriculum, declared his personal interest in enhancing RE and the spiritual and moral dimension across the curriculum. He set in motion the consultative process for establishing nationally agreed RE model syllabuses to guide LEA Agreed Syllabus Conferences and, at the final launch on 5 July, reiterated his 1993 recommendation for a minimum of 5 per cent curriculum time to be devoted to RE. Expressing his satisfaction that the faith groups were helping to stem 'the ebb tide of religious knowledge', he commended what he saw were the 'great purposes' of RE:

> to learn about and to understand others, to learn about and understand ourselves, to ponder the great question about life and the universe, to develop understanding throughout the land between people of different faiths and culture; and, above all, to know and understand the core elements of the Christian and other main faiths of this country.

John Patten, as Secretary of State for Education, went on to emphasize the centrality of RE to a school's life, justifying its inclusion primarily as an opportunity for discussion of moral principles and values 'such as goodness, responsibility, fairness and duty, as well as care and compassion'. The Archbishop of Canterbury welcomed the prime place given to Christianity 'because of its formative influence in our society' but also 'the importance of understanding the other principal religions'; he described this as a 'sensible balance', even though it would not please everyone. Bishop David Konstant insisted that RE is not just a syllabus but 'an educational process; it's not merely instruction and it's not indoctrination – what we are concerned with is the growth of people as persons in their religious, moral and spiritual sensitivities'. He went on to plead for proper training for RE teachers and the accreditation of short courses for RE at Key Stage 4 (i.e. GCSE) and at Sixth Form level to enhance the subject's status.[45] The spokesman for the Muslim Education Forum, Mohammed Khan-Cheema, warned that people could use the SCAA guidelines either 'to emphasize excluding the already excluded by talk of dominance and predominance', or 'to foster a genuine effort towards inclusiveness'.

Such wide-ranging consensus might have lulled the government into a false sense of security. The right-wing Christian traditionalists were furious that the model syllabuses had failed to retain at least 51 per cent of RE time for Christianity.[46] Lady Olga Maitland MP described the guidelines as 'multicultural mish-mash': 'our leading churchmen have not stood up for Christianity' (*The Times*, 6 July 1994). Although Christianity would be taught at every stage of school education, it would normally be taught alongside at least one other world religion for children aged 5–7 and two other religions for 7–11-year-olds. Colin Hart, director of the Christian Institute, felt that this was 'too many too soon: young children cannot grasp so many religions so easily' (*Independent on Sunday*, 3 July). The *Daily Telegraph* (6 July) commented: 'In modern Britain, ignorance of Islam is a pity, but ignorance of Christianity is an educational and moral calamity'. In July 1994, Hart circulated a pamphlet entitled *RE: Changing the Agenda* to MPs and Synod members, accusing Anglican representatives on local agreed syllabus conferences of failing to veto syllabuses which presented Christianity as just one of a kaleidoscope of religions, and the Church of running down its school provision.

The Anglican director of the National Society's RE Centre rebutted the allegations, suggesting that Hart's figures were inaccurate; the Evangelical Alliance had welcomed the SCAA syllabuses and he should stop 'sniping at others toiling in the same vineyard' (*TES*, 28 April 1995). In 1995, a Culham report had shown that 31 out of 39 Anglican diocesan boards of education provided a diocesan RE syllabus for their aided schools; 5 of the other 8 offered guidelines on how aided schools might use or adapt the LEA agreed syllabus; 10

additionally gave advice to their controlled schools. As LEA support for RE reduced, a few boards were even considering offering their services to county schools (*Culham College Institute*, 1995a, pp. 9–10).

Meanwhile in 1993 the Vatican had finally approved the publication in English of *The Catechism of the Catholic Church*, which many Catholics thought would provide an appropriate framework for RE in Catholic schools, complementing or replacing the more open-ended *Weaving the Web* (Lohan and McLure, 1988). In response, the Catholic bishops issued *What Are We to Teach?* (1994), approved by the Committee of Catechetics to guide teachers through the catechism: 'Throughout the school years, the presentation of the whole Christian message must grow and develop so that it becomes ever more challenging and central to the lives of our young people' (pp. 7–8). Similarly the National Board of Religious Inspectors and Advisers produced a statement about Catholic religious teaching at the key stages entitled *Broad Areas of Attainment in RE* (1994). This defined the twofold aims of RE as 'learning about religion according to the Catholic faith and reflecting on the ultimate questions of life' (p. 10) and set out the framework of skills, attitudes and attainment targets, following closely the design of the SCAA model syllabuses. This was followed in 1996 by the bishops' *Curriculum Directory*, emphasizing both the teaching of formulas of Catholic belief and the need for pupils' active participation and response.

COLLECTIVE WORSHIP

Issues around collective worship also proved divisive. In November 1994 the Churches' Joint Education Policy Committee (by now representing Anglican, Roman Catholic, Orthodox and Nonconformist Churches, including the Evangelical Alliance) argued in a press release that the DFE's Circular 1/94 definition, 'worship of a Supreme Being, with special reverence being accorded to Jesus Christ', should be broader; it feared irrelevant and hypocritical acts of worship and drew attention to recent OFSTED reports:

> Heads and governing bodies are frequently disturbed by an inspection report which praises the quality of spiritual and moral education in their schools, but reminds them that they must cease to break the law on daily worship by all pupils in attendance.

Nevertheless, the committee made it clear that, until there was consensus on an alternative, daily worship should be retained to provide schools with at least one non-secular occasion. The Anglican Board of Education of the General Synod discussed the issue at its autumn meeting, and the NAHT conducted a survey which showed that 85 per cent of secondary and 65 per cent of primary heads felt they could not comply with the law. Meanwhile John Hull's Templeton Lecture 'Collective worship: the search for spirituality', given at the Royal Society of Arts on 12 December 1994, insisted that the requirement that school worship should be distinctively Christian should be dropped: 'Spirituality in schools is being throttled by a theological noose fashioned by civil servants'. Coincidentally on the same day, even the Evangelical Alliance suggested that schools stood a better chance of providing worship of real quality if such occasions were limited to only two a week and parents should 'opt in' instead of 'out'; but this led other evangelical groups (including Hart) to dissociate themselves from this view, considering that the Alliance had 'run up the white flag of surrender'. *Education*'s headline (16 December) read 'Radicals and Conservatives attack daily assembly'.

The debate gathered momentum in the New Year. At the 1995 North of England Education Conference, the Archbishop of York, John Habgood, was asked about collective worship. He publicly admitted that it was not working well, that fewer occasions might lead to better quality and that a review might be helpful. His remarks were seized upon by the media, alleging that 'senior clerics want to banish God from schools'. The *The Times* leader was headed 'The Church Unmilitant' (7 January) and subsequent press coverage fuelled the controversy over the next two months.

Habgood clarified his views in the *TES* (17 February 1995):

> The Department for Education, in trying to define more precisely what the content of worship should be in its Christian references, has made it more exclusive ... Previously there was more flexibility, which enabled schools to be more sensitive to where the pupils actually were in terms of their own faith or lack of it. The enormous problem which faces schools is, how can you fulfil the requirement to do something which is specifically Christian without dividing the community? ... There is another form of assembly, one which is concerned with the development of spirituality ... It needs to be related to more specific aspects of worship in different traditions ... What I have been suggesting could be done under the Act but not under the present regulations.

Traditionalist Anglicans, however, had by now rallied to the cause.

A former education minister and headteacher, Sir Rhodes Boyson MP, argued that morning assembly provided 'discipline for the day'. Baroness Cox wrote to Geoffrey Duncan at the Board of Education expressing 'deep concern' at the Church of England's 'retreat' on the issue. Arthur Pollard, an Anglican Board of Education member and contributor to the 'Black Papers' of the 1970s, which advocated 'back to basics', insisted that the law offered sufficient flexibility in timing, place and people to lead worship, for the head's duty in arranging it to be fulfilled; local clergy could always be called upon to help. He continued:

> For some of us on the Board, it is completely appropriate that the Church of England should stand foursquare in support of the law of the land ... Denominations may say and do what they please, but the Church of England is the church of the nation responsible for every soul in every community throughout the country. We cannot afford to neglect that responsibility. (*Education*, 20 January 1995)

Responses came thick and fast. 'The Archbishop of York's view that worship has a legitimate place in education where it is voluntary and carried through by believers, should be welcomed by Anglicans, not pilloried', wrote one headteacher (*Education*, 27 January). Another commented that, 'while worship should remain central to the life of Church schools, it is entirely without educational, moral or theological justification that county schools ... should be required to hold acts of worship' (*Education*, 3 February). A church historian noted that 50 years of compulsory school assemblies had not halted the decline in religious observance and pleaded for an ecumenical approach in 'introducing children to the rich diversity of Christian traditions' (*Church Times*, 10 February). An Anglican diocesan director of education argued, 'There must be a relaxation in the law, however unpalatable to the diehards in church and politics, ... to free school communities to work out their own patterns within some legal minima', e.g. three worship experiences a week for primary schools (at least two of which would be broadly Christian) and two a week (with one broadly Christian) for secondary schools (*Education*, 10 February). Even OFSTED's list of 53 'beacons of excellence' schools published in February 1995 was found to include only 4 which complied fully with the worship requirements.

The government, however, was prepared to stand its ground. Speaking in an adjournment debate sponsored by Michael Alison MP, Schools Minister Eric Forth argued:

We want greater compliance – happier compliance – with the law so that the great religious tradition of this country can benefit pupils up and down the land, regardless of their personal, parental or family religion. Pupils must benefit from the core beliefs of the Christian religion, which is, and continues to be, so important to our society and education system.

Alison dismissed the 1994 NAHT survey as 'bogus', insisting that fewer than 300 schools had significant numbers from non-Christian backgrounds and around 70 per cent of parents favoured collective worship. He disparaged John Hull's suggestion of 'collective spirituality' rather than 'collective worship' as 'nothing less than a call for the restoration of the full-blown, multi-faith mish-mash that was so vigorously criticised when the 1988 Act was put on the statute books' (*Education*, 24 February). Common ground, let alone consensus, seemed as far away as ever.

On 7 March 1995, the Churches' Joint Education Policy Committee issued an expanded version of its November consultation statement, emphasizing that 'School worship must allow pupils to respond personally or collectively in their own way' or 'it will be counter-productive and divisive'; 'We all agree with many teachers that one of the major stumbling blocks has been the attempt at tighter definitions in Circular 1/94'. In June, the bishops called an open meeting at the House of Commons on 'Collective Worship and the Law', to enable MPs to hear the views of teachers and religious leaders on the subject; HMI David Trainor regretted that schools' efforts to comply with the spirit of the law were not being recognized because their acts of worship were not held 'daily', but one head-teacher commented, 'More people are prepared to lead assembly than to teach physics, but we don't consider abolishing the latter'.

Throughout 1995 a series of seminars was organized by the Anglican Board of Education (sponsored by St Gabriel's Trust) to draw together views on collective worship from across the country; the responses from diocesan boards, while wishing daily worship in church schools to continue, generally thought collective worship arrangements needed more flexibility, particularly for secondary schools. The seminars found that most participants considered the 1988 legislation, albeit contentious at the time, had in practice provided a flexibility which was now being undermined by Circular 1/94; why was school worship not counted as 'curriculum time'[47] nor proper training provided? The survey[48] considered that a change in the law was unlikely while the objectives of collective worship remained debatable, but the Board hoped to continue discussions with the DFEE and OFSTED to agree a workable framework.

NATIONAL COLLABORATION IN RE

Meanwhile in 1995 the RE debate gathered momentum again. Three years on from the 1992 Culham and St Gabriel's conference, when the Archbishop of York had argued for RE to be included in the National Curriculum, Habgood reopened the issue at a follow-up conference on 8 March entitled 'National Collaboration in Religious Education'. The SCAA model syllabuses, he insisted, were not going to change

> the endemic problems of not enough specialist staff, not enough time for teaching and not enough resources ... Things are likely to get worse if LEAs can no longer afford RE advisers or resource centres, if the contribution of colleges to teacher training is diminished and if schools find themselves more and more subject to market pressures.

The Archbishop argued that RE's place in the curriculum was justified by the need to guide a 'morally bewildered generation'; to encourage a rational understanding of religion (to counter the influence of more irrational religious movements); and to appreciate religious issues underpinning international politics. He described religion as 'an essential part of knowledge and of human experience'; 'it is uniquely capable of relating all other subjects to some vision of the whole, and drawing out their practical implications for human life and community'.

Alongside the widespread media coverage of the conference,[49] a significant move by government ministers was also announced: from September 1996 public examination boards would offer a 'short course' for RE at GCSE level, appropriate to the 5 per cent of curriculum time recommended by Dearing at Key Stage 4. SCAA's professional officer for RE acknowledged the importance of syllabuses which would be 'challenging and intrinsically interesting' (*TES*, 8 December 1995).[50] At the national launch of the GCSE courses in June 1995, the chief executive of SCAA, Nick Tate, welcomed the development but highlighted the danger of too utilitarian a view of the curriculum: 'It is a disturbingly narrow, secularist view of the world that leads some people in our educational system to regard the dispassionate study of religion as something peripheral to the main purposes of schooling' (*TES*, 30 June 1995).[51]

Tate's concern that Britain was becoming a 'religiously illiterate society' was shared by John Gay in his RSA lecture of November 1994, which reported a Gallup poll in 1992 that 76 per cent of 16–24-year-olds had never heard of the Ascension. The director of the National Society's RE Centre, Alan Brown, acknowledged that children no longer understood religious references in art or literature (*TES*, 30 June 1995). Linda Edwards of King's College London, at the Anglican Secondary Heads' conference (September 1995), noted that in her research 80 per cent of children could not name two of the ten commandments or even one parable. The Secondary Heads Association survey published in 1996 showed that 64 per cent of grammar and 48 per cent of comprehensive schools had less that 3.5 per cent curriculum time allocated to RE, and at least 4 per cent of comprehensives were not offering RE to all students.

Concern was expressed by the *Times* leader-writer:

> The truth is that while we may reject or ignore Christianity, we can never escape its power over us. To teach it poorly in our schools is to rob children of the most essential education of all: the knowledge of who and what we are. (30 June 1995)

Clifford Longley went further: the Churches have some responsibility for RE's decline, since they had taken the best RE expertise into church schools rather than county schools, creating a secularized education system which might eventually turn against church schools.

> The argument concerns the Churches' self-interest. They also have a responsibility towards the whole nation. The Church of England admits as much without being sure what to do about it. But the Catholic Church can no longer isolate itself from what is happening in the rest of the school system ... The only strategy likely to reverse the trends Dr Tate has identified would be a combined RC and C of E effort to 'rescue' RE in the non-denominational sector. (*Daily Telegraph*, 30 June 1995)

Such recognition by this influential Catholic writer that Roman Catholics should feel confident enough to involve themselves beyond the enclave of their own school system showed how far the Church had come since 1944; it was also significant that ecumenical co-operation was seen as the best way forward.

The development of the GCSE 'short courses' was widely welcomed and renewed the call for RE to be declared a 'shortage subject'. In 1995, the Culham Institute published a survey on *Religious Education in Secondary Schools*, showing the highest priority being the need for more RE specialists; 'no other curriculum area would be exposed to an army of non-specialist teachers', said one respondent. However, in 1995 the Government's new Teacher Training Agency (TTA) still allocated fewer places for intending secondary RE specialists than any other subject (only 510 out of 16,630). While many of the church colleges, as Institutes of Higher Education, still retained RE teacher training, they had generally diversified their portfolios away from teacher education when they linked up with the larger secular universities, following the 1992 Act incorporating the polytechnics into the university sector.[52] The TTA's chief executive found difficulty in meeting a delegation from the RE Council (despite three months' notice) in May 1995 and a report from the National Foundation for Educational Research (published in January 1996) revealed that, although the decline in RE advisory posts appeared to have been halted, 35 per cent of LEAs still had no RE specialist or adviser. By October 1995, after constant lobbying (and even though no bursaries like those for physics teachers were to be available), the TTA was finally obliged formally to acknowledge RE as a 'shortage subject'.

Meanwhile the DFE's policy from 1992 of shifting substantially into school-based training (or wholly in 1994, under the School-Centred Initial Teacher Training (SCITT) scheme)[53] and of reducing the number of primary training places by 20 per cent in three years, threatened the future viability of many church colleges, to which church schools had traditionally looked for well-trained Christian teachers.[54] Especially following the 1995–6 budget cuts in higher education, college departments risked penalties for under-recruitment if RE targets were not met. In May 1995, Anglican and Roman Catholic church leaders put the case to the DFEE and the Committee of Vice-Chancellors and Principals (CVCP) that church colleges should be allowed to adopt the title 'University Colleges' to enhance their status and future prospects.

RE: THE SECTARIAN DIVIDE?

Just as it might be assumed that RE in schools was beginning to move into less troubled waters, the spectre of religious fragmentation reappeared on the scene. John Hull and Michael Grimmitt had already warned that the emphasis on the 'integrity' of religions, with the content owned by each separate faith tradition, as demonstrated in the SCAA model B syllabuses, could be 'antithetical to the development of a society in which religious tribalism is replaced by religious dialogue' (Grimmitt, 1995, p. 82). Trevor Cooling (1996) criticized the polarization between Grimmitt's view (prioritizing RE as 'educational' to enhance pupils' personal development) and that of the religious communities (emphasizing primarily pupils' 'religious' development). Cooling suggested that 'learning about' and 'learning from' religion (cf. SCAA syllabuses) could achieve both personal and religious development: 'To overemphasize one is to endanger the fine balance that makes religious education such a valuable subject.'[55]

Hull traced how the conservative Christian lobbyists, having been disappointed that the 1988 Act (Section 8.3) had not in reality reinstated pride of place to Christianity, began to argue that the integrity of each religion should be safeguarded to avoid a 'mish-mash' in RE and that Muslim parents should be encouraged to seek 'determinations' to allow Muslim acts of worship:[56] it seems they hoped that if each religion was distinctly separate, Christianity could once more become predominant. These traditionalist groups ranged from 'staunch supporters of the rights and privileges of the established Church' to 'those whose emphasis is more cultural than religious'.[57]

It did not take long for Muslim parents to seize their opportunity, particularly after their bids for a voluntary-aided Muslim school had again been refused. In 1996, two significant developments hit the headlines. First, at Batley in West Yorkshire, the Muslim community protested against the 'predominance' of Christianity in their schools by withdrawing 1500 pupils from RE in January; by June this had increased to 2400. The spokesman for the Muslim parents warned that, although Muslims had helped draw up the local agreed syllabus for Kirklees LEA, they still felt their children would be confused by, for example, the Nativity story's teaching because 'Islam teaches that God cannot be incarnated in human form'. The LEA's chief education officer felt 'the basic problem is a confusion between religious instruction in schools and religious instruction with which Muslims are more familiar' (*Education*, 26 January 1996). Nevertheless, as the Muslim pupils were mainly Asian, the withdrawal could be seen as a racial rather than a religious divide. Even the Anglican-controlled primary school was affected when 17 of the 37 Muslims withdrew: the head commented, 'Very rarely do we have difficulties because of

cultural differences, but this action has singled out certain young-
sters as being different' (*Church Times*, 14 June 1996).

The second development took place in Birmingham, where Birch-
field Primary School parents were offered, as an alternative to the
multi-faith RE, a Muslim RE class taught by a Muslim RE teacher; with
70 per cent of the 640 pupils from Muslim families, the arrangement
by which denominational RE could be provided at the request of
parents was deemed to be legal under the 1944 and 1988 Acts.
Concerned that this precedent might pave the way for the more
evangelical Christians[58] to insist on 'single-faith' RE for their children, Stephen Orchard of the Christian Education Movement
warned that 'separate RE could unpick the compromise reached
with the churches in the 19th century which had also been applied to
multi-faith RE. This would ultimately be to everyone's disadvantage'
(*Education*, 16 February 1996). Margaret Holness in the *Church Times*
noted that many Anglican 'controlled' primary schools, particularly
in Muslim inner-city areas, 'could be vulnerable to pressure from
activists' (16 February).

However, she also reported (*Church Times*, 14 June) that areas like
Kirklees' neighbouring LEA Bradford had few withdrawals from RE,
although many more schools had sought determinations on worship.
The Bradford Inter-Faith Centre put these better relations down to
the community's efforts on multi-faith issues in the 1980s. The
Anglican diocesan director of education reaffirmed the Church's
mission as the Established Church to serving its community, even
deciding to rebuild an Anglican school in an area where about 80 per
cent were Muslim; the RE in this school focused mainly on Christianity and Islam, but succeeded in keeping all the children together in
the classroom. Critical of the more secular 'liberal studies' approaches to RE of previous decades, a Muslim spokesman insisted, 'we
need to strive for a formula which is inclusive of all pupils and which
does not exclude any of the cultural traditions represented in our
school communities' (*Church Times*, 14 June).

Nevertheless this 'Pandora's box' had been threatening to open
for some time. The confusion between religious instruction in a
particular faith and a wider understanding of religious education was
never far from the surface, even through the debates in 1988 after 44
years of operating within the 1944 compromise. On 21 June 1988 in
the Lords, Bishop Leonard had been careful to deny that 'mainly
Christian' meant 51 per cent in every school rather than across the
country, or that a 'mishmash' of different religions would be taught

(*Hansard*, 717). Those who had expressed concern that the more 'aggressive' advocates of teaching predominantly Christianity to underpin Britain's cultural heritage could capsize the fragile boat, seemed to be proved right. Powerful lobby groups had rallied support to try to guarantee that explicit Christianity was taught in every school; thus, as Muslim leaders became more confident, they understandably modelled their approach on such Christian pressure groups. 'Sectarian' RE seemed to be moving closer.

THE SPIRITUAL AND MORAL DIMENSION

The 1988 Education Reform Act had stated that the purpose of education was 'to promote the spiritual, moral, cultural, mental and physical development of pupils at school and of society ... and to prepare pupils for the opportunities, responsibilities and experiences of adult life'. Such wide-ranging aspirations seemed impressive until the reality became clearer, that schools struggling just to comply with the law on National Curriculum attainment targets had little scope to reflect on these broader cross-curricular 'themes' and 'dimensions'.[59] Despite the government's apprehension that such areas might encourage pupils to question too critically, the House of Lords (after 'enormous battles', one HMI recalled)[60] insisted that the 1992 Schools Act reiterated the importance of the 'spiritual, moral, social and cultural development' of all pupils and required these areas to be inspected by OFSTED as outlined in the 1992 *Framework for Inspection*.[61] In 1993 that Framework was revised to combine all four areas of 'personal development' while retaining distinctive evaluative criteria, but OFSTED inspections continued to be focused primarily on 'outcomes' rather than 'process'. The 1995 revision asked inspectors to judge the extent to which a school was providing 'its pupils with knowledge and insight into values and beliefs and enables them to reflect on their experiences in a way which develops their spiritual awareness and self-knowledge' (Section 5.3).

Meanwhile in April 1993 the NCC produced a discussion document on *Spiritual and Moral Development*, in order 'to guide schools in their understanding of spiritual and moral development and to demonstrate that these dimensions apply not only to RE and collective worship but to every area of the curriculum and to all aspects of school life'. The document emphasized that

> the potential for spiritual development is open to everyone and is not confined to the development of religious beliefs or conversion

> to a particular faith ... It has to do with relationships with other
> people and ... the search for meaning and purpose in life and for
> values by which to live.

Such language was not dissimilar from the 1970 Durham Report
(para. 107). This NCC document was widely circulated to schools
and reissued in 1995 under Sir Ron Dearing as a SCAA discussion
paper (No. 3) to assist schools in preparation for OFSTED inspections. The issues it raised were taken up by OFSTED in a paper of
February 1994 written by HMI David Trainor. It noted that

> spiritual development is emphatically not another name for reli-
> gious education, although there are close connections, and
> spiritual development may be both an aim for religious education
> and an outcome of it ... spiritual development is a responsibility of
> the whole school and the whole curriculum, as well as activities
> outside the curriculum. (OFSTED, 1994c, p. 8)

Taking into account the views of those with or without a specific
religious belief, the inspection framework must 'press towards a
common currency of shared understandings'. The four aspects of
personal development should be taken seriously both in personal
relationships across the school and in all curriculum subjects.[62]

The Catholic bishops also recognized (in *Spiritual and Moral Development across the Curriculum: a discussion paper*, 1995) that, although
the NCC document had not expressed 'the meaning of the spiritual
in our Catholic tradition', it did 'usefully sketch out some common
starting points. In the Catholic tradition, spiritual development is
inseparable from growth in faith' (p. 11). On moral development,
'we must make it clear to the children and their parents that, in
advocating certain moral values, we are presenting a distinctive vision
of human life' (p. 21). 'In the Catholic school, we see the inter-
dependence of spiritual and moral development' (p. 27). The
Islamic Academy also welcomed the NCC publication: 'It is gratifying
that the importance of the spiritual and moral dimensions of education is being increasingly recognised.'[63]

Nevertheless, confusion remained. If inspections reported an
'orderly atmosphere', did that mean schools were good 'morally'?
Was social compliance evidence of moral development or an ethical
framework? Was there a danger in trying to structure the 'spiritual'
dimension? Could pupils be spiritually developed without any knowledge of God? If questions were more important than answers, would
this open-endedness leave pupils cynical? Taking up Milbank's analy-

sis[64] that 'policing the sublime begins with that tendency in secular thought to exclude God from the realms of meaningful discourse', Adrian Thatcher criticized the NCC document for its apparent reductionism, 'assumed searches for meaning, emphases on interiority, generalised awe, personal identity, and borrowings from literature and art'; nevertheless he acknowledged the opportunity to clarify 'more religiously adequate models of spirituality'.[65]

Unlike most primary class teachers, secondary teachers were seldom able to have a curricular overview; this often led to the 'affective' domain being sidelined in the pressure to complete the prescribed syllabus. OFSTED found that personal and social education (PSE) was the subject most criticized in its reports for lack of motivated staff and pupils (like RE, it had no accreditation), whereas when RE was taught well by specialists, values issues could be explored professionally and 'legitimized'. There seemed to be a fear among staff of contravening 'political correctness' in classroom discussions and therefore a reluctance to stray into the territory of 'values',[66] despite the view that 'the unfolding of a learning society will depend upon the creation of a more strenuous moral order'.[67] As Christopher Price commented,

> Throughout a century of argument between church and state about the 'dual' system of secular and religious schools in England, the rhetoric assumed the centrality of moral and religious education in both traditions. Now with the churches and the great education authorities sidelined, such arguments are no longer deployed: when the grant-maintained system was set up, the schools were given no hint that they should have any particular ethic beyond individuality, the market and competition – the secular religion of the 1980s ... The 1988 Act was grossly unbalanced; it led to too much testing and too little space for values. (*TES*, 'Opinion', 20 October 1995)

One head of RE, questioning the impact on pupils of moral education, wrote in reply: 'The overwhelming message they receive from the media is that money is the god and the National Lottery is hope ... Survival of the fittest is illustrated in league tables' (*TES*, 3 November 1995). Even John Patten joined in the debate from the backbenches, arguing that 'we need the help of religious education in order to underpin a re-born theology of work, which in its turn can be the foundation for the moral legitimacy of the free market' (1995 lecture on 'Christian values in education').

Growing concern led to a major National Symposium on 15 January 1996 entitled 'Education for adult life with particular reference to the spiritual and moral dimensions of the curriculum', its high profile enhanced by the presence of Sir Ron Dearing and Dr Nick Tate, respectively the Chairman and Chief Executive of SCAA. Dearing noted the public's 'distress' about moral standards in the face of 'evil'[68] and Tate criticized 'moral relativism', encouraging schools and society to be more explicit about teaching 'right and wrong'. He recognized the 'crucial' role of RE in moral development and announced an SCAA National Forum (including parents, teachers, industrialists, police and youth workers) to take these ideas further. In October, their discussion document on *Values in Education and the Community* was published, receiving widespread media coverage.[69]

At the same time, the Catholic Church contributed to the discussion with a statement by the Bishops' Conference on *The Common Good*, encouraging Catholics to examine political policies in the light of the Catholic Church's social teaching. It suggested (pp. 25–6) that

> the nation's real crisis is not economic, but moral and spiritual ... loss of confidence in the concept of the common good is one of the primary factors behind the mood of pessimism ... Young people [should] be encouraged to ... see that the good of society as a whole deserves their commitment and idealism.

Meanwhile, on 5 July 1996, the Archbishop of Canterbury had welcomed the SCAA initiative and launched a special debate in the House of Lords on moral values in society, ironically coinciding with the announcement of the royal divorce settlement between the Prince and Princess of Wales. He criticized the apparent privatization of religion, insisting on its central role in the education of young people:

> Under this tendency, God is banished to the realms of the private hobby and religion becomes a particular activity for those who happen to have a taste for it ... I believe that there is a great deal to be done here in teacher-training to help to give teachers greater confidence, skills and techniques in bringing out the moral and spiritual aspects of many different subjects.

In the debate, peers across the political spectrum fulminated about the harmful influence of the media, the lack of support from parents and the poor moral standards of the business world. Viscount Tony-pandy pleaded, 'If society has gone wrong, don't put the blame on the schools. If society has lost its way, it's because it's lost its faith.' Several reiterated the importance of RE and collective worship in schools to help pupils consider the fundamental questions of life and welcomed the inspection of moral and spiritual development in schools.

The importance attributed to the teaching of moral and spiritual values in schools, however, was always going to depend less on society's public 'breast-beating' than on the confidence of teachers and the seriousness with which they viewed such issues in the class-room. While OFSTED reports or the media generally might be critical of their efforts or lack of them, teachers' hesitation in advocating unequivocal moral standpoints or spiritual guidance seemed to reflect the uncertainty of a society which paid mere lip-service to its Christian heritage, whose moral values had been steadily undermined by moral relativism and in which teachers, faced with a diversity of school pupils' religious beliefs or life-stances, felt con-fused and unsupported. With schools increasingly the only secure place for children whose homes had been turned upside-down by divorce or deprivation, Nick Tate of SCAA acknowledged their role as havens of security and explicit moral values in an ever-changing world.[70] Yet schools needed more than public rhetoric to support them in encouraging pupils' moral and spiritual development.

CHURCH SCHOOL INSPECTION

Like county schools, church schools were subject to independent inspection under Section 9 of the Education (Schools) Act 1992, as amended in 1993, for the quality of their education provision, the educational standards achieved, the efficient management of resour-ces and the spiritual, moral, social and cultural development of their pupils. They were also to be inspected under Section 13 by an inspector for 'Denominational Religious Education' chosen by the governors, which could take place at the same time.

In 1992, the Churches had 'insisted that knowledge of the philoso-phy of Church education is required if inspectors are to judge the spiritual and moral development of pupils competently' (*TES* front-page headline 'Church's threat to inspection timetable', 30 October); they insisted that Section 9 teams should include a

Church-appointed lay inspector, although this had not been specified in the legislation. OFSTED was concerned that such concessions
would open the way for other religious groups to make similar
demands. However, amendments in 1993 did allow for the content
of a school's collective worship to be inspected and clarified that
voluntary-controlled schools were also to be subject to Section 13
denominational inspection (Section 259). The Section 13 inspector
was also to report on the pupils' spiritual, moral, social and cultural
development, the government belatedly realizing this could not be
separated under Section 9 from the RE provision of the school under
Section 13. This legislation provided the first opportunity for the
Churches to assess through inspection the service their schools were
offering; until the 1992 Act, the Churches had only had the right,
rather than the responsibility, to inspect their schools denomination-
ally.[71] The subsequent DFE Circular 7/93 required both inspection
on a four-yearly cycle and a post-inspection action plan including RE
to be drawn up. If a school was deemed to be 'failing' even after the
action plan had been implemented, the government could appoint
an 'Education Association' (without church representatives) to take
over (although it should act in accordance with any existing trusts),
and in the last resort the Secretary of State could order the school's
closure. The Churches were understandably concerned that the
secular power of the State had invested itself with direct control over
the provision of church schools.

Following the first 100 inspections, OFSTED reviewed the new
system in *A Focus on Quality* (1994). It reported the Anglican Board of
Education's regret that even OFSTED's trainers appeared ignorant of
the voluntary sector's distinctive legal framework and also its concern
about inspecting spiritual and moral development within the 'Framework's emphasis on learning outcomes rather than the experience of
the child'. The Catholic Education Service also wished for greater
clarity in the relationship between Section 9 and 13 inspections.

Both Churches produced guidelines[72] and support materials[73] on
inspection for their schools, but the issue of most significance
seemed to be the governors' appointment of Section 13 inspectors.
In the negotiations for the 1992 Act, the Churches had tried unsuccessfully to insist that, as for Section 9 appointments, appropriate
Section 13 training should be made mandatory; the government had
teasingly replied to Church representatives, 'Don't you trust your
governors?' The original OFSTED specification (cf. DFE Circulars
7/93 and 1/94) had stated:

Ofsted encourages the governing body to arrange inspection of denominational education at the same time as the Ofsted inspection and invites it to consider contracting with the Registered Inspector or one of his/her team for the inspection and report as required under Section 13 of the Act.

However, Catholic guidelines were unequivocal: 'Under Canon Law, the RE inspector must be acceptable to the Bishop of the Diocese.' The Church objected strongly to secular inspectors writing reports on the quality of the spiritual and moral education in a Catholic school and wished to retain control. One sceptical Catholic teacher even surmised that denominational inspectors could be used by the Catholic Church to impose traditional views and curtail more radical RE teaching: 'Inspectors are hand-picked to "follow Peter"' (*TES*, 11 October 1996).

Similarly, Anglican diocesan boards drew up lists of approved inspectors, specifically trained by the National Society for Section 13 contracts; a few dioceses established their own inspection teams, believing that at least some inspectors should understand the aims of church schools, whilst others felt they were more useful to their schools in a supportive advisory capacity following an inspection (see Gay, 1995, pp. 11–12).

In March 1996 the issue was headlined in reports that the governing body of St Marylebone Anglican secondary school in the London diocese had appointed a Jewish Section 13 inspector (who had not attended the National Society's training course) with the support of its diocesan RE adviser; the latter acknowledged that the diocesan guidelines were 'unenforceable'. This prompted the General Synod Board of Education RE Officer to write to all diocesan directors of education, suggesting that the appointment of non-Christians as denominational inspectors for church schools 'raises questions about the integrity and probity of the whole exercise. The person involved should be familiar with Anglican schools and be a practising Christian'. The diocesan director for Blackburn commented, 'The Church fought hard to ensure that denominational inspections were included in the 1992 Act: St Marylebone's choice makes us look very foolish' (*Church Times*, 22 March 1996).[74]

Despite such problems, the Churches seemed overall to accept that their denominational interests were being served by the Section 13 framework. The Anglicans were generally satisfied as long as their schools' Section 13 inspectors had been trained by the National Society, although Jane Lankshear's 1996 research suggested that 12 per cent of 504 Anglican primary school inspections had been conducted by untrained inspectors; she nevertheless found that worship in the majority of Anglican schools complied with their trust deed.[75] Similarly the CES, reporting in 1995 on *Quality of Education in Catholic Secondary Schools* from the results of over 80 inspections, indicated (p. 8) that

> senior staff and governors successfully promote the Catholic ethos within their schools ... Religious education departments are generally well-organised ... The schools are seen as an important and integral part of the wider Catholic community ... Prayer, in the form of collective worship, liturgical celebration and private reflection, is an integral part of the life of the schools.

CONCLUSION

The government had come a long way since 1988. The marked contrast between the 'hands-off' statements of Kenneth Baker in 1987, anxious not to stir the sleeping Leviathan and only reluctantly squeezing RE into the 'basic' curriculum, and the recognition under Sir Ron Dearing that RE should have a national 'model' framework supported by accreditation and training, showed how much the climate had changed. The important contribution of RE to the 'spiritual and moral' development of the nation's children was now publicly acknowledged by OFSTED inspectors and SCAA, while schools were responding to the challenge of providing effective RE teaching as more classroom resources became available.[76]

Bearing in mind not just their own schools, the Churches had made commendable efforts to enhance RE, the subject many educationists had expected (or perhaps hoped) would die of neglect and inertia. Stronger ecumenical partnerships between Anglican and Roman Catholic church leaders had enabled them to achieve far more together than would have been likely if central government had been able to 'divide and rule'. Religious values were once again on the political agenda. They had much about which to be gratified.

NOTES

1 *The Fourth R* (Durham Report 1970), paras 26–7; Lord Butler, speaking later in a debate on RE on 15 November 1967, remarked: 'I shall listen with respect to those who have doubts about religious instruction being compulsory, but I am convinced of the principle which animated us in the flush of war-time.'

2 Kenneth Wolfe noted: 'Christianity was undocked from its ecclesial craft' ('Religion and the 1944 Education Act: education and engineering', paper to the British Sociology Society, 1995).

3 See Institute of Christian Education (1954) *Religious Education in Schools* (London: National Society and SPCK).

4 University of Sheffield Institute of Education (1961) *Religious Education in Secondary Schools* (London: Nelson), p. 44.

5 Wolfe described it as 'the 1944 liturgical warhead' (*ibid.*).

6 By the 1970s, comprehensive schools were generally catering for around 1500 to 2000 pupils. Few had assembly halls large enough to accommodate the whole school for collective worship even if they wanted to.

7 E.g. J. Hull (1975) *School Worship: an obituary* (London: SCM).

8 H. Loukes (1961) *Teenage Religion* and (1965) *New Ground in Christian Education* (both London: SCM).

9 R. Goldman (1964) *Religious Thinking from Childhood to Adolescence* and (1965) *Readiness for Religion*, p. 8 (both London: Routledge).

10 Chapter 7 was entitled 'Spiritual and moral development'; RE was seen to be about more than ethical teaching (p. 59).

11 C. Alves (1968) *Religion and the Secondary School* (London: SCM). Further research on pupils' attitudes to RE can be found in L. Francis and J. Lewis (1995) 'Who wants RE?' in J. Astley and L. Francis (eds) (1996) *Christian Theology and Religious Education* (London: SPCK).

12 Described by Norman as 'doctrinaire politics'; he observed, 'The Church has given a generous hearing to radical views on education' (1977, pp. 452–3).

13 P. Friere (1972) *The Pedagogy of the Oppressed* (London: Penguin).

14 A. Wright (1993) *Religious Education in the Secondary School* (London: Fulton), p. 17. Ninian Smart's work on world religions was particularly influential.

15 Cf. E. G. Parrinder (1967) *Comparative Religion* (London: Allen & Unwin). The danger with this comparative approach was, e.g. that while Christianity and Islam

might both identify their founders in Jesus and Muhammad respectively, the theological understanding of each was profoundly different.

16 S. and B. Sutcliffe (1994, 1995) *Faith and Commitment* series (Norwich: RMEP). These booklets, including interviews with specific religious communities, 'offer students insight into spirituality in the context of real individuals, their experiences, feelings and values'.

17 E.g. Committee 1 of the 1982 Inner London Education Authority's Conference included one Muslim, Hindu, Sikh, Jew, Humanist, Methodist, Baptist and Pentecostal representative, and two Roman Catholics, who struggled to come to the unanimous agreement required. Even then the Muslim community felt their different traditions (e.g. Sunni and Shiite) should have separate representation: a compromise was reached by offering the additional Muslim 'observer' status. Also note that no Committee 2 was required in Wales.

18 E.g. J. Hull (1975).

19 National Association of Headteachers (1985).

20 Back in 1942, a Christian group (basing its practical ideas on the work of Karl Mannheim) advocated compulsory technical and vocational education from 14 to 18, the replacement of classics by a National Curriculum of science and technology, and the inculcation of public spirit through the teaching of Christian doctrine. This was rejected by the Conservative Party's Central Council in September 1942 as, among other things, 'Christian fascism'.

21 Clarke (described by Thatcher, 1993, p. 835 as 'an energetic and persuasive bruiser') had hoped his objections to 'vouchers' would preclude his appointment, but his disagreement with Thatcher later became public (A. McSmith (1994) *Kenneth Clarke: a political biography* (London: Verso), p. 172). Vouchers for nursery education were eventually piloted in 1996.

22 The right wing's ideological influence is discussed in K. Crawford, 'A History of the Right; the battle for control of National Curriculum History', *British Journal of Educational Studies* **xxxxiii**(4), December 1995.

23 This point was made in the statement from the Catholic Teachers' Federation in February 1988 and reiterated in the Hierarchy's letter read in all parish churches on 27 February 1991.

24 The controversy over West Sussex's RE syllabus in 1981, however, suggested that the DES was most reluctant to exercise this power.

25 It did not go unnoticed that, comparing the 1944 and 1988 legislators with reference to Genesis 40, it was the butler who was rewarded and the baker who was hanged.

26 Although agreed syllabuses have been required since the 1944 Act, they have not always been updated nor have all LEAs established a Standing Advisory Committee on RE (SACRE); the writer was instrumental in persuading one LEA in 1985 that its 1948 syllabus (even though legally binding) was wholly inappropriate for its by then multicultural community.

27 Cf. Colin Alves's article in the *British Journal of Religious Education* **13**(3), Summer 1992, p. 174.

28 *Hansard*, 502 (4 May) and 1343–44 (12 May).

29 *Ibid.*, 505, 510 (4 May).

30 In 1996, 1500 Muslim parents exercised this right in Batley, West Yorkshire (*TES*, 26 January 1996), when they considered their official primary schools' RE programme was 'insufficiently Islamic'.

31 An amendment incorporated into Section 7 of the 1988 Act.

32 Thatcher 'had a high regard for Caroline Cox and had been briefed to support her by Brian Griffiths. But Margaret agreed that these latest demands were going too far ... and gave her support to Graham Leonard's proposals' (Baker, 1993, p. 209).

33 *Hansard*, 432, 434.

34 Bishop Leonard sensed differences of approach between the Catholic Education Council (mainly concerned with legal matters and trustees) and the Catholic Education and Formation Council (concerned with RE and catechesis).

35 A MORI poll in 1991 stated that 84.5 per cent of the nation had some Christian allegiance.

36 Baroness Cox in *Hansard*, 17 June 1992, 259.

37 *Sunday Telegraph*, 21 June 1992. *Hansard* also reported information from the Christian Institute that only 15 out of 117 LEAs had produced new RE syllabuses (17 June, 261).

38 The Conservative-controlled Westminster Council only allowed three non-Christian representatives, together with one each from the Roman Catholic, Orthodox and Nonconformist Churches, on Committee 1 of its Agreed Syllabus Conference in 1993; unlike other LEAs, it had little contact with its SACRE until its Education Committee chairman resigned over the 'homes-for-votes' scandal.

39 Key Stage tests for 7, 11, and 14 year olds in 1992 were at the pilot stage or beyond. National league tables of examination results began in September 1992.

40 The DES Secondary School Staffing Survey (1988) showed that only 44 per cent
   of RE teachers had any post-school RE qualification; few could choose to
   specialize in a subject outside the National Curriculum.

41 The HM Senior Chief Inspector's *Fourth Annual Report* had previously warned in
   1992 that 'the entitlement of some pupils to religious education was not being
   met' (p. 17). The 1997 OFSTED report was no better (pp. 17, 25).

42 A *Church Times* article on Young's appointment commented: 'Educational controversies are as numerous as the snakes in Medusa's hairdo, with religious
   education and collective worship potentially the most poisonous' (25 March
   1994).

43 B. Gates (1993) *Time for Religious Education and Teachers to Match: a digest of under-
   provision* (Lancaster: Religious Education Council). This report revealed that
   over 50 per cent of secondary school RE staff had no formal RE qualifications
   and only a quarter had degrees in the subject.

44 SCAA was created in autumn 1993 by the amalgamation of the National
   Curriculum Council (NCC) and the Schools Examination and Assessment
   Authority (SEAC).

45 The poor status of RE was reconfirmed by Francis and Lewis, who found that
   only 35.6 per cent of Year 9 and 10 pupils in secondary schools thought RE had
   a place in the school curriculum. Even among Roman Catholic and Anglican
   pupils, only 49.6 per cent and 42.6 per cent respectively supported RE. Interestingly the research showed that pupils in favour of RE 'hold a more positive
   attitude towards school and towards work in general'(1995, pp. 230–1).

46 The original draft models had allowed up to 75 per cent for Christianity.

47 There remained a legal anomaly that church services for voluntary-controlled
   church schools were not deemed 'collective worship', whereas they were for
   aided or special agreement schools.

48 Alan Brown described it as 'a very comprehensive exercise, certainly the largest
   on the issue of collective school worship in the recent history of the Board'
   (*Between a Rock and a Hard Place* (1996) (London: National Society), p. 5).

49 Reports on 9 March included: 'Archbishop warns schools over religious education' (*Daily Telegraph*); 'RE decline threatens moral confusion' (*Independent*);
   'Habgood urges support for RE' (*The Times*).

50 In 1996 the Northern Examination and Assessment Board offered courses in
   'Thinking about God' (e.g. discussion on the nature of the universe and the
   problem of suffering) and 'Thinking about Morality' (e.g. absolute and relative
   morality and the relationship betweeen belief and behaviour).

51 Wolfe wrote to *The Times*: 'the young should know how religions were born and shaped; how they are the product of historical influences, all of which are the stuff of religious studies. Only thus will the formality and academic reputation of the subject be established as an indispensable ingredient in our education system at all levels' (11 July 1995).

52 For discussion of the implications for church colleges, see J. Gay and P. Chadwick in the *Tablet* (10 and 17 February 1995). The debate continued in *An Excellent Enterprise*, a report for Anglican General Synod (GS 1134, 1994), and *Partnership in the Training of Teachers for Catholic Schools* (CES, 1995).

53 Thatcher (1993, p. 598), concerned about teacher competence and 'socialist' ideology (e.g. multiculturalism and equal opportunities), insisted that 'the effective monopoly exercised by the existing teacher-training routes had to be broken'. The school-based training scheme was incorporated into the 1994 Education Act under John Major.

54 In May 1996, after receiving a poor OFSTED report on its teacher training, Lancaster University announced the closure of Charlotte Mason College, an Anglican foundation in Ambleside which had merged with Lancaster in 1992 (*Times Higher Education*, 31 May 1996). Edward Norman, noting the secularization and expansion of the church colleges, regretted that in the process they seemed to have lost their Christian identity (*Church Times*, 14 June 1996).

55 'Education is the point of RE – not religion? theological perspectives on the SCAA model syllabuses', in J. Astley and L. Francis, 1996, p. 180.

56 The Parental Alliance for Choice in Education, chaired by Baroness Cox, supported this Muslim request in Birmingham in 1994.

57 J. Hull (1996) 'A critique of Christian religionism', in J. Astley and L. Francis, 1996, p. 145).

58 Fred Naylor supported the Muslims' case on Channel 4 News (22 February); it was argued that Muslim children want to distance themselves from 'spectator religion'.

59 One HMI described 1988–93 as the 'wilderness period'. The NCC published a range of guidelines on cross-curricular themes, e.g. economic and industrial awareness, citizenship, health education.

60 These battles were commented on by G. Walford in 'The Northbourne Amendments: is the House of Lords a garbage can?', *Journal of Educational Policy* 10(4), July 1995. Lord Northbourne's amendments were intended to ensure that school inspectors should assess more than just league-table positions.

61 OFSTED training courses for new inspectors in 1992 revealed concern about inspecting such ill-defined concepts as 'spirituality'; some more cynical participants argued that perhaps the newly appointed lay inspectors should be members of the clergy so this dimension could be left to them.

62 During the Dearing review of the National Curriculum in 1994, science teachers were concerned that an over-emphasis on technical skills and knowledge would remove the important moral/social aspects of their subject.

63 Islamic Academy (1993) *Spiritual and Moral Development: a response to the NCC discussion paper*, p. 5.

64 J. Milbank (1990) *Theology and Social Theory: beyond secular reason* (Oxford: Blackwell).

65 'Policing the sublime and the spiritual development of children' in J. Astley and L. Francis, 1996, pp. 134–6.

66 In a survey of pupils' values, most thought sniffing glue or using heroin was wrong; but the overwhelming majority found drunkenness morally acceptable, though Free Church pupils continued to reflect traditional disapproval and Roman Catholics showed significantly greater tolerance (L. Francis and B. Kay (1995) *Teenage Religion and Values* (Leominster: Gracewing).

67 S. Ranson (1993) 'Markets or democracy for education', *British Journal of Educational Studies* **xxxxi**(4), p. 344.

68 In the light of the serial murders by the Wests in Gloucester, the death of 2-year-old James Bulger by two primary school pupils and the fatal stabbing of Catholic headteacher Philip Lawrence outside his own school gate in London.

69 This coincided with the conviction of the teenager responsible for the murder of headteacher Philip Lawrence and the plea by Lawrence's widow for a more explicit debate on the moral values underpinning our society; as a result, politicians from all parties vied with each other to occupy the moral high ground in the run-up to the election.

70 In January 1996, attacking the 'all-pervasive moral relativism', he noted that schools were among the few organizations attempting to 'shore up the moral fabric of our society' (*TES*, 19 January).

71 For further discussion, see J. Lankshear ('The inspection of collective worship in Anglican primary schools: an analysis of Section 13 reports', paper given to the International Symposium on Church School Studies, Durham, 3 July, 1996).

72 CES (1994) *The Inspection of Catholic Schools: guidelines for governing bodies, headteachers and staff* suggested it should be used with diocesan support and guidance.

The Anglican National Society produced an *Inspection Handbook* in 1995 (A. Brown and D. Lankshear).

73 L. Louden and D. Unwin (1993) *Church School Inspection* offered a practical training manual 'to locate inspection firmly in the context of the basic purposes and distinctiveness of Church schools'.

74 The debate further revealed a Hindu who had inspected Anglican denominational worship in a controlled school and an evangelical Christian who had inspected denominational RE in the Jewish Free School.

75 J. Lankshear, p. 6; 81 per cent of aided and special agreement and 63 per cent of controlled schools were reported to have worship reflecting the 'Anglican tradition'.

76 In 1995 the Culham Institute (supported by the Jerusalem Trust of the Sainsbury family) produced a multi-media CD-Rom, *Living Stones*, on the history of Christianity in Britain. In 1996 the BBC announced a major new five-year investment in RE, entitled *Worlds of Belief*, offering television programmes and support materials for all Key Stages in both primary and secondary sectors.

5

THE FUTURE OF THE CHURCH–STATE
PARTNERSHIP IN EDUCATION

This survey of the constant fluctuations in the relationship between the Churches and central or local government over more than a century has raised important questions about the future of the Church–State partnership in education. Like any human relationship, there have been times of disagreement, impatience, frustration or downright hostility from one or other party during this period, as well as times of constructive compromise and harmonious co-operation to enable education reform to progress in the interests of the nation as a whole. From the beginning of the twentieth century, 'there was a reversion to the vision of a close partnership between Church and State in which religious and moral education would be the Church's most important contribution' (Kent, 1992, p. 37). R. A. Butler noted the intention of the 1944 legislation 'to bring the Church schools along with us in as close a degree of partnership as possible and to eliminate as much of the friction involved in the operation of the dual system as we can' (*Hansard*, 5th Series, cccxcvi 227, 19 January 1944).

The mainstream Churches continued to have an influence on education policy through their official representation on government committees and working parties and an effective contribution through the practical experience of implementing those policies in their own schools. As *The Fourth R* recommended, the Church's involvement

> shall be of as high a quality and over as wide an educational range as possible, giving the Church both direct experience of the different types and contexts of education and also full opportunity for expressing its beliefs about education in practical terms at all levels. (Durham Report, 1970, para. 517)

Governments have come and gone subject to the will of the electorate and church schools have adapted to the vicissitudes of the political climate. Cruickshank's comprehensive account of Church–State relations in education, published in 1963, was written as post-war developments were leading to a more pragmatic, 'consensus' approach to education policy. She concluded:

> It may well be that some future Minister will be able to merge the two systems on terms which will ensure the distinctive character of denominational schools. Indeed, such a unification may seem to him [*sic*] a necessary political expedient, the only way of securing equality of opportunity for all the nation's children. Native empiricism may in the end ... reconcile the claims of Church and State. (1963, p. 178)

The upheavals of the Thatcher years could not then have been imagined but, by 1984, the Anglican Robert Waddington warned that

> one end of the political spectrum still seemed hypnotised by a sort of sanctified dull uniformity under the guise of equality of opportunity and continued to view any kind of power-sharing with the gravest suspicion as a denigration of due democratic process ... The other end of the spectrum threatens to spoil an admirable insistence on diversity in schools and on the exercise of parental preference by suggestions that market forces can be allowed to operate within the educational partnership. (1984, p. 19)

Certainly after 1988, the Churches found their loyalty to their traditional partners divided: central government expected church schools to be at the forefront of their new policies, while LEAs hoped that the Churches would prove an ally in their defence of local control and accountability. It is interesting to speculate whether in fact the Conservative government's radical proposals from 1979 had behind them the deliberate intention of demolishing the consensual framework of the dual system.

THE THATCHER LEGACY

Margaret Thatcher's impact on British politics dominated the late twentieth century. Her 'conviction' style of government would not allow anybody, the Churches[1] or the teaching profession, let alone her own Cabinet, to stand in her way or mitigate her zeal for education reform. Discussion leading to consensus was not seen to be helpful and therefore any real debate on the issues was impossible.[2]

Her view that the post-war settlement had led to a 'dependency culture' fired her enthusiasm for a 'survival of the fittest' social Darwinism, which excluded ideas of co-operating in the interests of the 'common good' or to support the disadvantaged.[3] As John Kent observed,

> By the 1980s, the bourgeois hero had resurrected himself, was boasting about his superior cunning and the virtues of making money; he stood on everyone else's feet and flatly denied the moral and social value of the Welfare State. There was still no question of a 'Christian-democratic' party, but instead religious pressure groups such as the anti-abortion groups appeared ... Temple's vision of a single Christian ideological movement working through the establishment to bring rational pressure to bear on the law-makers had been lost. (1992, p. 140)

Taking up Adam Smith's argument that all professions are a conspiracy against the laity,[4] Thatcher also considered that professionals, be they educationists, lawyers or broadcasters, were characterized by vested interests rather than objective, informed judgement and were therefore not to be trusted. The teachers' disputes of the mid 1980s convinced her that their power and influence should be curtailed, if not eliminated. Even officers in the DES felt that the government

> failed to treat education as a system in which ministers, bureaucrats, the teachers themselves and the students and/or their parents are all stakeholders, all interacting upon each other and all deserving respect ... Senior officials, rather than being managers of a system and partners of a vision, could easily come to feel like overworked ... 'hired guns'. (Woollard, 1996)

At the same time, Thatcher's circle of advisers became tighter and more incestuous. Ministers (known as 'wets') who disagreed with her policies were weeded out and 'the conduct of business turned on personality and faction'. After 1988, still more influence was 'syphoned inside the tight little No. 10 circle' which she used 'as a counter-Whitehall backed by her patronage and her will'.[5] The Carlton Club seminar on education (31 January 1991) was dominated by the right-wing views of Robert Balchin on GMS and Michael Fallon, then the Schools Minister, and led to a confidential paper (March 1991) criticizing the influence of LEAs and diocesan boards (para. 4.3.); perhaps not surprisingly, many of its recommendations found their way into government policy within six months. The Centre of Policy Studies, chaired by Brian Griffiths, encouraged radicals like Robert Skidelsky in advocating free-market education policies.[6]

Yet the centrally determined framework gave the Secretary of State for Education 175 extra powers under the 1988 Act and another 50 under the 1993 Act.[7] Observers were not slow to notice that 'While employing the rhetoric of the market-place, the Conservative administration has in fact imposed the heaviest centralized controls that the school system in England and Wales has ever experienced' (Bridges and Husbands, 1996, p. 2).

With the removal of local autonomy, 'services which have remained in public-sector hands have beeen increasingly subject to standardized central control' (Cloke, 1992, p. 81). GM schools were consistently used as 'trail-blazers' or 'guinea-pigs' in piloting central government initiatives such as bank borrowing, raising capital from private industry through the Private Finance Initiative (PFI) and recreating grammar schools by increasing pupil selection by ability (cf. DFEE, 1996). This accretion of power to the centre prompted Bishop Konstant to warn in 1993,

> If the schools of a diocese are predominantly GM, it could in time become impossible for a bishop to ensure Catholic schooling for all the Catholic pupils in his diocese. The Secretary of State has very considerable powers over a GM school. He can open, close, enlarge, reduce, move, and inspect it; he can change its character (not religious), its teachers, its governors and its curriculum. (Address to Salford diocese, 29 June)

To implement its policies, Thatcher's government advisers felt they could no longer rely on civil servants, especially those in the DES, to carry them through with sufficient conviction. After 1988, the DES had created an administrative framework to assess the benefits of greater autonomy for schools but, in doing so, had minimized the differences in order to create a 'level playing field': GM status should confer no financial advantage over schools with delegated LMS budgets, all schools still had to teach the National Curriculum, and none could change their admissions policy (e.g. introduce selection) for five years. The government was left with the embarrassment that schools were not rushing to climb aboard the GM 'bandwagon' as ministers had anticipated.[8]

Their concern about DES caution led to the creation of a 'new magistracy' of 'quangos', for example the Funding Agency for Schools (FAS), thereby increasing the capacity of the centre to drive policy. Often the chairmen of quangos were 'captains of industry'[9] whose part-time commitments meant they would provide only a 'light touch' in steering government policy and, as they were unaccountable to the electorate, a 'democratic deficit' was built into the process. As Jenkins noted, 'What was extraordinary was the lengths to which ministers went to ensure that the membership of these bodies was loyal to them, and distant from any link with local democracy' (1996, p. 264).[10]

The Director of the Catholic Education Service regretted the effect of this on the Churches: 'Until recently, we could rely on ministers and civil servants' understanding of our "historic share" in education. Chief executives of quangos do not have this understanding, nor are they necessarily concerned about the political implications of their decisions' (*Tablet*, 18 May 1996).

The Schools Officer for the Anglican Board of Education confirmed that 'partnership' had become more complex because of 'quangos'; with each new organization created, the Churches have had to educate its members about the framework of the dual system (interview, July 1996). The appointment of church representatives, for example, on to the FAS in 1994 proved controversial, since none of the people originally proposed by the Churches was deemed to be sufficiently enthusiastic about the policy of GMS.

Such developments have been analysed by academics interested in educational policy-making. Charles Raab, for example, has shown how concepts of network, market and hierarchy[11] have been applied to education. Hierarchical measures of control can be seen in the provisions for the National Curriculum; yet the decentralized 'market' of parental choice and financial delegation was intended to leave the State with a mainly strategic role; thus restructured 'networks' at national, local and school levels would implement policy with less resistance to central initiatives. This resulted in

> the uprooting of old 'partnership' understandings ... Older patterns of trust have been eroded and newer ones are intended to take their place, although the mistrust and conflict that also inhered in the complexity of 'partnership' may be reproduced in the contemporary conditions. (Raab, 1994)

Not surprisingly perhaps, the Churches' position in the restructuring of the partnerships was some way from the top of the government's agenda of change and the 'gratifying tributes to the work of the Churches in education', for example in the 1992 White Paper *Choice and Diversity*, contrasted with clauses seen to be inimical to the Churches' interests.[12]

There have been different interpretations of the implications of the 'market' in education. In Sir Keith Joseph's view, 'the blind, unplanned, uncoordinated wisdom of the market ... is overwhelmingly superior to the well-researched, rational, systematic respectable plans of governments' (Joseph, 1976). This contrasted with the scepticism of Stewart Ranson, who considered that

> The market entrenches the powerful beyond control ... While indicating radical change, it actually entrenches a traditional order of authority and power ... The market polity, by reinforcing only the interests of a minority, rests on a limited and thus vulnerable democracy. (1993, p. 339)

He went on to argue,

> An internal educational market will ensure selection to match a pyramidal, hierarchical society ... It is underpinned by a political system which encourages passive rather than active participation in the public domain ... Education needs to be a local *democratic* system because it must be a public service responsive and accountable to the community as a whole. (*Ibid.*, pp. 348–9)

Denis Lawton also traced how 'the unfettered market ran counter to traditional, paternalistic, one-nation Toryism' and suggested that 'the market has tended to replace notions of "fairness" which is the traditional community value'.[13] He noted that 'morality has become more a question of individual beliefs (even taste) than consensus or community norms', a situation viewed with particular concern by the Churches.[14] As Leslie Griffiths of the Free Churches reflected,

> Our systems of governance must not keep power at a distance in Whitehall or else unaccountable in the hands of faceless quangos. If hope is to surge in our hearts then it will be on the basis both of solidarity with our neighbour and a subsidiarity which encourages and motivates our participation in the affairs which govern us. (*The Month*, May 1995)

RUMOURS OF CONSPIRACY

Church schools appeared to have hidden 'adversaries' in the system. The DES civil servants as much as LEA officers were not always sympathetic to a specific denominational framework and the management issues it raised. Just as Fisher had tried to create a 'single system of elementary schools' in the early twentieth century, when the National Society had been ready to give up the separate status of church schools 'in return for a guarantee of conditions permitting denominational teaching in county schools, given as an integral part of the timetable',[15] so at one point the 1944 negotiations had seemed to consider dismantling the 'dual system'. However, the final settlement recognized the importance of a realistic 'compromise', if not always a tidy or manageable one, particularly when it later came to school reorganization plans as pupil rolls fell in the 1980s. Unsympathetic LEAs might conceal inequalities in school budgets across their local authority, resulting in serious underfunding for church schools until the financial delegation of LMS from 1990 corrected the imbalance by introducing more open 'per pupil' formula funding.[16] There could be officers in local or central government who might argue that the weaker the influence of the Churches in education policy the better, more especially if church leaders were seen to be openly critical of government policy.[17] The government's declared intention of weakening LEAs and strengthening schools' independence could mean there would be less opposition, since individual schools would be less able to exert significant influence on national policy.

What seemed to irk the government was the Churches' insistence that they should be appropriately consulted and their views taken into account as key stakeholders in the state education system, whereas Thatcher seemed adamant her policies were inherently sound and that further debate would have the unfortunate consequence of delaying or even diluting their effectiveness. One example was the announcement of the extension of the GMS option to primary schools with less than 300 pupils, which had not been previously discussed with the Churches, despite the fact that many of the smaller primary schools were rural Anglican parish schools (Adie, 1990a). Under John Major, the Churches first learned about the GM fast-track proposals for church schools through the media.

Church schools also had considerable difficulty in gaining their share of capital funding from the DES for additional buildings or improvement to bring them up to the DES's 1981 specified standards by 1991 (in fact the DES found it had insufficient resources to meet its own targets). The voluntary contribution of 15 per cent from the church foundation should have allowed the DES to be more generous to aided schools, but the Churches had to compete with each other in a smaller 'pot' than county schools, prioritized by their

LEA on a separate list before submission to the DES or its successors. The government seemed unsympathetic to the needs of over-subscribed church schools to expand to meet parental demand, despite its rhetoric about enhancing 'parental choice'. By 1989 a new GM list had increased the competition for capital funding, as so many schools were 'opting out' specifically in order to improve their chances of capital building improvement, and church GM schools had to join yet another, if initially more generous, queue. By 1996, even that was drying up[18] and church schools' frustration at the lack of funding continued. Indeed, although the 1996 Nursery and Grant-Maintained Schools Act[19] allowed GM schools to borrow money on their assets, the church GM schools faced additional restrictions since their buildings were owned by the trustees.

The publication on the first day of the long summer holiday of Baker's 1987 Education Reform Bill (with a six-week consultation period) was indicative of the government's high-handed approach. The relegation of RE to its 'Cinderella' position outside the National Curriculum seemed to imply that the DES had warned Baker to leave RE well alone within the local agreed syllabus framework, since any interference might open up debates that had brought down governments in the past. There was increasing influence from the evangelical lobby in Conservative circles (for example, Griffiths, Maitland and Cox), not to mention the right-wing views of Roman Catholics like Sheila Lawlor, as the legislation continued through 1988 to 1993. There appeared to be a move to 'privatize' religious education, that is, to acknowledge its importance for an individual's personal faith development but to question its role in educating pupils about religion, particularly if that included non-Christian faiths. The lobbyists wanted children of so-called Christian families to be taught more undiluted Christian RE in county schools, in order to preserve their British cultural heritage. As we have seen, the Churches refused to be restricted to commenting on their own school sector, because they were convinced that the wider interests of good 'academic' RE teaching in all schools had to be defended, thus again bringing them into conflict with powerful Conservative interest groups. The government's consistent refusal to accept the reality of RE's 'Cinderella' status, whatever the statistics said[20] and ignoring HMI warnings that RE was desperately under-resourced, also suggested the DES's priorities lay elsewhere.[21]

But it was the issue of grant-maintained status which revealed, perhaps more than anything else, a sense of 'conspiracy' and collusion in sidelining the Churches' influence. The government consistently ignored the concerns of the Churches over 'opting out', particularly the arguments that the distinctive nature of the schools' foundations and the responsibilites of trustees should be acknowledged. Their protests at the inequality of funding and the self-centredness of a policy which encouraged schools to enhance their own funding regardless of any effect this might have on other schools in the community or diocese[22] were deliberately discounted. John Patten wrote to Cardinal Hume in May 1992, following the Catholic Bishops' Conference Low Week statement on GMS, noting their concerns about inequity but justifying the policy, since these increased resources were 'being directly applied to pupils' education' and more generous capital funding was needed to set up GM schools 'on a sound basis'. He insisted that the role of the diocese and the ethos of Catholic schools was in no way threatened by GMS. Yet the dioceses were, like the LEAs, not even permitted to have a mailing list of parents eligible to vote in the GM ballot for church schools in case they circulated views unsympathetic to GMS.[23] There appeared to be mixed messages.

More seriously, the future of the dual system appeared in doubt if GM church schools were in danger of losing their distinctive Christian status. In theory, the foundation governors of a church school had more control as the number of 'first' or foundation governors increased on a GM governing body; this could be particularly helpful for Anglican voluntary-controlled schools since, by going GM, the Church would once again take overall control of its school. But again there seemed to be mixed messages. In 1992 the DFE denied any knowledge of which GM schools originally had denominational foundations, and proposals in the 1992 White Paper that all GM schools (church or county) should have common Articles of Government were strongly challenged by the Churches. In 1995 both the Grant-Maintained Schools Foundation and the Grant-Maintained Schools Centre insisted that 'once a school is GM, it's only GM', its previous status being irrelevant. Even the lists of all schools in the 1996 *LEA Handbook* identifying LEA schools as voluntary-controlled or aided, did not distinguish within the GM sector schools with church foundations. We have already noted that the only record of previous allegiances was retrieved as a result of a parliamentary question from Labour MP Andrew Smith on 11 May 1994, prompting a DFEE database to be established.

The Churches' fears were exacerbated by John Major's GM 'fast-track' proposals in autumn 1995 and the lack of consultation even on a policy that was explicitly aimed at the denominational sector. Whereas in the past ministers would have sounded out church opinion privately to ensure reasonable support before going public, the government seemed uninterested in seeking any such agreement, hoping that church school governors would jump at the chance to be independent of their diocese and LEA. The fact that the 2000 responses were overwhelmingly negative probably confirmed the government's worst suspicions that the church school system only caused problems and that the quicker it could be dismantled the better. The Anglican Schools Officer commented,

> The Churches may one day pay the price for their opposition to 'fast-track'; the government has always seen church schools at the forefront of GM policy, suggesting the logical thing to do was for voluntary-aided schools to go GM. The 100 per cent capital funding was only a bribe. Labour LEAs were furious about 'fast-track', thinking it was a church plot, until they realized the Churches too opposed it. (Interview, July 1996)

The additional accusations by churchmen that the government was extolling advantages of a 'self-governing status' which were inherently selfish exacerbated the tension. The Church argued that the diocesan family of schools should resist government pressure for increased competition and co-operate in partnership with their Christian community.

MISUNDERSTANDINGS

The antagonisms between Church and State were, however, not entirely justified. Church schools, as Baker and Burt acknowledged in 1987, had already put into practice many of the policies which Thatcher had then been advocating: for example, their very rationale as denominational schools was predicated on the principle of parental choice; their parents and foundation sponsors made considerable financial contributions to the capital development and improvement of school buildings; they already worked independently (if still in partnership) with their LEAs; aided schools had always been 'self-governing' in appointing their own staff and admitting their own pupils; and they placed a high premium on moral and spiritual values in the ethos of their schools.

The government from 1979 seemed schizophrenic about church schools. On the one hand, it welcomed them as making a valuable contribution to the diversity of provision from which parents could make their own choice for their children's education, a view reiterated by a later Secretary of State, Gillian Shephard (*On the Record*, BBC1, 28 April 1996). At the same time, it found difficulty in understanding church schools' reluctance to compete with other schools in local and national league tables, if such self-promotion at others' expense was out of step with the church schools' ethos of placing priority on service to their wider community.

There appeared to be several misunderstandings, particularly over the interpretation of such concepts as 'competition', 'parental choice', 'independence' or 'academic success'. At first sight, the increasing drive towards 'consumerism' and 'competitive market-forces' in education was not in itself problematic. Church schools were used to competing for pupils, particularly in the more diverse market of the secondary sector, where church-going parents might place other criteria (e.g. academic selection) above the importance of a Christian ethos. They were accustomed to making their case in the constant battle for scarce resources and often proficient in advertising their pupils' achievements in the local press. They placed a high priority on their own pupils' needs[24] and encouraged them to compete to achieve high standards, believing competition to be important for individual growth. Many church schools performed creditably in the national league tables from 1992 onwards,[25] increasing the pressure of over-subscription on pupil admissions. As Patten argued in an interview for *The Universe* (2 January 1993), in a competitive world the idea of 'competitiveness and market forces' should be strategies for 'raising standards'.

Yet the concept of 'competition' could be understood in different ways; church schools might see themselves as complementary to county schools rather than in competition, and their nearest 'rival' was more likely to be another church school in a nearby LEA. While proud of pupils' examination success, they might also value their Christian mission to the poor and marginalized in society. Vatican II's *Declaration on Christian Education* (*Gravissimum Educationis*) §9 was reiterated in *The Catholic School* (1977), p. 21: 'first and foremost the Church offers its educational service to "the poor or those who are deprived of family help and affection or those who are far from the faith"'. In 1995, ten Catholic secondary schools in Birmingham funded their own 'Zacchaeus Centre' to provide support for the needs of difficult children, as a distinctly Catholic response of 'forgiveness and compassion' (*TES*, 10 May 1996). Meanwhile in 1991

Anglican secondary heads had issued an agreed Allington statement confirming their commitment to disadvantaged pupils; and in 1992 the Anglican Church, supported by its church colleges, had opened a new centre for its Urban Learning Foundation in the East End of London to train teachers to work in deprived inner-city schools. Similarly, church schools might consider 'special needs' pupils an integral part of their school rather than a drain on limited resources or a disadvantage in the statistical league tables. Few would criticize the additional resource needs of neighbouring schools with particular specializations (e.g. facilities for the disabled), as long as such funding was openly accountable through the agreed formula. 'Survival of the fittest'[26] had not yet become the accepted 'gospel truth'.

Back in 1912, in a lecture on 'The Kingdom of God', William Temple had asserted that 'Competition is simply organised selfishness. It is sometimes said that if you want to get the best out of a man [*sic*], you must appeal to his own interest ... The whole gospel rests on the denial of that statement' (1914).

Eight decades later, the Churches' response to Patten's White Paper argued that 'competition is not a panacea for failings in education nor are market forces acceptable as a fundamental principle in the provision of educational opportunity' (*Education*, 16 October 1992). The work of Bryk *et al.* in the USA, where Catholic schools receive no support from government funds and have to compete in the educational market-place, recognized that

> Market forces cannot explain the broadly shared institutional purpose of advancing social equity or account for the efforts of Catholic educators to maintain inner-city schools (with large non-Catholic enrolments) while facing mounting financial woes. Likewise, market forces cannot easily explain why resources are allocated within schools in a compensatory fashion in order to provide an academic education for every student. Nor can they explain the norms of community that infuse daily life in these schools. (Bryk *et al.*, 1993, p. 300)

Speaking to Catholic independent schools on 18 January 1996, Bishop Konstant reflected:

> Competition is of itself neither inherently good or bad ... The search for excellence is a profoundly Christian quest, since it means striving to make the best possible use of God's gifts. But if the search for excellence is seen as a means of weakening or destroying others,

then it is morally evil. In the school context, where governors, parents and teachers are trying to do the best for their school, raising standards, improving resources and accommodation, expansion, selection, all these are generally seen as benefits for the pupils and their teachers ... However there may be occasions where, for example, expansion or change of status will, inevitably, harm a neighbouring school.[27]

Richard Pring, a Roman Catholic professor of education, went on to explore the distinctive view of human nature underlying the 'market' in education; as 'enterprise becomes an important virtue', so 'competition' regulated by the State determines educational aims: 'The authority of the teacher in matters concerning what is worth learning gives way to the authority of consumer choice ... performance indicators replace the judgement of educated persons ... diversity and choice are justified in terms of client satisfaction'.[28] However, Pring argued, what is the quality of life worth living?

> Since each person is of equal value and equally deserving of recognition, then it is difficult to see how a Catholic school could reject people on grounds of inability, poverty, social background or ethnicity. Such attributes are irrelevant to the value of a person. (*Ibid.*, p. 68)

Professor Gerald Grace, criticizing moral worth justified through individual merit as 'a reinvigorated version of the Protestant ethic', also noted that 'The moral economy of schooling is in the process of losing other moral commitments ... to community, collegiality, social justice and public good' (Grace, 1993).

On the publication of the 1996 White Paper advocating increased pupil selection by ability, the *Tablet*'s editorial (29 June) was entitled 'Citizens or Consumers':

> Citizenship involves the crucial principle of solidarity: each citizen weighing up the common good, judging the interests of the community as a whole. Market consumerism means each individual acting only out of self-interest, which used to be called mere selfishness. There can be little doubt which of these sharply contrasting philosophies a Catholic Christian must prefer.

This shared concern among church spokespersons and educationists suggested that the values underpinning Christian schools, while aware of and responsive to market forces, were not primarily driven by self-interest and competition.

Secondly, just as the concept of 'competition' could be interpreted in different ways, so also could that of 'parental choice'. The Churches had traditionally claimed to provide schools because parents desired them: 'The Catholic community as a whole has been accustomed to call its schools "our schools", because they have originated from the demand of Catholic parents for a Catholic education for their children' (Bishops' Conference statement, November 1992). Indeed the role of parents in educating their children has been paramount: as the *Declaration on Christian Education* (§ 3) from the Second Vatican Council stated, 'the first and primary educators of children are their parents'. Catholic schools were established to support them in this task: 'Parents and teachers have to rely on one another: they are in a partnership of care.'[29] Anglicans were committed to similar principles: 'It is where the shared assumptions of the members of a school's staff coincide with the assumptions of the parents of the pupils that the educational opportunities of a Church school can become most fully realized' (Durham Report, 1970, para. 484).

While church schools held fast to the principle of parental choice, however, this was not to be at the expense of the Christian community as a whole, as shown in Cardinal Hume's attempts in 1989 to persuade Catholic schools in the Westminster diocese to take a broader view, rather than merely to consider their own interests: 'we must balance the freedom and initiative of the individual against the needs and requirements of the community'.[30] As Bishop Konstant (1991a) noted, 'Choice is a fundamental value ... however our choices are never absolute, because one person's choice invariably restricts someone else's choice.' The Director of the CES, interviewed in 1996, contrasted the short-term involvement of parents while their children attended as pupils, with the much longer-term responsibilities of church school trustees. Even before the publication in 1992 of John Major's *Parent's Charter*, Anglicans had also noted with concern the reduction of the role of parents to 'mere consumers' and the emphasis on parental rights at the expense of responsibilities (Waddington, 1984, pp. 20, 75). *The Fourth R* had already insisted that Anglican aided schools were not dependent on 'denominational demand' *per se*, because the criteria for membership of the Church of England were ill-defined; aided schools could provide a 'real focus of the community' even if the traditional local Church itself was poorly supported (para. 524). However, if church schools were over-subscribed, the schools were in practice more likely to be choosing the parents than the other way round; middle-class parents, as Ball has shown, were similarly able to manipulate the admission system to their advantage.[31]

Thirdly, the concept of 'independence' proved equally ambiguous. The government was keen to extend the privilege of independence from LEAs enjoyed by church schools to all the nation's schools. It argued that headteachers should not under-estimate the extra responsibilities involved in the autonomous running of their own schools under GMS, but implied that good senior managers would relish the prospect. Thatcher had hoped to recreate the 'direct-grant grammar schools' in her proposals for 'independent state schools' – or 'grant-maintained' as the DES insisted on describing them, much to her annoyance (Thatcher, 1993, p. 570).[32]

Some Catholic independent schools which had lost their 'direct grant' under the Labour government in 1976 saw GMS as a way back into the state sector.[33] Other Catholic GM headteachers argued that their chief incentive to opt out was less the desire for more funding than for greater freedom; Brother Francis Patterson, head of St Francis Xavier GM School in Liverpool, first chairman of the Association of Catholic Maintained Schools and a member of the Funding Agency for Schools, insisted 'with opting out we are convinced that we can enhance the Catholic character because we can control resources' (*TES*, 22 January 1993). As we have noted, the percentage of Catholic schools going GM by 1994 was at least twice that of Anglicans. The then Director of the CES commented in 1993 that 'We share a belief in the value and importance of independence for schools in the conduct of their affairs and the development of their activities – and that this independence should continually increase and improve' (Price, 1993). However, he went on,

> the faith and values of our shared mission ... provide a balance of liberty and restraint which are the disciplines of any freedom we seek ... In the current debate we seem to be asked to believe that independence for schools and people was discovered in devolved budgets and ballots and only exists in regard to power, money and resource management ... These characteristics of independence are not central to Catholic distinctiveness. (*Ibid.*)

Although Roman Catholic schools placed particular store on their independence from state interference, having struggled to safeguard their voluntary-aided status after 1944 at considerable financial sacrifice, the bishops were concerned that GMS would reduce their autonomy rather than increase it. Archbishop Derek Worlock noted in 1995 that, in that earlier era, 'we battled for the rights of parents. More recently and no more successfully in the Education Reform Act we battled for the rights of Trustees' (1995, p. 24).

At the DFEE's 'Going GM' conferences for church schools from 1994, many delegates questioned GM speakers about the benefits of GMS compared to those of LMS delegated budget management. Several expressed the view that LMS offered them sufficient independence from LEAs to identify and resource their own priorities, whilst retaining that valuable support to call on in emergencies. The kind of independence that severed links with local colleagues might be ultimately disadvantageous. Simon Jenkins also questioned the apparent 'independence' under GMS, arguing that, with a centralized curriculum and assessment, a national funding formula and the FAS's power to expand or create new schools and summarily remove school governors, 'self-governing' status under the control of the Secretary of State seemed a misnomer (1996, pp. 129–30). Bishop Konstant reflected that

> schools will stand more and more alone, in one sense independent, yet wholly dependent upon their merits in the market place ... Any new independence and authority given to our schools to determine their own future must be seen as part of a coherent philosophy and theology of education.[34]

Fourthly, church schools were committed to high standards of academic attainment.[35] In fact the 1996 OFSTED Annual Report confirmed their notable achievements across the country, particularly at secondary level. Nevertheless, as Cardinal Hume had recognized back in 1988, there was the risk of placing academic and material success on a pedestal to the detriment of other values, such as the spiritual and moral dimensions of the curriculum: 'we must avoid the trap of treating the "spiritual and moral" as religious extras which are bolted onto an otherwise secular educational process' (Hume, 1995). Similarly, national accolades for league table positions were not to be won at the cost of excluding other areas of pupils' achievement like sport, the arts or community service, for which no league tables existed:

> Great emphasis is placed on meeting curriculum needs, on the acquisition of skills ... These are essential. But ... education is not primarily for work but for life. What we should value most in

education is the cultivation of all those elements of human activity
... which make all the difference to human happiness and flourish-
ing. The ability to form stable, trusting and self-giving relationships
as adults and parents; the appreciation of music and drama; the
exercise of artistic creativity; the enjoyment of sport and leisure
activities, and above all the development of an inner spiritual
life.[36]

Governors of church schools, while responsible for implementing
the National Curriculum, faced the dilemma of ensuring a distinctive
Christian ethos: 'As new subjects come on board, the governors of
Church schools have to be aware of these strains, particularly as they
affect the teaching of religious education. We have to make sure it
does not get squeezed', said one governor (*TES*, 30 October 1992).
The Archbishop of Canterbury, opening a key debate on 5 July 1996
in the House of Lords on moral values, insisted

It would be a failure if our schools were to produce people with the
right skills and aptitudes to take on our economic competitors, but
who cannot string two sentences together about the meaning and
purpose of life or who have no idea what it means to be a moral
person ... What we have to combat is the idea that spiritual and
moral matters are add-on extras, contingent on giving overwhelming priority to more utilitarian goals.

The post-1988 debates showed how, faced with a number of key
principles fundamental to Conservative educational and political
philosophy, the Churches found themselves questioning the direction their schools were following. The distinctive contribution that
church schools brought to the educational market-place was valued
by government ministers, but managing that diversity was less
straightforward in the light of the complexities of Church–State
relationships.

THE FUTURE: THE CHURCHES' COMMON INTERESTS

We have seen how the mainstream Churches have had distinctive
approaches to Christian education in schools. The Nonconformists
were satisfied that their Sunday schools could supplement the non-
denominational RE teaching of the state schools; the Anglicans were
content that their denominational interests could be met in parish
schools reflecting the tradition of the Church of England as the
Established Church of the nation; and Roman Catholics were insistent on all their children having access to a full Catholic education in

a Catholic school. The strategic alliances, for example between the Nonconformists and Anglicans in 1902 and 1944 to defend the Cowper-Temple clause,[37] led to government endorsement of religious education for all children. Roman Catholics defended their own interests vigorously after the 1944 Act when Catholic schools were needed for an expanding population, while Anglicans generally caught the mood of greater openness to their local communities. Prior to 1944, the arguments centred on the appropriateness of the catechism or Bible teaching in schools; since then the debate has been more about the place of Christianity in an increasingly multicultural and multi-faith society. Similarly, up to 1944, the main concern was about church school buildings but, as the Churches' financial contribution reduced, so the government tightened its central control over national education provision.

In the 1970s, as the influence of Vatican II began to percolate into Catholic education, so a less defensive tone became evident; meanwhile Anglican schools, faced with increasing secularization of the school environment, started to reassess their distinctively Christian mission. In 1988, the increasingly confident liaison between Anglicans and Roman Catholics to strengthen their interests in the face of a concerted attempt by government to divide them, showed how far the Churches had come in recognizing the benefits of ecumenical co-operation.[38] Although John Patten consulted the Churches separately in 1992 over issues such as sex education in the light of the 'Aids' crisis,[39] on most matters the Churches anticipated joint meetings with ministers. The strengthening of the Churches Joint Education Policy Committee[40] in the 1990s also provided an effective forum to develop a coherent Christian alliance in education.

Yet there have been indications of disunity and competition between church schools themselves. The tensions remain in the debate over whether church schools should be primarily for practising church-going families (where the priest's reference may be critical for gaining admission to over-subscribed schools), for any baptized Christian pupil, or even more open to their local communities whatever their religious allegiance.[41] The GMS debate has added another dimension: whether a church school should have as a priority the education of its own children rather than those in the area as a whole. Should any additional resources gained be seen as one's entitlement, even if they may mean others' loss? Or should the church school still see itself in partnership with its local authority and neighbouring county schools? Despite the pleas from dioceses for schools, GM or not, to continue in Christian partnership, since 'no useful purpose will be served by the Diocese castigating either group for their lack of Christianity',[42] Dennis Richards argued from an Anglican perspective that 'the community of Church schools remains divided on the GM principle itself' (*Church Times*, 14 June 1996). Roman Catholics also had polarized views:

> For some Catholics, the grant-maintained option appeared to be a form of manna from heaven, providing extra resources to build upon and expand the excellence of Catholic education. For other Catholics, the financial inducements were the equivalent of thirty pieces of silver, encouraging Catholic schools to abandon community values for individual self-interest. In other words, the Catholic education community was deeply divided as to what course of action would be in the best interests of the pupils, the future of Catholic schooling and of the integrity of its special mission. (Grace, 1995, p. 170)

There were those who claimed to foresee the end of the partnership between Church and State. James Arthur warned in 1991:

> The survival of the partnership on which the 'dual system' was based now appears doubtful. Ten years of Conservative government, culminating in the Education Reform Act, have eroded the statutory rights built up since 1870. Further moves in this direction will have to be resisted by the bishops if anything significant is to be left of the Catholic schools system in England and Wales. (Arthur, 1991)

By 1995, nothing had happened to change his mind:

> The government decided to ignore the traditional pattern of power-sharing in the partnership with the Church ... Voluntary-aided schools have found themselves with no satisfactory alternative to falling in with schemes that they had played little part in formulating and have found impossible to influence. (Arthur, 1995b, pp. 453–4)

It might be that the Conservative government's drive to offer parents a wide diversity in their choice of school as customers in the education 'market-place' encouraged the view of church schools as one particular 'brand-name product' among others.[43] Therefore the concept of 'partnership' no longer seemed to have meaning to secular policy-makers. In this diversity, church schools were just another category of educational institution teaching the National

Curriculum, but with a 'niche-market' offering a distinctively Christian ethos to parents who chose it. As if to show that the Churches were not to be treated differently, central government refused, for example, to intervene in the clash between Catholic authorities and LEAs which failed to fund home–school transport, implying that as this was discretionary (under Section 55 of the 1944 Act) it should be subject to market forces. The Churches counter-argued that the siting of many Catholic schools had only been agreed with LEAs on the basis of the provision of free transport. Another aspect of the church school 'market' was that by May 1996, three independent Catholic schools had taken up the chance to opt into the state system as free GM schools with no requirement for them to ballot parents.

Alternative markets might be schools run by 'new religious movements', Muslims or the Seventh-day Adventists[44] or even technological industrialists (cf. city technology colleges). The 1993 Education Act permitted applications for GMS from 'faith-based' or other independently sponsored schools. Although one fundamentalist Christian school, Oakhill in Bristol, received no government support since there was already a surplus of school places in the area, the successful CTC in Gateshead, Emmanuel College, sponsored by an industrialist, prided itself on its fundamentalist Christian ethos. Geoffrey Walford[45] showed how, although the Christian evangelical schools were often supported by the 'New Right', they were not necessarily exclusive and could be sited in socially deprived areas.

In this 'free market' environment, the historic partnership between Church and State appeared increasingly irrelevant and outdated. The mainstream Churches were no longer seen as the traditionally respected partners who had made great sacrifices to establish and enhance their educational provision over the centuries. Although the Churches might still own one in five of the nation's schools, the government seemed to treat them more like any other sectarian interest group to be taken into account as and when necessary.[46] Instead of 'partnership', the more appropriate concept might be at best one of intermittent mutual 'collaboration' in areas of common interest.

While much of the evidence before the reader would support this view of disillusionment with the relationship, it may be that the partnership model of Church and State should not be so easily jettisoned. Marjorie Cruickshank had reflected that 'for our own age, which is struggling to preserve and uphold moral standards, no tradition is so vital as that of the Church schools which link faith and practice' (1963, p. 177). Such words were reiterated in 1995 by MP Frank Field, who acknowledged that 'the gloves were now off' and church schools should be proactive and positive, prepared to go on the attack; education had a key role in 'keeping the rumour of God alive' and teaching values to a society that has lost its moral certainties. He thought LEAs would continue because they were wanted by schools, but recognized that parents expected more say. The State may not be interested in the Church any more, but neither were MPs particularly antagonistic, merely expecting church schools to linger to a slow death. Instead the Churches should go on the offensive, harnessing the support of parents: 'we're on a winner to extend our influence' (speech to the Anglican headteachers' conference, September 1995).

We have noted the increasing concern about a society whose moral values are based on the principle of 'survival of the fittest'. The once inexorable rise of the New Right under Thatcher could yet be replaced by a more consensual approach. As John Gray reflected,

> A liberal civil society cannot hope to be stable if political life is polarised between ideological extremes ... For conservatives in Britain, such a move entails abandoning the simplistic formulae and utopian panaceas of the libertarian New Right and recognising the dependency of the market economy on a common culture which contains institutions that protect those whom the unconstrained market would neglect ... For British social democrats, the move toward a new consensus means shedding the disabling illusions of egalitarianism in order to consider the detailed failings of the market and of the current welfare state. (Gray, 1993, p. 122)

Just as T. S. Eliot had argued that, since 'political philosophy derives its sanction from ethics, and ethics from the truth of religion' (*The Idea of a Christian Society*, p. 63), it is difficult for the State to assert itself as wholly 'secular', so the education system, based on religious values, cannot easily renounce its Christian heritage. Archbishop Habgood considered that the growth in tolerance of pluralism has always depended on 'a residual sense that there are some things which hold us together as a nation'; Peter Cornwell went on to suggest that 'the National Church could become both the articulator and supporter of those common values which are present but submerged beneath the free-for-all of the pluralist society' ('The Church of England and the State', in Moyser, 1985, p. 54). The Churches, both Roman Catholic and Anglican, and their schools have a critical role to play in supporting a society 'that is deeply troubled by the level of violence, anxieties about standards in public life, a general lack of discipline and self-control' (Bishop Konstant, paper to SCAA conference on 'Education for Adult Life', 1996), a society which 'seems to be losing its awareness that there are truths and values and responsibilities which transcend our individual opinions, our selfish desires and the mad scramble for personal fulfilment' (J. Habgood, Gerald Priestland Memorial Lecture, 1995).

The challenge to this country, as Bishop David Young pleaded on the fiftieth anniversary of the 1944 Education Act,

> is to articulate a vision for our nation in a fast-changing world, a vision which embraces the pluralism of multi-culture and multi-faith, which builds on values shared, which gives energy and purpose to our economic and social life. Such a vision was there in 1944. It cannot simply be replicated; a new vision must be discerned. (*Fifty Years Forward, TES* and Institute of Education Conference, May 1994)

The issue of ecumenical Christian education has a bearing on the questions we have discussed. This is especially important at a time when ecumenical relations seem strained by the consequences of the ordination of women to the priesthood and the episcopate in some provinces of the Anglican Communion, and the unattractiveness to Anglicans (and many Catholics) of a highly ultramontane and seemingly autocratic style at the Vatican.[47] There remain major areas where it is possible for the two bodies to co-operate in a common cause for the gospel. In the area of religious education in schools, both communions in England find themselves drawn together in defending their common interests, particularly in ensuring a secure place for RE in curriculum and assessment. The Churches expressed the hope that schools, both Anglican and Roman Catholic, would continue to reflect the wider Christian community and not retreat into a ghetto of self-interest if adopting grant-maintained status. The government's proposals in autumn 1995 for a GM 'fast-track' for church schools had the unexpected consequence of uniting the Churches, voluntary schools and most GM church schools in opposition.

Common cause by the Churches can also be made where political or economic decisions may have damaging effects on church schools, for example the abolition of discretionary school transport or the DFE 'clawback' on the sale of aided school buildings.[48] In this process it may well turn out that ecumenical co-operation at diocesan level, already established in governor training,[49]could prove invaluable and may provide the impetus for creating more joint educational ventures in situations where diocesan boards, perhaps on both sides, have hitherto been suspicious of each other's interests and reluctant to work together in schools.

The greater autonomy given to individual schools, rather than creating a narrow 'ghetto' mentality, may encourage more ecumenical co-operation than would previously have been possible in dioceses where episcopal influence has brought ecumenical dialogue to a standstill. Even where relationships between local Anglican and Roman Catholic schools have been cordial but held on a tight rein from the top, governing bodies might find that the greater freedom given to them under legislation could enable them to build more ecumenical bridges. As things now stand, this can be no more than speculation. Ecumenism is too important to be left entirely to the bishops, but obviously it cannot be successful without them or in defiance of them. Suffice it to say, in conclusion, that the changing roles in the partnership between Church and State are likely to have an influence on the future development of church schools and to make a difference to possible moves in ecumenical co-operation in education.

Church voluntary schools, once 'designed largely as a bargain with Churches to enable them to sustain their institutional presence',[50] have a responsibility to articulate their distinctive mission within a Christian framework. In so far as the government wants the nation to have a strong moral sense, it tends to look to the Churches to form consciences, so that some urge to partnership may survive the depersonalizing effect of secularism. There can be little doubt that the rise of parental consumerism and central government control marked the demise of the universalist 'one nation' assumptions of the Butler Act of 1944[50] which, with the increasing pressures of secularism and sectarianism in the 1990s, has important consequences for the Churches' role in education in the twenty-first century.

Looking to the future, Roman Catholic and Anglican spokesmen confirmed their respective commitment to their church schools and Christian education:

> The purpose of education is to develop integrated human beings. Disputes over the purpose of education reflect a much deeper conflict in our society over what it is to be human . . . The task of the Church can rarely have been more urgent or more difficult.[52]

The concept of partnership in education is more than just a cliché or bureaucratic device ... The Christian vision of education ... sees human beings as partners with God in the work of creation ... For the Church to be able to exercise its important responsibility in education, we may have to disturb and invigorate the present ecclesiastical and educational structures and expectations.[53]

NOTES

1 The relationship between Thatcher and the Church of England began to deteriorate after the Falklands War Memorial Service (1982); she cultivated the 'bourgeois virtues' of self-reliance and personal salvation, while the Churches expressed concerns about social reform. For further discussion, see H. Clark (1993) *The Church Under Thatcher* (London: SPCK).

2 It was said that she conducted 'a species of guerrilla war'; visitors left feeling 'they had somehow been prevented from doing themselves justice' (P. Cradock (1994) *Experiences of China* (London: John Murray), pp. 175–6). 'She ruled by force of argument as well as by fear ... but fear was often uppermost when she controlled the career prospects of so many under her command' (Jenkins, 1996, p. 17).

3 Patrick Bateson, Professor of Ethology at Cambridge, questioned the assumption that the natural order was based on individualism, pointing out that 'those that team up are more likely to survive than those who do not' (University Sermon, 19 May 1985).

4 A. Smith (1776, 1961) *An Enquiry Into the Nature and Causes of the Wealth of Nations,* Book 1, 10 (London: Methuen), p. 144.

5 J. Vincent (1987) 'The Thatcher government 1979–1987', in P. Hennessy and A. Seldon (eds) *Ruling Performance: British governments from Attlee to Thatcher* (London: Blackwell), p. 288.

6 In 1996, Lord Skidelsky published *A Question of Standards: raising standards through choice* (London: Politeia), advocating the privatization of all state schools and limiting state intervention only to requiring a fixed school-leaving age and health and safety standards.

7 Simon Jenkins described Patten's 1993 Act as 'more gargantuan and certainly more centralist than Baker's "Gerbil 1988" ' (1996, p. 129).

8 Conservative MPs were rumoured to favour an end to parental ballots when at least 60 per cent of schools were GM, which on current progress was then estimated to take 42 more years (*TES,* 29 January 1993). The head of one of the first Catholic schools to opt out in 1992, interviewed in October 1996, felt that GM was 'no longer a useful policy' since it was being hijacked by government pressures for pupil selection on ability. Such views were also reflected in a *TES* survey of GM heads (19 January 1996).

9 We have already noted the appointment of a BP executive to run the National Curriculum Council and Sir Ron Dearing, then Chairman of the Post Office, to chair SCAA. The chairman of the National Council for Vocational Qualifications (NCVQ) had been the managing director of Unilever and that of the FAS the chairman of the Sun Alliance Group.

10 For further discussion of quangos, see Will Hutton's (1995) *The State We're In* (London: Vintage), p. 38. The issue of 'democratic deficit' is developed in J. Stewart (1990).

11 For further discussion of these concepts, see Rod Rhodes' paper 'The New Governance: governing without government' in *The State of Britain Seminars* (24 January 1995), Economic and Social Research Council.

12 Cf. Bishop Konstant, 1993.

13 D. Lawton (1994) *The Tory Mind on Education 1979–1984* (London: Falmer), pp. 147, 143. For further discussion, see also C. Knight (1990) *The Making of Tory Education Policy in Post-War Britain 1950–1986* (London: Falmer).

14 Cf. The Bishops' Conference of England and Wales, 1996a, pp. 18, 26.

15 *The Fourth R*, 1970, para. 472.

16 When the LMS funding per pupil was published in 1990, one Anglican secondary church school in West London discovered that its pupils had up to 50 per cent less funding than some neighbouring county schools. A Catholic school in Lambeth found its pupil–teacher ratio was a third worse than its county neighbours. The Roman Catholic diocesan director of education for Southwark acknowledged: 'no-one should underestimate the fury of schools at the huge financial discrimination against us revealed when LEAs published their school budgets'; however, the Anglican Board's Schools Officer thought that LMS had 'corrected the worst excesses' (interviews, July 1996).

17 The newly appointed Archbishop of Canterbury, George Carey, gave his first speech on education to the Anglican secondary heads conference in September 1991, but the Conservative press were incensed by his passing comment about the link between the Newcastle street riots and social deprivation. Melanie Phillips regretted the way the Church's authority to speak about the problems in society was undermined by government criticism (1996, *All Must Have Prizes* (London: Little, Brown & Co.), p. 298).

18 In 1996 the DFEE published *National Funding for GM Schools*, predicting that 'GM schools will increasingly be funding capital projects out of recurrent income' (p. 11).

19 This 1996 Act also intended to introduce nursery vouchers across the system, which was of concern especially to church primary schools, as it affected their provision for children below statutory school age.

20 The RE Council produced a pamphlet in 1991 entitled *What Conspired Against RE Specialist Teacher Supply?*, arguing that the low priority given to RE 'is so blatant that it cannot be an accident'; the TES reported the 'RE shortage "conspiracy" claim' (15 March).

21 In autumn 1990, the DES offered funding to LEAs for in-service training in National Curriculum subjects and RE, but its offer of classroom resources excluded RE.

22 See M. Walsh (1993) 'Schools at the crossroads', *Tablet*, 13 February.

23 At an RC 'Going GM' conference in January 1995, one GM Catholic head dismissed this as 'a strange little quirk: that's the way things are'.

24 *The Fourth R*, 1970, para. 453: 'A school's first duty is to meet the needs of its own pupils. It is a task which will take us well into the twenty-first century.'

25 Their success in the primary school league tables first published in March 1997 prompted front-page headlines (e.g. *Independent*, 11 March 1997).

26 Hywel Thomas discussed this balance in (1994) 'Markets, collectivities and management', *Oxford Review of Education* **20**(1). Cordingley and Wilby (1987) predicted two sectors of education: 'market-based provision for the majority; a safety-net service for those who cannot survive in the market' (p. 15). The reality was shown on *Panorama* (BBC1, 4 November 1996) where a Halifax school in competition with grammar and GM schools closed after discipline broke down.

27 Bishop Konstant's theme was also evident in the 1996 Bishops' Conference report on *The Common Good.*

28 'Markets, education and Catholic schools', in T. McLaughlin, J. O'Keefe and B. O'Keeffe (eds), 1996, pp. 66–9. See also Will Bartlett on 'Quasi-markets and educational reforms' in J. Legrand and W. Bartlett (eds) (1993) *Quasi-markets and Social Policy* (London: Macmillan).

29 Cardinal Hume's speech to the National Conference on Catholic Education, 10 April 1995.

30 'Education since the 1944 Act', lecture by Cardinal Hume, Institute of Education, 5 May 1994.

31 S. Ball, R. Bowe and S. Gewirtz (1996) 'School choice, social class and distinction: the realization of social advantage in education', *Journal of Educational Policy* **11**(1). A Channel 4 television documentary 'School prayers' (2 October 1996) followed the pupil admissions process of an oversubscribed GM church secondary school in Bolton, showing the lengths to which parents were prepared to go to persuade the school to select their child.

32 The centrepiece of the Tory Right's education policy was 'independent education for all' (cf. A. Flew (1987) *Power to the Parents* (London: Sherwood Press)). Roger Scruton argued that in order for autonomous schools to enhance standards, they must select pupils by ability or aptitude (1980, 2nd edition, 1984, *The Meaning of Conservatism* (London: Macmillan)).

33 Two Catholic independent schools were the first to become GM in July 1995: St Anselm's and Upton Hall Convent School, both in the Wirral (*TES*, 6 July 1995).

34 'Catholic schools and market forces', address to headteachers in the Westminster and Brentford dioceses, 25 September 1991.

35 Cf. A. B. Morris, who noted the apparent success of Catholic schools in the first published sets of examination league tables in 1992: (1994) 'The academic performance of Catholic schools', *School Organisation* **14**(1).

36 Hume, 1994. Fifty-nine church schools were placed in the top 100 primary schools listed in the first league tables of tests for 11-year-olds in 1997: Church leaders commented that their schools benefited from both being 'an integral part of the community' linked to parishes and also having the support of the diocese and LEA (*TES*, 14 March 1997).

37 Butler asked the House of Commons in 1944, 'Is it too much to hope that our discussions will help remove the historic grievances dating from the Act of 1902? It is indeed a happy augury to note the coming together of those between whom a gulf has been fixed for so long' (*Hansard*, cccxcvi, 229–30, 19 January).

38 These trends are more fully analysed in P. Chadwick (1994).

39 The government launched a major advertisement campaign to educate people on the risks from the Aids virus involved in unprotected sexual intercourse; the widespread advocacy of the value of condoms could have been offensive to Catholics.

40 The CJEPC had been used by Graham Leonard as Bishop of London to develop an agreed strategy for the Churches in the 1988 debates. As the Conservative government's legislative programme gathered momentum in the 1990s, the CJEPC had to agree a joint policy (e.g. on collective worship) despite the historical differences in their denominational approaches to church schools.

41 These tensions are well articulated in Waddington, 1984, chapter 4.

42 Blackburn Diocesan Board of Education (1993) *Grant Maintained Status* 2.2.6.

43 Sir Malcolm Thornton, previously Conservative chairman of the Select Committee on Education, expressed his concern at a system of schools 'like 24,000 corks

bobbing around in a market sea'; parental choice and vouchers would lead to 'administrative chaos' rather than a 'levering up of standards' (*Education*, 8 March 1996).

44 The John Loughborough School in Tottenham, e.g., as a fee-paying Seventh-day Adventist school for 170 pupils, in 1996 proposed to opt-in to the state sector as a free GM school.

45 G. Walford (1994) 'The new religious grant-maintained schools', *Educational Management and Administration* 22(2); and (1995) 'The Christian Schools Campaign: a successful pressure group?', *British Educational Research Journal* 21(4).

46 Back in 1942, C. K. Francis Brown had written: 'The Churches distrusted, and with reason, the state and quite rightly fought against being reduced to the level of one amongst so many competing sects' (pp. 125–6). Expressing caution in 1943 about 100 per cent government funding leading to loss of Church control, the Methodist MP, Mr Magnay, warned: 'Methodist and Baptist schools would soon be multiplying, spiritualist or Christadelphian in some places perhaps, no doubt Communist schools under some religion-of-humanity camouflage' (*Hansard*, cccxcvi, 300–1).

47 The causes for this drifting apart are briefly studied by Father Edward Yarnold SJ (1989) in *In Search of Unity* (Slough: St Paul Publications).

48 The DFE 'claw back' their 85 per cent of capital expenditure from the sale of an aided school site; the diocese therefore may not be able to afford to build a replacement aided school, although under the 1973 Education Act (Section 2) the Church is entitled to the proceeds. A DES circular restricting limited funds for nursery provision to county schools prompted a meeting between the Minister (then Tim Eggar) and both Anglican and Roman Catholic bishops in 1991.

49 E.g. joint governor training courses have been run by the Anglican diocese of London and the Roman Catholic diocese of Westminster for several years.

50 Waddington, 1984, p. 29.

51 The *TES* recognized that the fiftieth anniversary of the Butler Education Act was more 'a wake than a celebration' (26 March 1993, p. 11).

52 Hume, 1995.

53 Speech to General Synod by Bishop Graham Leonard, 3 July 1985.

BIBLIOGRAPHY

Adie, M. (1990a) 'Restoring responsibility', *Education*, 14 December.
Adie, M. (1990b) 'Basic or marginal', *Education*, 21 December.
Adie, M. (1993) 'Value inadequate', *Education*, 29 January.
Aldrich, R. (1982) *An Introduction to the History of Education*, London: Hodder and Stoughton.
Aldrich, R. and Leighton, P. (1985) *Education: time for a new act?*, London: Bedford Way Papers 23.
Alison, M. and Edwards, D. L. (eds) (1990) *Christianity and Conservatism*, London: Hodder and Stoughton.
Alves, C. (1968) *Religion and the Secondary School*, London: SCM.
Alves, C. (1991a) *Free to Choose*, London: National Society.
Alves, C. (1991b) 'Just a matter of words? The religious education debate in the House of Lords', *British Journal of Religious Education* 13(3).
Anglican Consultative Council (1984) *Towards a Theology for Inter-faith Dialogue*, London: Church House Publishing.
Angus, L. B. (1988) *Continuity and Change in Catholic Schooling*, London: Falmer.
Archbishop's Commission on Urban Priority Areas (1985) *Faith in the City*, London: Church House Publishing.
Arnold, T. (1833) *Principles of Church Reform*, London: B. Fellowes.
Arthur, J. (1988) 'Catholic schools: rhetoric or reality?', *The Sower* 11(4).
Arthur, J. (1991) 'Catholic responses to the 1988 Education Act: problems of authority and ethos', *British Journal of Religious Education* 13(3).
Arthur, J. (1992) *Policy and Practice of Catholic Education in England and Wales Since the Second Vatican Council*, D.Phil. thesis, University of Oxford.

Arthur, J. (1994) 'Admissions to Catholic schools: principles and practice', *British Journal of Religious Education* **17**(1).

Arthur, J. (1995a) *The Ebbing Tide: policy and principles of Catholic education*, Leominster: Gracewing.

Arthur, J. (1995b) 'Government education policy and Catholic voluntary-aided schools', *Oxford Review of Education* **21**(4).

Ashraf, A. (1987) 'Education of the Muslim community in Great Britain', *Muslim Education Quarterly* **5**(1).

Aspin, D. N. (1983) 'Church schools, religious education and the multi-ethnic community', *Journal of Philosophy of Education* **17**(2).

Association of Anglican Headteachers (1995) Annual Conference report.

Association of Metropolitan Authorities (1988) *Grant-maintained Schools: independence or isolation?*, London: AMMA.

Astley, J. (1984) 'The role of worship in Christian learning', *Religious Education* **79**(2).

Astley, J. (1988) 'Theology and curriculum selection: a theoretical problem in teaching Christianity in religious education', *British Journal of Religious Education* **10**(2).

Astley, J. et al. (1991) *How Faith Grows: faith development and Christian education*, London: National Society.

Astley, J. and Day, D. (eds) (1992) *The Contours of Christian Education*, London: McCrimmons.

Astley, J. and Francis, L. (eds) (1994) *Critical Perspectives on Christian Education*, Leominster: Gracewing/Fowler Wright.

Astley, J. and Francis, L. (eds) (1996) *Christian Theology and Religious Education*, London: SPCK.

Attfield, D. G. (1991) 'The challenge of the Education Reform Act to Church schools', *British Journal of Religious Education* **13**(3).

Audit Commission (1991) *Home to School Transport: a system at the crossroads*, London: HMSO.

Ayel, V. (1981) 'Shifts in catechesis 1950–1980' (trans. Rummery), *Word in Life*, August 1981.

Baker, K. (1988) 'In the moral dimension', *The Times*, 1 February.

Baker, K. (1993) *The Turbulent Years*, London: Faber.

Balen, M. (1994) *Kenneth Clarke*, London: Fourth Estate.

Balfour, M. (1985) *Britain and Joseph Chamberlain*, London: Allen and Unwin.

Ball, S. and Troyna, B. (1987) 'Resistance, rights and rituals: denominational schools and multicultural education', *British Journal of Education Policy* **2**(1).

Ball, S., Bowe, R. and Gerwitz, S. (1996) 'Social choice, social class and distinction: the realization of social advantage in education', *Journal of Educational Policy* **11**(1).

Bander, P. (ed.) (1968) *Looking Forward to the Seventies*, London: Colin Smythe.

Barber, M. (1994) *The Making of the 1944 Education Act*, London: Cassell.

Barber, M. (1996) 'Why are you still smiling, Kenneth?', *TES*, 31 May.

Bartlett, W. (1993) 'Quasi-markets and educational reforms', in Legrand, J. and Bartlett, W. (eds) *Quasi-markets and Social Policy*, London: Macmillan.

Bayly, W. D. (1820) *The State of the Poor and Working Classes*.

Beales, D. and Best, G. (1985) *History, Society and the Churches*, CUP.

Beck, G. A. (ed.) (1950) *The English Catholics 1850–1950*, London: Burns and Oates.

Beck, G. (1955) *The Case for Catholic Schools*, London: Catholic Education Council.

Bell, G. K. A. (1952) *Randall Davidson*, 3rd edn, OUP.

Birmingham (1975) *Agreed Syllabus of Religious Education*, City of Birmingham Education Committee.

Birrell, A. (1937) *Things Past Redress*, London: Faber.

Bishops' Conference of England and Wales (1981) *Signposts and Homecomings: the educative task of the Catholic community*, London: St Paul Publications.

Bishops' Conference of England and Wales (1987) *Education Reform Bill: a commentary for Catholics*, London: CEC.

Bishops' Conference of England and Wales (1988) *Evaluating the Distinctive Nature of the Catholic School*, London: St Paul Publications.

Bishops' Conference of England and Wales (1994) *What Are We to Teach?*, London: CES.

Bishops' Conference of England and Wales (1996a) *The Common Good and the Catholic Church's Social Teaching*, Manchester: Gabriel Communications.

Bishops' Conference of England and Wales (1996b) *Religious Education: curriculum directory of Catholic schools*, London: CES.

Blackburn Diocesan Board of Education (1993) *Grant Maintained Status*.

Blackburn Diocesan Board of Education (1994) *Going Grant-Maintained ??*

Blake, N. (1983) 'Church schools, religious education and the multi-ethnic community: a reply to David Aspin', *Journal of Philosophy of Education* **17**(3).

Board of Education (1943) *Educational Reconstruction*, White Paper, Cmnd 6548.

Board of Education (1988) *Children in the Way: new directions for the Church's children*, London: National Society and Church House Publishing.

Board of Education (1991) *All God's Children*, London: National Society.

Board of Education (1992) *Response to the Department for Education Consultation on RE and Collective Worship*, London: General Synod of the Church of England.

Boyd, C. W. (ed.)(1914) *Mr Chamberlain's Speeches*, London: Constable.

Boyle, J. J. and Francis, L. J. (1986) 'The influence of differing church aided school systems on pupil attitude towards religion', *Research in Education* 35.

Bridges, D. (1985) 'Non-paternalistic arguments in support of parents' rights', *Journal of Philosophy of Education* **18**(1).

Bridges, D. and Husbands, C. (eds) (1996) *Consorting and Collaborating in the Education Market Place*, London: Falmer.

British Council of Churches (1976) *The Child in the Church*, London: British Council of Churches.

British Council of Churches (1981) *Understanding Christian Nurture*, London: British Council of Churches.

British Council of Churches (1989) *Worship in Education*, London: British Council of Churches.

Brooksbank, K. (ed.) (1980) *Educational Administration*, London: Councils and Education Press.

Brown, A. (1988) 'Church, school and ecumenism', in McClelland, V. A. (ed.) *Christian Education in a Pluralist Society*, London: Routledge.

Brown, A. (1996) *Between a Rock and a Hard Place*, London: National Society.

Brown, A., Barrett, V., Cole, O. and Erricker, C. (1987) *The Shap Handbook on World Religions in Education*, London: CRE.

Brown, A. S. (1987) *Religious Education and the Pupil with Learning Difficulties*, Cambridge: Cambridge University Press.

Brown, P. and Sparks, R. (eds) (1989, 2nd edn 1990) *Beyond Thatcherism: social policy, politics and society*, Milton Keynes: Open University Press.

Bryk, A. S., Lee, V. E., and Holland, P. B. (1993) *Catholic Schools and the Common Good*, Cambridge MA: Harvard University Press.

Butler, R. A. (1971) *The Art of the Possible*, London: Hamish Hamilton.

Butler, R. A. (1982) *The Art of Memory*, London: Hodder and Stoughton.

Byrne, A. and Malone, C. (1992) *Here I Am*, London: Collins.

Caldwell, B. J. and Spinks, J. M. (1988) *The Self-managing School*, London: Falmer.

Cambridgeshire (1949) *The Cambridgeshire Syllabus of Religious Teaching for Schools* 1949, CUP.

Carlisle Commission (1971) *Partners in Education: the role of the diocese*, London: National Society and SPCK.

Carpenter, E. (1991) *Archbishop Fisher*, Norwich: Canterbury Press.

Carpenter, S. C. (1933) *Church and People 1789–1889*, London: SPCK.

Catechism of the Catholic Church (1993), London: Chapman.

Catechism of Church Law (1984), London: Catholic Truth Society.

Catholic Commission for Racial Justice (1984) *Learning from Diversity*, London: Catholic Media Office.

Catholic Education Service (1989) *The Education Reform Act and Catholic Schools*, London: CES.

Catholic Education Service (1993) *The Education Act* 1993, London: CES.

Catholic Education Service (1994) *The Inspection of Catholic Schools: guidelines for governing bodies, headteachers and staff*, London: CES.

Catholic Education Service (1995a) *Partnership in the Training of Teachers for Catholic Schools*, London: CES.

Catholic Education Service (1995b) *Quality of Education in Catholic Secondary Schools*, London: CES.

Catholic Education Service (1995c) *Spiritual and Moral Development Across the Curriculum*, London: CES.

Catholic Poor School Committee Reports (1849, 1850), Appendix K.

Chadwick, P. (1994) *Schools of Reconciliation*, London: Cassell.

Chadwick, P. and Gladwell, M. (1987) *Joint Schools*, Norwich: Canterbury Press.

Chadwick, W. O. (1957) *From Bossuet to Newman*, CUP.

Chadwick, W. O. (1970) *The Victorian Church*, London: A. & C. Black.

Chapman, C. (1990) 'Pluralism and British schools: asking the right questions', *Spectrum* **22**(1).

Christian Education Movement (1991) *Planning RE in Schools*, Derby: CEM.

Clark, H. (1993) *The Church Under Thatcher*, London: SPCK.

Clegg, A. (1980) *About Our Schools*, Oxford: Blackwell.

Cloke, P. (ed.) (1992) *Policy and Change in Thatcher's Britain*, Oxford: Pergamon.

Coke, Sr. M. (1983) 'Recent historical summary of catechetical renewal and its implications for R.E.', *British Journal of Educational Studies* **31**(1).

Cole, W. O. (ed.) (1978) *World Faiths in Education*, London: Allen and Unwin.

Cole, W. O. (ed.) (1986) *Religion in the Multi-faith School*, London: Hulton.

Coleman, M., Bush, T. and Glover, D. (1993) 'Researching autonomous schools: a survey of the first 100 GM schools', *Educational Research* **35**(2).

Congar, Y. M. J. (1967) *Priest and Layman*, London: Darton, Longman and Todd.

Congregation for Catholic Education (1988) *The Religious Dimension of Education in a Catholic School*, London: Catholic Truth Society.

Connelly, G. (1984) 'The transubstantiation of a myth', *Journal of Ecclestiastical History* **35**(1).

Cooling, T. (1996) 'Education is the point of RE – not religion?', in Astley, J. and Francis, L. (eds.) *Christian Theology and Religious Education*, London: SPCK.

Cooling, T. and Oliver, G. (1989) *Church and School*, Nottingham: Grove Books.

Copley, T. (1997) *Teaching Religion: religious education in England and Wales 1944–1994*, Exeter: University of Exeter Press.

Cordingley, P. and Wilby, P. (1987) *Opting out of Mr. Baker's Proposals*, Ginger Paper One, London: Education Reform Group.

Cornwell, P. (1985) 'The Church of England and the State', in Moyser, G. (ed.) *Church and Politics Today*, Edinburgh: T. & T. Clark.

Cox, E. (1983) *Problems and Possibilities for Religious Education*, London: Hodder and Stoughton.

Cox, E. (1987) 'The relation between beliefs and values', *Religious Education* **82**(1).

Cox, E. and Cairns, J. M. (1989) *Reforming Religious Education: the religious clauses of the 1988 Education Reform Act*, London: Kogan Page.

Cox, E. and Skinner, M. (1990) 'Multi-faith religious education in church primary schools', *British Journal of Religious Education* **12**(2).

Cox, H. (1965) *The Secular City*, London: SCM.

Cracknell, K. and Lamb, C. (1984) *Theology on Full Alert*, London: British Council of Churches.

Cradock, P. (1994) *Experiences of China*, London: John Murray.

Craft, M. (1984) *Education and Cultural Pluralism*, London: Falmer.

Crawford, K. (1995) 'A history of the Right: the battle for control of National Curriculum History', *British Journal of Educational Studies* **43**(4).

Credo: a Catholic catechism (1983), London: Chapman.

Crowther Report (1959) 15–18, vol. 1, London: HMSO.

Cruickshank, M. (1963) *Church and State in English Education*, London: Macmillan.

Cruickshank, M. (1972) 'The denominational school issue in the twentieth century', *History in Education* 1, pp. 200–13.

Culham College Institute (1987) *The Way Ahead?* (17 November) Conference Report, Abingdon.

Culham College Institute (1995a) *Diocesan Boards of Education*, Abingdon.

Culham College Institute (1995b) *Religious Education in Secondary Schools*, Abingdon.

Culham College Institute (1996) *National Collaboration in Religious Education* (8 March) Conference Report, Abingdon.

Culham College Institute and St Gabriel's Trust (1992) *RE – the Way Ahead?* (29 June) Conference Report.

Cunningham, R. F. (1989) *The Education Reform Act 1988 and Catholic Schools*, London: Catholic Education Council for England and Wales.

Dale, A. T. (1972) *The Bible in the Classroom*, OUP.

Davies, B. and Anderson, L. (1992) *Opting for Self-management: the early experiences of grant-maintained schools*, London: Routledge.

Davies, J. (1994) 'L'Art du possible', in *Recusant History*, London: Catholic Record Office.

Day, D. (1985a) 'Religious education forty years on', *British Journal of Religious Education* **7**(2).

Day, D. (1985b) 'Suspicion of the spiritual; teaching religion in a world of secular experience', *British Journal of Religious Education* **7**(3).

Deakin, R. (1989) *New Christian Schools: the case for public funding*, Bristol: Regius.

Denison, G. A. (1878) *Notes of my Life*, Oxford and London: James Parker.

Dent, H. C. (1971) *Educational Systems in England and Wales*, University of London Press.

Dent, H. J. (1947) *The Education Act 1944: provisions, possibilities and some problems*, University of London Press.

Department for Education (1992a) *Choice and Diversity: a new framework for schools*, DFE White Paper, London: HMSO.

Department for Education (1992b) *Religious Education and Collective Worship: a consultation paper*, London: DFE.

Department for Education (1994) *Religious Education and Collective Worship*, Circular 1/94, London: HMSO.

Department for Education and Employment (1995) *Consultation Paper on Self-government for Voluntary-aided Schools*, London: DFEE.

Department for Education and Employment (1996a) *National Funding for GM Schools*, London: DFEE.

Department for Education and Employment (1996b) *Self-government for Schools*, White Paper Cmnd 3315, London: HMSO.

Department of Catholic Education and Formation (1991) *On Appraisal in Catholic Schools*, 2nd edition, London: CES.

Department of Education and Science (1981) *The School Curriculum*, London: HMSO.

Department of Education and Science (1985) *Better Schools*, London: HMSO.

Department of Education and Science (1987) *Grant-maintained Schools: a consultative document*, London: HMSO.

Department of Education and Science (1988) *School Governors: a guide to the law: aided schools*, London: DES.

Department of Education and Science (1989) *The Education Reform Act 1988: religious education and collective worship*, London: DES Circular 3/89.

Department of Education and Science (1991) *The Parent's Charter: you and your child's education*, London: DES.

Dickens, A. G. and Tonkin, J. (1985) *The Reformation in Historical Thought*, Oxford: Blackwell.

Dummett, A. and McNeal, J. (1981) *Race and Church Schools*, London: Runnymede Trust.

Duncan, G. (1990) *The Church School*, London: National Society.

Durham Report (1970) *The Fourth R: the report of the commission on religious education in schools*, London: National Society and SPCK.

Earl, W. J. H. (1984) 'The 1944 Education Act: forty years on', *British Journal of Religious Education* **6**(2).

Edwards, D. (1974) *Religion and Change* (rev. edn) London: Hodder and Stoughton.

Egan, J. (1988) *Opting Out: Catholic schools today*, Leominster: Fowler Wright.

Egan, J. and Francis, L. J. (1986) 'School ethos in Wales: the impact of non-practising Catholic and non-Catholic pupils on Catholic secondary schools', *Lumen Vitae* **41**(3).

Eliot, T. S. (1939, 1982) *The Idea of a Christian Society*, London: Faber and Faber.

Evans, A. (1994) 'Acts of worship in secondary schools', *Education Today* **43**(4).

Fahy, P. S. (1980) 'The religious effectiveness of some Australian Catholic high schools', *Word in Life* **28**(2).

Fahy, P. S. (1992) *Faith in Catholic Classrooms*, London: St Paul Publications.

Felderhof, M. C. (ed.) (1985) *Religious Education in a Pluralistic Society*, London: Hodder and Stoughton.

Ferguson, J. (ed.) (1981) *Christianity, Society and Education*, London: SPCK.

Field, F. (1989) *Opting Out: an opportunity for Church schools*, London: The Church in Danger.

Flannery, A. (ed.) (1981) *Vatican Council II: the Conciliar and Postconciliar documents*, 5th edition, Leominster: Fowler Wright.

Fletcher, J. (1994) 'Research, education policy and the management of change', *Oxford Review of Education* **20**(1).

Flew, A. (1987) *Power to the Parents*, London: Sherwood Press.

Flude, M. and Hammer, M. (eds) (1990) *The Education Reform Act 1988: its origins and implications*, London: Falmer.

Flynn, M. F. (1975) *Some Catholic Schools in Action*, Sydney: Catholic Education Office.

Flynn, M. F. (1985) *The Effectiveness of Catholic Schools*, Homebush NSW: St Paul Publications.

Fowler, G., Morris, V. and Ozga, J. (eds) (1973) *Decision-making in British Education*, Milton Keynes: Heinemann and Open University.

Francis, L. J. (1983) 'The logic of education, theology and the church school', *Oxford Review of Education* **9**(2).

Francis, L. J. (1986a) *Partnership in Rural Education*, London: Collins Liturgical Publications.

Francis, L. J. (1986b) 'Denominational schools and pupil attitudes towards Christianity', *British Educational Research Journal* **12**(2).

Francis, L. J. (1986c) 'Roman Catholic secondary schools: falling rolls and pupil attitudes', *Educational Studies* **12**(2).

Francis, L. J. (1987a) *Religion in the Primary School*, London: Collins Liturgical Publications.

Francis, L. J. (1987b) 'Measuring attitudes towards Christianity among 12- to 18-year old pupils in Catholic schools', *Educational Research* **29**(3).

Francis, L. J. (1987c) 'Catholic schools and the communication of faith', *Catholic School Studies* **60**(2).

Francis, L. J. (1987d) 'The decline in attitudes towards religion among 8–15 year olds', *Educational Studies* **13**(2).

Francis, L. J. (1990) 'Theology of education', *British Journal of Educational Studies* **38**(4).

Francis, L. J. and Egan, J. (1987) 'Catholic school as "faith community": an empirical enquiry', *Religious Education* **85**(4).

Francis, L. J. and Kay, B. (1995) *Teenage Religion and Values*, Leominster: Gracewing.

Francis, L. J. and Lankshear, D. (1993) *Christian Perspectives on Church Schools*, Leominster: Gracewing/Fowler Wright.

Francis, L. and Lewis, J. (1995) 'Who wants RE?', in Astley, J. and Francis, L. (eds) *Christian Theology and Religious Education*, London: SPCK.

Francis, L. J. and Thatcher, A. (1990) *Christian Perspectives for Education: a reader in the theology of education*, Leominster: Gracewing/ Fowler Wright.

Francis Brown, C. K. (1942) *The Churches' Part in Education 1833–1941*, London: National Society/SPCK.

Friere, P. (1972) *The Pedagogy of the Oppressed*, London: Penguin.

Gallagher, J. (1986) *Guidelines: living and sharing our faith*, London: Collins.

Gallagher, J. (1988) *Our Schools and Our Faith*, London: Collins.

Gardner, P. (1988) 'Religious upbringing and the ideal of autonomy', *Journal of Philosophy of Education* **22**(2).

Gates, B. (1993) *Time for Religious Education and Teachers to Match: a digest of under-provision*, Lancaster: Religious Education Council.

Gay, J. D. (1994) *Compulsory RE: is it a benefit?*, Templeton Lecture, Royal Society of Arts, 28 November.

Gay, J. D. (1995) *Diocesan Boards of Education*, Abingdon: Culham College Institute.

Gay, J. D. *et al.* (1982) *The Debate About Church Schools in the Oxford Diocese*, Abingdon: Culham College Institute.

Gay, J. D., Kay, B., Newdick, H. and Perry, G. (1991a) *A Role for the Future: Anglican primary schools in the London diocese*, Abingdon: Culham College Institute.

Gay, J., Kay, B., Newdick, H. and Perry, G. (1991b) *Schools and Church:*

Anglican secondary schools in the London diocese, Abingdon: Culham College Institute.

General Synod of the Church of England (1994) *An Excellent Enterprise: the Church of England and its colleges of higher education*, London: Board of Education.

General Synod of the Church of England Board of Education (1984) *Schools and Multi-cultural Education*, London: Board of Education.

Gilmour, I. (1992) *Dancing with Dogma: Britain under Thatcherism*, London: Simon and Schuster.

Goldman, R. (1964) *Religious Thinking from Childhood to Adolescence*, London: Routledge.

Goldman, R. (1965) *Readiness for Religion*, London: Routledge.

Goodall, B. (1972) *Ecumenical Progress 1961–71*, OUP.

Gordon, P. and White, J. (1979) *Philosophers as Educational Reformers*, London: Routledge.

Gordon, P., Aldrich, R. and Dean, D. (1991) *Education and Policy in England in the Twentieth Century*, London: Woburn Press.

Grace, G. (1993) 'Beyond educational management', *British Journal of Educational Studies* **xxxxi**(4).

Grace, G. (1995) *School Leadership: beyond education management*, London: Falmer.

Graham, D. with Tytler, D. (1993) *A Lesson for Us All: the making of the National Curriculum*, London: Routledge.

Gray, J. (1993) *Beyond the New Right*, London: Routledge.

Greeley, A. M. (1982) *Catholic High Schools and Minority Students*, New Brunswick: Transaction Books.

Greeley, A. M. and Rossi, P. H. (1966) *The Education of Catholic Americans*, Chicago: Aldine.

Greeley, A. M., McCready, W. C. and McCourt, K. (1976) *Catholic Schools in a Declining Church*, Kansas City: Sheed, Andrews and McMeel.

Green, R. H. (1982) *Church Schools: a matter of opinion*, London: Southwark Diocesan Board of Education.

Griffiths, L. (1995) 'The survival of hope' (The R. H. Tawney Memorial Lecture), *The Month* **28**(5).

Grimmitt, M. (1995) 'The use of religious phenomena in schools', *British Journal of Religious Education* **13**(3).

Groome, T. H. (1980) *Christian Religious Education*, San Francisco: Harper and Row.

Groome, T. H. *et al.* (1988) 'The spirituality of the religious educator', *Religious Education* **83**(1).

Habgood, J. (1990) 'Are moral values enough?', *British Journal of Educational Studies* **38**(2).

Hadow Report (1926) *The Education of the Adolescent*, London: HMSO.

Haldane, J. (1986) 'Religious education in a pluralist society: a philosophical examination', *British Journal of Educational Studies* **34**(2).

Haldane, J. (1988) 'Religion in education: in defence of a tradition', *Oxford Review of Education* **14**(2).

Halévy, E. (1926, 1951, 1987) *History of the English People 1895–1905*, (trans. E. Watkin), London: Ark.

Halpin, D., Fitz, J. and Power, S. (1993) *The Early Impact and Long Term Implications of the Grant-maintained Schools Policy*, University of Warwick: Trentham Books.

Halstead, J. (1994) *Parental Choice and Education: principles, policy and practice*, London: Kogan Page.

Hammersley, P. (1989) 'Development in faith development theory', *British Journal of Religious Education* **11**(3).

Hammond, P. E. (1988) 'Religion and the persistence of identity', *Journal for the Scientific Study of Religion* **27**(1).

Hampshire (1978) *Religious Education in Hampshire Schools*, Winchester: Hampshire Education Committee.

Hargreaves, D. (1984) *Improving Secondary Schools*, London: ILEA.

Harris, K. (1988) *Thatcher*, London: Weidenfeld and Nicolson.

Hart, C. (1991) *From Acts to Action*, Newcastle upon Tyne: CATS Trust.

Hastings, A. (1968, 1969) *A Concise Guide to the Documents of the Second Vatican Council*, vols 1 and 2, London: Darton, Longman and Todd.

Hastings, A. (1986) *The History of English Christianity 1920–1990*, London: Burns and Oates.

Hastings, A. (ed.) (1991) *Modern Catholicism: Vatican II and after*, London: SPCK.

Hastings, A. (1993) 'Catholicism and Protestantism', *One in Christ*, 1993(1).

Haviland, J. (ed.) (1988) *Take Care Mr. Baker!*, London: Fourth Estate.

Hayden, G. (ed.) (1987) *Education and Values*, University of London, Institute of Education.

Heenan, J. (1944) *Cardinal Hinsley*, London: Burns and Oates.

Heenan, J. (1971) *Not the Whole Truth*, London: Hodder and Stoughton.

Hennessy, P. (1996) 'A tigress surrounded by hamsters', Gresham Lecture, 20 February.

Hennessy, P. and Seldon, A. (eds) *Ruling Performance: British governments from Attlee to Thatcher,* London: Blackwell.

Henson, H. H. (1939) *The Church of England,* CUP.

Her Majesty's Chief Inspector of Schools (1993) *Grant-maintained Schools 1989–92,* London: HMSO.

Her Majesty's Inspectors (1977) *Curriculum 11–16,* London: HMSO.

Her Majesty's Inspectors (1993) *Report on the Introduction of the National Curriculum,* London: HMSO.

Her Majesty's Senior Chief Inspector (1992) *Fourth Annual Report,* London: HMSO.

Heywood, D. (1988) 'Christian education and enculturation', *British Journal of Religious Education* **10**(2).

Hibbert Lectures 1965 (1966) *Christianity in Education,* London: Allen and Unwin.

Higgins, A. (1979) *Teaching about Controversial Issues in Catholic Schools,* Norwich: CARE Occasional Paper 7, UEA.

Higgins, J. (1989) 'Gender and Church of England diocesan syllabuses of religious education', *British Journal of Religious Education* **12**(1).

Hill, B. V. (1989) 'Spiritual development' in the Education Reform Act: a source of acrimony, apathy or accord', *British Journal of Educational Studies* **37**(2).

Hill, B. V. (1990) 'Will and should the religious studies appropriate to schools in a pluralist society foster religious relativism?', *British Journal of Religious Education* **12**(3).

Hirst, P. H. (1972) 'Christian education: a contradiction in terms?', *Learning for Living* **11**(4).

Hirst, P. H. (1974a) 'Moral education in a secular society', *British Journal of Educational Studies* **24**(2).

Hirst, P. H. (1974b) *Knowledge and the Curriculum,* London: Routledge.

Hirst, P. H. (1976) 'Religious beliefs and educational principles', *Learning for Living* **15**(4).

Hirst, P. H. (1981) 'Education, catechesis and the church school', *British Journal of Religious Education* **3**(3).

HMSO (1992) *Diocesan Boards of Education Measure 1991,* London: HMSO.

Holland, G. (1996) *Alas Sir Humphrey, I Knew Him Well,* Royal Society of Arts lecture, 3 May.

Holm, J. (1975) *Teaching Religion in School,* OUP.

Holm, J. (1977) *The Study of Religions,* London: Sheldon Press.

Holmes, J. D. (1978) *More Rome than Rome*, London: Burns and Oates.

Holt, M. (1978) *The Common Curriculum*, London: Routledge.

Holtby, R. (1986) 'Duality: the National Society 1934–1986', in Yates, J. (ed.) *Faith in the Future*, London: National Society.

Hornsby-Smith, M. P. (1978) *Catholic Education: the unobtrusive partner*, London: Sheed and Ward.

Hornsby-Smith, M. P. (1991) *Roman Catholic Beliefs in England*, CUP.

Hornsby-Smith, M. P. and Lee, R. (1980) *Roman Catholic Opinion: a study of Roman Catholics in England and Wales in the 1970s*, University of Surrey.

Howard, A. (1987) *RAB: the life of R. A. Butler*, London: Jonathan Cape.

Hudson, A. (1978) *Wycliffite Writings*, CUP.

Hudson, W. D. (1973) 'Is religious education possible', in Langford, G. and O'Connor, D. J. (eds) (1973) *New Essays in the Philosophy of Education*, London: Routledge.

Hughes, F. (1990) 'Christian education in recently established Christian schools', *Spectrum* **22**(2).

Hull, J. M. (1975) *School Worship: an obituary*, London: SCM

Hull, J. M. (1976) 'Christian theology and educational theory: can there be connections?', *British Journal of Educational Studies* **24**(2).

Hull, J. M. (1980) 'The value of the individual child and the Christian faith', *British Journal of Educational Studies* **28**(3).

Hull, J. M. (1984) *Studies in Religion and Education*, London: Falmer.

Hull, J. M. (1989a) 'Editorial: school worship and the 1988 Education Reform Act', *British Journal of Religious Education* **11**(3).

Hull, J. M. (1989b) *The Act Unpacked*, Derby: Christian Education Movement.

Hull, J. M. (1990) Editorials, *British Journal of Religious Education* **12**.

Hull, J. M. (1993) *The Place of Christianity in the Curriculum: the theology of the Department for Education*, Hockerill Lecture, 19 November.

Hull, J. M. (1994) *Collective Worship: the search for spirituality*, Templeton Lecture, Royal Society of Arts, 12 December.

Hull, J. M. (1996) 'A critique of Christian religionism', in Astley, J. and Francis, L. (eds) *Christian Theology and Religious Education*, London: SPCK.

Hulmes, E. (1979) *Commitment and Neutrality in Religious Education*, London: Chapman.

Hulmes, E. (1989) *Education and Cultural Diversity*, London: Longman.

Hulmes, E. (1992a) 'Christian education: an instrument of European unity?', in Astley, J. and Day, D. *The Contours of Christian Education*, London: McCrimmons.

Hulmes, E. (1992b) 'Unity and diversity: the search for common identity', in Watson, B. *Priorities in Religious Education*, London: Falmer.

Hulmes, E. and Watson, B. (eds) (1980) *Religious Studies and Public Examinations*, Oxford: Farmington Institute.

Hume, B. (1987) 'No room for religion', *The Times*, 13 January.

Hume, B. (1988a) *Towards a Civilization of Love: being Church in today's world*, London: Hodder and Stoughton.

Hume, B. (1988b) *The Future of Catholic Schools*, address to Catholic Headteachers, 19 September 1988.

Hume, B. (1989) *Catholic Schools Today*, address to National Conference of Priests, 5 September 1989.

Hume, B. (1990a) *Building Bridges*, address to the North of England Education Conference, 3 January 1990.

Hume, B. (1990b) *Transforming the World: a pastor's viewpoint*, Toronto, 1990.

Hume, B. (1991a) *Recapturing the Vision*, address to the conference on the Future of Post-16 Education in Catholic Schools and Colleges, 27 June 1991.

Hume, B. (1991b) Address to Catholic Secondary Headteachers in the Archdiocese of Westminster, 24 September 1991.

Hume, B. (1994) *Education Since the 1944 Act*, lecture (5 May), Institute of Education, London.

Hume, B. (1995) *The Church's Mission in Education*, address to the National Conference on Catholic Education, 10 April 1995.

Hunter, J. (1991) 'Which school? A study of parents' choice of secondary school', *Educational Research* **33**(1).

Hutton, W. (1995) *The State We're In*, London: Vintage.

Inge, W. R. (1911) *Speculum Animae*, London: Longman.

Inner London Education Authority (1968) *Learning for Life*, London: ILEA.

Inner London Education Authority (1984) *Religious Education for Our Children*, London: ILEA.

Institute of Christian Education (1954) *Religious Education in Schools*, London: National Society and SPCK.

Iremonger, F. A. (1948) *William Temple*, OUP.

Islamic Academy (1993) *Spiritual and Moral Development: a response to the NCC discussion paper*, London.

Jackson, R. (1995) 'Religious education's representation of "religions" and "cultures" ', *British Journal of Educational Studies* **43**(3).

James Report (1972) *Teacher Education and Training*, London: HMSO.

Jamison, C. (1991) 'Catholic schools under fire', *Priests and People* 5(8).

Jebb, P. (ed.) (1968) *Religious Education: the downside symposium*, London: Darton, Longman and Todd.

Jefferys, K. (1984) 'R. A. Butler, the Board of Education and the 1944 Education Act', *History* 69.

Jefferys, K. (ed.) (1987) *Labour and the War-time Coalition: from the diary of James Chuter Ede*, London: Historians' Press.

Jenkins, S. (1996) *Accountable to None: the Tory nationalisation of Britain*, London: Penguin.

Jennings, R. E. (1977) *Education and Politics*, London: Batsford.

Jerusalem Bible (edns 1968, 1985) Darton, Longman and Todd/ Doubleday.

Jones, M. (1938) *The Charity School Movement*, CUP.

Joseph, K. (1976) *Stranded on the Middle Ground*, London: Centre of Policy Studies.

Kay, W. K. (1975) *Moral Education*, London: Allen and Unwin.

Keegan, W. (1995) 'Smiles from the fat cats', *Tablet*, 22 July.

Kent, J. (1992) *William Temple: church, state and society in Britain 1880–1950*, CUP.

Ker, I. T. (ed.) (1990)*Newman the Theologian*, London: Collins.

Kirk, K. E. (1937) *The Story of the Woodard Schools*, London: Hodder and Stoughton.

Knight, C. (1990) *The Making of Tory Education Policy in Post-war Britain 1950–1986*, London: Falmer.

Kogan, M. (1975) *Educational Policy-making*, London: Allen and Unwin.

Konstant, D. (1976) *Religious Education for Secondary Schools*, London: Search Press and Macmillian.

Konstant, D. (1991a) *Catholic Schools and Market Forces*, address to headteachers in Westminster and Brentford dioceses, 25 September.

Konstant, D. (1991b) 'Roots in religious education', in Watson, B. *Priorities in Religious Education*, London: Falmer.

Konstant, D. (1993) *Education: church and state*, address to Salford diocese (29 June).

Konstant, D. (1996) *The Church and Catholic Independent Schools*, address to the Catholic Independent Schools' Conference, 18 January.

Labour Party (1995) *Diversity and Excellence*, policy document on education.

Lankshear, D. W. (1992a) *A Shared Vision*, London: National Society.

Lankshear, D. W. (1992b) *Governing Church Schools*, London: National Society.

Lankshear, D. W. (1992c) *Looking for Quality in a Church School*, London: National Society, Southwark Diocesan Board of Education and Culham College Institute.

Lankshear, D. W. (1996) *From Research to Policy 1980–1996: the case of the Church of England school*, paper to the International Symposium of Church School Studies, Durham, 3 July.

Lankshear, J. (1996) *The Inspection of Collective Worship in Anglican Primary Schools: an analysis of Section 13 reports*, paper to the International Symposium on Church School Studies, Durham, 3 July.

Lawlor, S. (1988) *Opting Out – a guide to how and why*, London: Centre of Policy Studies.

Lawson, N. (1992) *A View from No.11*, London: Bantam.

Lawton, D. (1980) *The Politics of the School Curriculum*, London: Routledge.

Lawton, D. (ed.) (1989) *The Education Act: choice and control*, London: Hodder and Stoughton.

Lawton, D. (1992) *Education and Politics in the 1990s: conflict or consensus?*, London: Falmer.

Lawton, D. (1994) *The Tory Mind on Education 1979–1984*, London: Falmer.

Leahy, M. (1990) 'Indoctrination, evangelization, catechesis and religious education', *British Journal of Religious Education* 12(2).

Legrand, J. and Bartlett, W. (1993) *Quasi-markets and Social Policy*, London: Macmillan.

Leonard, G. and Yates, J. (eds) (1986) *Faith for the Future: essays on the Church in education*, London: National Society.

Lima Declaration (1982) *Baptism, Eucharist and Ministry*, Geneva: World Council of Churches.

Lohan, R. and McClure, M. (1988) *Weaving the Web*, London: Collins.

London Diocesan Board for Schools (1992) *The Education Bill: brief summary and comments.*

London Diocesan Syllabus (1988) *Religious Education in the Diocese of London*, London: Diocesan Board of Education.

Louden, L. and Unwin, D. (1993) *Church School Inspection*, Abingdon: Culham College Institute and Southwark Diocesan Board.

Loukes, H. (1961) *Teenage Religion*, London: SCM.

Loukes, H. (1965) *New Ground in Christian Education*, London: SCM.

Lowndes, G. A. N. (1969) *The Silent Social Revolution: the expansion of public education in England and Wales 1895–1965* (2nd edn), OUP.

Mabud, S. K. (1992) 'A Muslim response to the Education Reform Act 1988', *British Journal of Religious Education* 14(2).

McCabe, H. (1985) *The Teaching of the Catholic Church: a new catechism of Christian doctrine*, London: Catholic Truth Society.

McClelland, V. A. (1988) *Christian Education in a Pluralist Society*, London: Routledge.

McClelland, V. C. (1988) 'Sensus Fidelium: the developing concept of Roman Catholic voluntary effort in education in England and Wales', in Tulasiewicz, W. and Brock, C. (eds) *Christianity and Educational Provision in International Perspective.*

McCloy, R. (1982) 'The Church and LEA partnership', *Crosscurrent* (October).

Macgregor, G. P. (1981) *Bishop Otter College and Policy for Teacher Education 1839–1980*, London: Pembridge Press.

Machin, G. I. T. (1977) *Politics and the Churches in Great Britain 1832–1868*, OUP.

McLaughlin, T. (1990) 'Peter Gardner on religious upbringing and the liberal ideal of religious autonomy', *Journal of Philosophy of Education* 24(1).

McLaughlin, T. (1992) *Christian Education and Schooling: a liberal perspective*, Conference paper, Nottingham, January 1992.

McLaughlin, T. (1994) 'Parental rights and the religious upbringing of children', *Journal of Philosophy of Education* 18(1).

McLaughlin, T., O'Keefe, J. and O'Keeffe, B. (eds) (1996) *The Contemporary Catholic School: context, identity and diversity*, London: Falmer.

McLeod, J. (1990) 'Church and state: the religious settlement in the 1988 Education Reform Act', in Morris, R. (ed.) *Central and Local Control of Education after the Education Reform Act*, BEMAS, Harlow: Longman.

Maclure, J. S. (1979) *Educational Documents*, London: Methuen.

Maclure, J. S. (1986) *Educational Documents, England and Wales 1816–1967*, London: Methuen.

Maclure, J. S. (1990) 'Parents and schools – opting in and opting out', in Lawton, D. (ed.) *The Education Act: choice and control*, London: Hodder and Stoughton.

Maclure, J. S. (3rd edn, 1992) *Education Reformed*, London: Hodder and Stoughton.

McSmith, A. (1994) *Kenneth Clarke: a political biography*, London: Verso.

Marquand, D. (1988) 'The paradoxes of Thatcherism', in Skidelsky, R. (ed.) *Thatcherism*, London: Chatto and Windus.

Marr, P. (1989) 'Denominational schools: some implications from ARCIC 1', *One in Christ* 25.

Marthaler, B. L. (1987) 'Dilemma for religious educators: indoctrination or indifference', *Religious Education* 82(4).

Martin, B. (1981) *A Sociology of Contemporary Cultural Change*, Oxford: Blackwell.

Martin, D. (1967) *A Sociology of English Religion*, London: SCM.

Mayfield, G. (1958, 1963) *The Church of England, its Members and its Business*, London: OUP.

Meakin, D. C. (1988) 'The justification of religious education reconsidered', *British Journal of Religious Education* 10(2).

Milbank, J. (1990) *Theology and Social Theory: beyond secular reason*, Oxford: Blackwell.

Mitchell, B. (1967) *Law, Morality and Religion in a Secular Society*, OUP.

Mitchell, B. (1968) *Neutrality and Commitment*, OUP.

Mitchell, B. (1970) 'Indoctrination', Appendix B in the Durham Report, *The Fourth R*, London: SPCK.

Mitchell, B. (1973) *The Justification of Religious Belief*, London: Macmillan.

Mitchell, B. (1980a) 'Religious education', *Oxford Review of Education* 6(2).

Mitchell, B. (1980b) *Morality: religious and secular*, Oxford: Clarendon.

Moran, G. (1966) *Catechesis and Revelation*, New York: Herder and Herder.

Moran, G. (1967) *God Still Speaks*, London: Burns and Oates.

Moran, G. (1968) *Visions and Tactics*, London: Burns and Oates.

Moran, G. (1989) *Religious Education as a Second Language*, Birmingham, Alabama: REP.

Morley, J. (1905) *Life of Gladstone*, London: Macmillan.

Morris, A. B. (1994) 'The academic performance of Catholic schools', *School Organisation* 14(1).

Morris, N. (1977) 'Public expenditure on education in the 1980s', *Oxford Review of Education* 3(1).

Moyser, G. (ed.) (1985) *Church and Politics Today*, Edinburgh: T. & T. Clark.

Murphy, J. (1971) *Church, State and Schools in Britain 1800–1970*, London: Routledge and Kegan Paul.

Murphy, J. (1972) *The Education Act 1870*, Newton Abbot: David and Charles.

Musty, E. (1991) *Opening Their Eyes*, London: National Society.

National Association of Head Teachers (1985) *Religious Education in Schools*, NAHT.

National Audit Office (1994) *Value for Money at Grant-maintained Schools: a review of performance*, London: HMSO.

National Board of Religious Inspectors and Advisors (1994) *Broad Areas of Attainment in RE*, London: Rejoice Publications.

National Curriculum Council (1991) *Religious Education: a local curriculum framework*, York: NCC.

National Curriculum Council (1993) *Spiritual and Moral Development: a discussion paper*, York: NCC.

National Foundation for Educational Research (1996) *Religious Education*, Slough: NFER.

National Pastoral Congress (1981) *Liverpool 1980*, London: St Paul Publications.

National Society (1973) *Voluntary Controlled Schools of the Church of England*, London: National Society.

National Society (1984) *A Future in Partnership*, London: National Society.

National Society (1985) *Positive Partnership*, London: National Society.

National Society (1988) *Children in the Way*, London: National Society.

National Society (1989) *Religious Education*, London: National Society.

National Society (1990a) *The Curriculum: a Christian view*, London: National Society.

National Society (1990b) *Staff for Church Schools: guidelines on appointment*, London: National Society.

National Society (1991) *Grant Maintained Status and the Church School*, London: National Society.

Newcastle Commission Report (1861).

Newman, J. H. (1852) *The Idea of a University*, 1976 edn by I. T. Ker, OUP.

Newsom Report (1963) *Half Our Future: a report of the Central Advisory Council for Education (England)*, London: DES/HMSO.

Niblett, W. R. (1960) *Christian Education in a Secular Society*, OUP.

Nichols, A. (1993) *The Panther and the Hind; a theological history of Anglicanism*, Edinburgh: T. & T. Clark.

Nichols, K. (ed.) (1974) *Theology and Education*, London: St Paul Publications.

Nichols, K. (1978) *Cornerstone*, London: St Paul Publications.

Nichols, K. (1979) *Orientations*, London: St Paul Publications.

Noble, A. and Wright, R. (1994) *To Ballot or Not to Ballot*, Northampton: JEMA.

Nordberg, R. B. (1987) 'Curricular integration in Roman Catholic education', *Religious Education* 82(1).

Norman, E. R. (1977) *Church and Society 1770–1970*, OUP.

Norman, E. R. (1985) *Roman Catholicism in England*, OUP.

Office for Standards in Education (OFSTED) (1994a) *A Focus on Quality*, London: OFSTED.

Office for Standards in Education (OFSTED) (1994b) *Religious Education and Collective Worship 1992–1993*, London: HMSO.

Office for Standards in Education (OFSTED) (1994c) *Spiritual, Moral, Social and Cultural Development: an OFSTED discussion paper*, London: OFSTED.

Office for Standards in Education (OFSTED) (1997) *The Annual Report of Her Majesty's Chief Inspector of Schools: Standards and Quality in Education 1995/6*, London: OFSTED.

O'Hare, P. (1978) *Foundations of Religious Education*, New York: Paulist Press.

O'Hear, A. (1981) *Education, Society and Human Nature*, London: Routledge.

O'Keeffe, B. (1986) *Faith, Culture and the Dual System*, London: Falmer.

O'Keeffe, B. (1988) *Schools for Tomorrow: building walls or building bridges*, London: Falmer.

O'Keeffe, B. (1992) 'A Look at the Christian Schools Movement', in Watson, B. *Priorities in Religious Education*, London: Falmer.

O'Leary, D. L. and Sallnow, T. (1982) *Love and Meaning in Religious Education*, OUP.

O'Leary, D. L. (ed.) (1983) *Religious Education and Young Adults*, London: St Paul Publications.

Orchard, S. (1991) 'What was wrong with religious education? an analysis of HMI reports 1985–88', *British Journal of Religious Education* 14(1).

Parrinder, E. G. (1967) *Comparative Religion*, London: Allen and Unwin.

Peters, R. S. (1966) *Ethics and Education*, London: Allen and Unwin.

Peters, R. S. (ed.) (1973) *Philosophy of Education*, OUP.

Phillips, M. (1996) *All Must Have Prizes*, London: Little, Brown and Co.

Platten, S. G. (1975) 'The conflict over the control of elementary education 1870–1902 and its effect upon the life and influence of the Church', *British Journal of Educational Studies* **23**(3).

Plowden Report (1967) *Children and Their Schools*, London: HMSO.

Price, A. (1993) *The Grant Maintained Option*, address to the Association of Catholic Schools and Colleges.

Price, C. (1995) 'Opinion', *TES*, 20 October.

Pring, R. (1976) *Knowledge and Schooling*, London: Open Books.

Pring, R. (1996) 'Markets, education and Catholic schools', in McLaughlin, T., O'Keefe, J. and O'Keeffe, B. (eds) *The Contemporary Catholic School: context, identity and diversity*, London: Falmer.

Purcell, E. S. (1973) *Life of Manning*, New York: Da Capo Press (First published 1896, London: Macmillan).

Purnell, P. (1985) *Our Faith Story*, London: Collins.

Quinton, A. (1978) *The Politics of Imperfection: the religious and secular traditions of conservative thought in England from Hooker to Oakeshott*, London: Faber and Faber.

Raab, C. (1994) 'Theorising the governance of education', *British Journal of Educational Studies* **42**(1).

Rahner, K. *et al.* (eds) (1968) *Sacramentum Mundi*, Burns and Oates.

Ranson, S. (1993) 'Markets or democracy for education', *British Journal of Educational Studies* **xxxxi**(4).

Raphael, T. (1991) *The Role of the Church School in a Multi-faith City*, London Diocesan Board for Schools.

Read, G., Rudge, J. and Howarth, R. (1986) *How Do I Teach RE?*, London: Mary Glasgow.

Regan, D. E. (1977) *Local Government and Education*, London: Allen and Unwin.

Religious Education Council (1989) *Handbook for Agreed Syllabus Conference, SACREs and Schools*, Lancaster: RE Council.

Robbins, K. (1985) 'Britain, 1940 and Christian civilization', in Beales, D. and Best, G. (eds) *History, Society and the Churches*, CUP.

Robinson, J. A. T. (1964) *Honest to God*, London: SCM.

Rogers, R. (1989) *Considering the Options: a guide on opting out*, London: Advisory Council for Education.

Rouse, R. and Neill, S. C. (eds) (1954) *A History of the Ecumenical Movement 1517–1948*, London: SPCK.

Sacks, B. (1961) *The Religious Issue in the State Schools of England and Wales 1902–1914*, Albuquerque: University of New Mexico.

Sacks, J. (1991) 'The persistence of faith: religion, morality and society in a secular age', *The Reith Lectures 1990*, London: Weidenfeld and Nicolson.

Sacred Congregation for Catholic Education (1971) *The General Catechetical Directory*, London: Catholic Truth Society.

Sacred Congregation for Catholic Education (1977) *The Catholic School*, London: Catholic Truth Society.

Sacred Congregation for Catholic Education (1979) *Catechesis in Our Time*, London: Catholic Truth Society.

Sacred Congregation for Catholic Education (1982) *Lay Catholics in Schools: witnesses to faith*, London: Catholic Truth Society.

Sacred Congregation for Catholic Education (1988) *The Religious Dimension of Education in a Catholic School*, London: Catholic Truth Society.

Sallis, J. (1977) *School Managers and Governors*, London: Ward Lock.

Salter, B. and Tapper, T. (1981) *Education, Politics and the State*, London: Grant McIntyre.

Schools Council (1971) *Religious Education in Secondary Schools*, Working Paper 36, London: Evans/Methuen.

School Curriculum and Assessment Authority (1996) *Education for Adult Life* (15 January), Conference report.

School Curriculum and Assessment Authority (1995) *Spiritual and Moral Development*, Discussion Paper No. 3 (reprint of NCC discussion paper), London: SCAA.

School Curriculum and Assessment Authority (1996) *Education for Adult Life: the spiritual and moral development of young people*, Discussion Paper No. 6, London: SCAA.

School Curriculum and Assessment Authority (1996) *Values in Education and the Community*, London: SCAA.

Scruton, R. (1980, 2nd edn, 1984) *The Meaning of Conservatism*, London: Macmillan.

Sealey, J. (1985) *Religious Education: philosophical perspectives*, London: Allen and Unwin.

Sedgwick, P. (1992) 'The sectarian future of the Church and ecumenical church schools', in Astley, J. and Day, D. *The Contours of Christian Education*, London: McCrimmons.

Selby, D. E. (1976) 'The Catholic teacher crisis 1885–1902', *The Durham and Newcastle Review* 37.

Sexton, S. (1987) *Our Schools: future policy*, Warlingham: Institute for Economic Affairs Education Unit.

Sharpe, E. (1988) *Understanding Religion*, London: Duckworth.

Sherratt, B. (1994) *Opting for Freedom*, London: Centre of Policy Studies.

Simon, B. (1974) *The Politics of Educational Reform 1930–1940*, London: Lawrence and Wishart.

Simon, B. (1988) *Bending the Rules: the Baker reform of education*, London: Lawrence and Wishart.

Simon, B. (1991) *Education and the Social Order 1940–1990*, London: Lawrence and Wishart.

Simon, B. (1992) *What Future for Education?*, London: Lawrence and Wishart.

Simon, B. and Chitty, C. (1993) *S.O.S. Save our Schools*, London: Lawrence and Wishart.

Slee, N. (1989) 'Conflict and reconciliation between competing models of religious education', *British Journal of Religious Education* 11(3).

Smart, N. (1968) *Secular Education and the Logic of Religion*, London: Faber.

Smart, N. (1979) *The Phenomenon of Christianity*, London: Collins.

Smith, A. (1776, 1961) *An Enquiry Into the Nature and Causes of the Wealth of Nations*, London: Methuen.

Smith, W. C. (1978) *The Meaning and End of Religion*, London: SPCK.

Snook, I. A. (ed.) (1972a) *Concepts of Indoctrination*, London: Routledge.

Snook, I. A. (ed.) (1972b) *Indoctrination and Education*, London: Routledge.

Socialist Education Association (1981) *The Dual System of Voluntary and County Schools*, London: Socialist Education Association.

Socialist Education Association (1986) *All Faiths in All Schools*, London: Socialist Education Association.

Spencer, A. E. C. W. (1968) 'Religious education today', in Jebb, P. (ed.) *Religious Education*, London: Darton, Longman and Todd.

Spinks, G. S. (1952) *Religion in Britain Since 1900*, London: Dakers.

Stewart, J. (1992) *Accountability to the Public*, paper to the European Policy Forum.

Strain, M. (1995) 'Autonomy, schools and the constitutive role of community', *British Journal of Educational Studies* **xxxxiii**(1).

Strudwick, V. (1986) *What Are Church Schools for?*, Oxford Diocesan Council for Education and Training.

Sutcliffe, S. and Sutcliffe, B. (1994, 1995) *Faith and Commitment* series, Norwich: RMEP.

Sutherland, G. (1973) *Policy-making in Elementary Education 1870–1895*, OUP.

Sutherland, S. (1986) 'Education and theology', in Yates, J. (ed.) *Faith for the Future*, London: National Society.

Sutherland, S. (1994) *The Spiritual and Moral Development of Children*, Templeton Lecture, Royal Society of Arts, 5 December.

Swann Report (1985) *Education for All: the report of the Committee of Inquiry into the education of children from ethnic minority groups*, Cmnd 9453, London: HMSO.

Talbott, J. (1707) *The Christian School-master or the Duty of Those Who Are Employed in the Publick Instruction of Children Especially in Charity Schools*, London: Joseph Downing.

Taylor, A. (1994) 'Arthur Balfour and educational change: the myth revisited', *British Journal of Educational Studies* **xxxxii**(2).

Taylor, J. (1664) *A Dissuasive from Popery* (ed. Heber and Eden, vol. 6, 1849), London: Longman.

Taylor, M. J. (1991) *SACREs: their formation, composition, operation and role in RE and worship*, Slough: NFER.

Taylor Report (1977) *A New Partnership for Our Schools*, London: HMSO.

Temple, W. (1914) *The Kingdom of God*, London: Macmillan.

Temple, W. (1942) *Christianity and the Social Order*, London: Penguin.

Thacker, J., Pring, R. and Evans, D. (eds) (1989) *Personal, Social and Moral Education in a Changing World*, Slough: NFER-Nelson.

Thatcher, A. (1996) 'Policing the sublime and the spiritual development of children', in Astley, J. and Francis, L. (eds) *Christian Theology and Religious Education*, London: SPCK.

Thatcher, M. (1993) *The Downing Street Years*, London: HarperCollins.

Thatcher, M. (1995) *The Path to Power*, London: HarperCollins.

Thiessen, E. J. (1985) 'A defense of a distinctively Christian curriculum', *Religious Education* **80**(1).

Thiessen, E. J. (1990) 'Indoctrination and religious education', in Francis, L. J. and Thatcher, A. (eds) *Christian Perspectives for Education*, Leominster: Gracewing, Fowler Wright.

Thomas, H. (1994) 'Markets, collectivities and management', *Oxford Review of Education* **20**(1).

Thornthwaite, S. (1990) 'School transport: the need to change', *British Journal of Educational Studies* **38**(2).

Tilby, A. (1979) *Teaching God*, London: Collins.

Tomlinson, S. (1990) *Multicultural Education in White Schools*, London: Batsford.

Tomlinson, S. (ed.) (1994) *Educational Reform and its Consequences*, London: IPPR/Rivers Oram.

Troyna, B. and Carrington, B. (1990) *Education, Racism and Reform*, London: Routledge.

Tulasiewicz, W. and Brock, C. (eds) (1988) *Christianity and Educational Provision in International Perspective*, London: Routledge.

University of Sheffield Institute of Education (1961) *Religious Education in Secondary Schools*, London: Nelson.

Unwin, R. W. (1984) *Charity Schools and the Defence of Anglicanism*, Borthwick Paper 65, University of York.

Vincent, J. (1987) 'The Thatcher government 1979–1987', in Hennessy, P. and Seldon, A. (eds) *Ruling Performance: British governments from Attlee to Thatcher*, London: Blackwell.

Waddington, R. (1984) *A Future in Partnership*, London: National Society.

Walford, G. (1993) *Choice and Equity in Education*, London: Cassell.

Walford, G. (1994) 'The new religious grant-maintained schools', *Educational Management and Administration* **22**(2).

Walford, G. (1995) 'The Northbourne Amendments: is the House of Lords a garbage can?', *Journal of Educational Policy* **10**(4).

Walkling, P. (1980) 'The idea of a multicultural education', *Journal of the Philosophy of Education* **14**(1).

Wallace, R. G. (1981) 'The origins and authorship of the 1944 Education Act', *History of Education* **10**(4).

Walsh, M. (1993) 'Schools at the crossroads', *Tablet*, 13 February.

Walsh, P. (1983) 'The church secondary school and its curriculum', in O'Leary, D. (ed.) *Religious Education and Young Adults*, London: St Paul Publications.

Walsh, P. (1993) *Education and Meaning*, London: Cassell.

Ward, J. T. and Treble, J. H. (1969) 'Religion and education in 1843: reaction to the Factory Bill', *Journal of Ecclesiastical History* xx.

Watson, B. (1987) *Education and Belief*, Oxford: Blackwell.

Watson, B. (ed.) (1992) *Priorities for Religious Education*, London: Falmer.

Watts, M. (1978) *The Dissenters*, OUP.

Webster, D. (1985) 'Commitment, spirituality and the classroom', *British Journal of Religious Education* **8**(1).

Wedderspoon, A. G. (ed.) (1966) *Religious Education 1944–1984*, London: Allen and Unwin.

Whitehead, A. N. (1932, 1970) *The Aims of Education*, London: Williams and Norgate.

Wilkins, R. (1992) 'Identifying the educators', in Watson, B. *Priorities in Religious Education*, London: Falmer.

Wilkinson, J., Wilkinson, R. and Evans, J. H. (1985) *Inheritors Together: black people in the C of E*, London: Board of Social Responsibility.

Wilson, B. (1966) *Religion in a Secular Society*, London: Pelican.

Wilson, B. (1982) *Religion in Sociological Perspective*, OUP.

Wilson, J. (1972) *Religion*, London: Heinemann.

Wolfe, K. (1995) *Religion and the 1944 Education Act: education and engineering*, paper given to the British Sociology Society.

Wood, P. (1990) 'Indoctrination and religious education in infant schools', *British Journal of Religious Education* 12(3).

Woollard, A. (1996) 'Bureaucrat's dilemma', *TES*, 23 February.

Worlock, D. (1995) *Briefing* (Education Special), June 1995.

Wright, A. (1993) *Religious Education in the Secondary School*, London: Fulton.

Yarnold, E. (1989) *In Search of Unity*, Slough: St Paul Publications.

Yates, J. (ed.) (1986) *Faith for the Future*, London: National Society and Church House Publishing.

Young, M. (1971) *Knowledge and Control*, London: Macmillan.

INDEX